The Rule of Law and Economic Reform in Russia

The John M. Olin Critical Issues Series

Published in cooperation with
The Harvard University Russian Research Center

The Rule of Law and Economic Reform in Russia, edited by Jeffrey D. Sachs
and Katharina Pistor

The Sources of Russian Foreign Policy After the Cold War, edited by
Celeste A. Wallander

Patterns in Post-Soviet Leadership, edited by Timothy J. Colton and
Robert C. Tucker

Central Asia in Historical Perspective, edited by Beatrice F. Manz

The Rule of Law and Economic Reform in Russia

EDITED BY
Jeffrey D. Sachs and
Katharina Pistor

Routledge
Taylor & Francis Group

NEW YORK AND LONDON

The John M. Olin Critical Issues Series

First published 1997 by Westview Press

Published 2018 by Routledge
605 Third Avenue, New York, NY 10017
4 Park Square, Milton Park, Abingdon, Oxon OX14 4RN

Routledge is an imprint of the Taylor & Francis Group, an informa business

Copyright © 1997 by The Harvard University Russian Research Center

Library of Congress Cataloging-in-Publication Data
The rule of law and economic reform in Russia / edited by Jeffrey D. Sachs and Katharina Pistor.
        p.   cm.—(The John M. Olin critical issues series)
    Includes bibliographical references and index.
    ISBN 0-8133-3313-X (hc).—ISBN 0-8133-3314-8 (pbk).
    1. Rule of law—Russia (Federation)   2. Privatization—Russia (Federation)   3. Russia (Federation)—Economic policy—1991–
I. Sachs, Jeffrey.   II. Pistor, Katharina.   III. Series.
KLB2020.R85   1997
340'.11—dc21   96-52474
                                                                                   CIP

ISBN 13: 978-0-8133-3314-4 (pbk)

Contents

Contents

Acknowledgments

The contributions in this book were first presented as part of the seminar series "The Rule of Law and Economic Reform in Russia" at the Kathryn W. and Shelby Cullom Davis Center for Russian Studies at Harvard University. We are grateful to the Davis Center for hosting the seminar series. Special thanks to the director of the Davis Center, Timothy J. Colton, and the associate directors, Marshall Goldman and Lisbeth T. Bernstein, for their support and encouragement. We also gratefully acknowledge the generous financial support provided by the John M. Olin Foundation for preparing this book. Our thanks to Michele W. Albanese and Anne Wildermuth for administrative and editing assistance. Joyce Wilson was superb in editing the final draft.

Jeffrey D. Sachs
Katharina Pistor

CHAPTER 1

Introduction: Progress, Pitfalls, Scenarios, and Lost Opportunities

Jeffrey D. Sachs and Katharina Pistor

The fundamental questions in this collection of essays are twofold: first, how Russia's distinctive traditions of law—and lawlessness—will shape, and perhaps cripple, Russia's struggle for economic reform; and second, what impact Russia's chosen path of reform had on the development of rule of law after the collapse of the communist regime. In 1992, at the initiation of radical market reforms, Russia differed in many ways from the reforming countries of Eastern Europe, and the lack of historical tradition of the rule of law was among the most important of these differences. Nonetheless, few observers guessed how large the lack of sound legal norms and principles, which governed the public and private actions as well as the issues of criminality and state corruption, would loom in the struggle over economic reform. At the outset of the transition process, all countries were confronted with the twin tasks of economic reform and reform of the political, constitutional, and legal order. Most of the Central and Eastern European countries managed to introduce political, legal, and economic reforms almost concurrently. In Russia, by contrast, constitutional and legal reforms were stalled or often simply ignored, while economic reforms were pushed forward.

Initial conditions may have been an important factor in determining Russia's distinctive reform path. Russia differed considerably from many countries of Central-Eastern Europe and the Baltic states with regard to political and constitutional conditions. While much of Central-Eastern Europe and the Baltic states had a pre-socialist constitutional and private legal tradition to return to or to build on, this was not the case in Russia. Also, communism had been forcibly imposed and maintained in the latter countries by an outside force (i.e., the Soviet Union), while Russian communism was essentially homegrown. As a result, the change of political leadership in Central Europe and the Baltic States was more thoroughgoing than it was in Russia. The generational change of leadership was also consequently greater.

Finally, given the ongoing struggles for power in Russia that followed the coup attempt in August 1991 and the dissolution of the Soviet Union itself in December 1991, it apparently seemed necessary to President Yeltsin and his newly chosen team to press ahead with radical economic reforms despite the fact that constitutional and legal problems were unresolved, and indeed heavily contested. Both political reforms and economic reforms became matters of improvisation, given the ongoing power struggle in Moscow and the provinces. Without question, though, the unresolved constitutional and political problems haunted the economic reform process, and continue to do so. The tension between the need for economic reform on the one hand and the weakness of legal and political institutions to implement reform in a transparent and equitable manner on the other hand has perhaps been the central problem of Russia's post-socialist development.

The present collection of essays, which were first presented in the 1994–95 Olin Seminar Series of the Davis Center for Russian Studies at Harvard University, explore different aspects of Russia's legal tradition and post-socialist legal development and their relation to the economic reform process.

The contributions by Thomas Owen and Michael Newcity give an account of Russia's pre-socialist legacy. Owen analyzes in detail the struggle for legal reform in the area of private law during the last decades of the Tsarist regime. He emphasizes the ambivalence of the autocratic state, including reform-minded politicians, to trade the wide discretionary powers of the bureaucracy for a legal framework that would be more conducive to market development, but would also impose constraints on the state. Newcity relates the roots of Russia's autocratic past to the orthodox church and the absence of competition among secular and religious legal systems.

The role of constitutionalism and the relationship between economic reform and criminality in the post-socialist environment are explored in the subsequent two chapters. Joel Hellman offers a comparative, empirical analysis of the relation between constitutional order and economic reform programs in transition economies. He concludes that the establishment of a constitutional order early in the reform process can be beneficial for, but the concentration of power in the hands of a president is detrimental to, the adoption of comprehensive and far-reaching economic reform programs. Anders Åslund analyzes the economic causes of crime and corruption. Using comparative data from several transition economies, he suggests that the extent of lawlessness in present-day Russia is exaggerated. In his view, successful economic reforms will lead to a stabilization, if not reduction, in crime rates and create the necessary constituencies for law and order.

This sets the stage for an investigation of legal institutions and substantive economic law in post-socialist Russia. Michael Waller analyzes the history and current role of securities forces, including the police. He argues that the *chekist* tradition and culture created serious obstacles for establishing effective and credible civil authority in post-socialist Russia. In the absence of structural reforms of the security forces and the police and the political will to control their actions, members of the security forces have infiltrated other parts of the state administration and have dampened the prospects for establishing credible civil authorities. Timothy Frye investigates the emergence and subsequent decline of non-state dispute settlement institutions at commodity exchanges. He relates their demise to the role of the state and argues that among the main causes for the weakness of private arbitration is state control and surveillance as well as arbitrary state interference and excessive taxation.

The final two contributions treat Russia's slow progress in economic law reform and discuss its implications for the success of economic reform. Cheryl Gray and Kathryn Hendley set out three basic conditions for law based private transacting, which are good laws, sound supportive institutions, and market based incentives that create a demand for law and legal institutions. Drawing from comparison with commercial law development in Hungary, they suggest that the development of effective judicial and administrative support institutions is the most difficult task to accomplish, not only in Russia but also in other transition economies. However, Russia still falls short of providing the first conditions for law based transactions: good laws that reduce transaction costs and enable private actors to mobilize their own rights. Katharina Pistor discusses the implications of the lack of a comprehensive corporate law at the outset of privatization for the development of property rights and corporate governance post-privatization. She traces the nature and quality of legal rules issued in post-socialist Russia, not only to Russia's legal tradition, but also to policy choices made by reformers during the course of economic reform. She argues that comprehensive legal reform was delayed in favor of speedy economic reforms based on *ad hoc* decisions and decrees with detrimental consequences for the development of property rights and governance structures.

As this overview suggests, this volume offers a host of different perspectives and views about the relationship between rule of law and economic reform in post-communist Russia. We have made no attempt to harmonize these views as this would have eliminated much of the richness of the debate. It would also do injustice to the complexity of the issues at hand, which are explored by a group of scholars who represent different disciplines, including law, economics, political science, and history. Nor does this volume aspire to offer a comprehensive account of all aspects related to rule of law and economic reform in Russia. Rather, it should be regarded as a first attempt to engage scholars from different disciplines in exploring a subject of great theoretical fascination and practical importance.

In this introductory chapter, we assess the state of the rule of law and of the economy at the outset of reforms in 1991/92 and in late 1996, five years into the reform process. We relate the outcome to Russia's pre-reform history as well as to the reform process, and propose some implications for the future of Russia's economic and legal development.

Initial Conditions

Russia faced enormous obstacles for creating a market economy and embarking on political and legal reforms aimed at establishing a democratic regime based on the rule of law. The roots of Russian exceptionalism in the rule of law and in the lack of economic freedom—in comparison with the rest of Europe—are deep. The exceptionalism far predates the 1917 Bolshevik Revolution, and indeed was already dramatic in the mid-nineteenth century, when Alexander II launched his attempts at the Great Reforms (described in detail by Owen). The exceptionalism can be traced back several centuries, plausibly to the start of the Muscovite state.

Following the emergence of Moscovy from more than two centuries of Mongol domination (1240–1480), law has played a conspicuously less important role than in Western Europe. The great formative stages of Western European law—the application of Roman Law throughout the dominions of the Roman Empire; the reception of Roman Law by medieval Europe; the struggle of the Emperor and the Papacy over political authority and legitimacy; the Renaissance; and the Enlightenment—touched Russia only indirectly. Perhaps equally important, after the sixteenth century, the Russian Orthodox Church was subsumed in state power. The Tsar was both the head of state and the head of the Russian Orthodox Church. This dual role eliminated one of Western Europe's key bulwarks against the concentration of power in the hands of a single ruler. Medieval Europe's prolonged struggle between Church and State over sovereign authority, natural law, and political legitimacy played a fundamental role in fostering law-bound state power and bolstering standards of political morality; in Russia, by contrast, the struggle ended in a dominant state and a politically subservient Church.

The Renaissance in Western Europe had profound and complex effects in furthering the Rule of Law in Western Europe. On the ideological level, mankind and the meaning of life itself were put at the center of renewed philosophic speculation. On the economic level, the rise of competing city states of Renaissance Italy spurred the role of international trade, with the attendant market institutions of banking, contract law, shipping law, and secured transactions. Political speculations, crowned by Machiavelli's *The Prince*, explored ways for the Prince to strengthen the state in competition with other states, including the role of the state in fostering economic prosperity.

At that time, Russia was still under Mongol rule. Moreover, Russia's international trade was greatly hampered by geography. With its vast overland distances, its paucity of roads (Russia has no roads, only directions, said Gogol), and its rivers running North-South rather than East-West towards Europe, Russia participated in international trade mainly through the export of few highly valued commodities, such as furs, which could be profitable despite the enormous transport costs. (While Russia's river systems allowed access to the Black Sea, Russia trade with Europe via the Black Sea was hampered for centuries by Ottoman domination.) Otherwise, Russia was not drawn deeply into the emerging European market economic system.

We can put the point more generally. Throughout European history, innovations in economic and political life have started in one region and then spread to others on the basis of their perceived or demonstrated advantages, or through conquest, colonization, or imperial rule. It was considerably more difficult for new European ideas and institutions to spread into Russia's vast continental expanse, especially in view of Russia's autocratic rule. Institutional innovations carry less well into continental, largely self-contained societies—China, India, Russia—than they do into small, open societies that are dependent for their very survival on international trade, international alliances, and the timely adoption of "best practices" from abroad. Perhaps "small is beautiful" in economic reform, if the small entity isn't simply gobbled up by a larger power. In any event, it is probably no accident that Russia, China, and India have had the most difficult time of all of the traditional societies in the world in adapting the new political and economic institutions from abroad, even when those institutions have an overwhelming track record of effectiveness.

By the mid-nineteenth century, the divergence in the rule of law between Western Europe and Russia was profound. In contrast with the emergence of parliamentary and constitutional limits on sovereign authority in Western Europe, the Russian Tsar was never constrained by constitutional limits, and the state administration before the mid-nineteenth century lacked minimal standards of rational bureaucracy, citizenship, and the application of law through a judicial system. Russia was the very last country in Europe to create a parliament as a check on the absolute power of the sovereign, and even lagged behind the Ottoman empire in this institutional change. And the new Russian Duma, granted reluctantly by the Tsar in 1906—following the debacles of a lost war to Japan, a failed revolution, and a deep fiscal crisis—had few powers to limit the sovereign. Extreme limits on suffrage, and on the Duma's institutional role vis-à-vis the Tsar's powers, left the Tsar and state bureaucracy with almost all of its traditional autocratic powers.

The Russian state administration failed the basic tests of a "rational" state, according to the classic definition of Max Weber. Until the emancipation of the serfs in 1861, the vast majority of Russians had no civil rights, were subjected to the violent and arbitrary rule of their lords, and had no recourse to the state for basic legal protections. The rural aristocracy, rather than a state bureaucracy, effectively governed Russia in its vast rural areas where the overwhelming majority of the Russian population lived. To the extent that the state bureaucracy functioned, it was notoriously free of rules, rational procedures, and effective administration, as captured in Gogol's devastating depictions in the 1830s.

The state's failure to establish basic principles of the rule of law is also reflected in the development of private law. Throughout Western Europe, basic notions of private property rights, and their exchange via voluntary contract, had deep roots in traditional practice and Roman law. By contrast, the vast majority of Russian households living as serfs had no notions or rights of private property. The most basic personal freedoms were denied them; even the right to decide on their own marriages depended upon the permission of the lord.

In continental Europe, it was not until the nineteenth century that many of the key economic laws underpinning a modern market economy were developed or adopted, such as laws governing limited liability joint-stock companies, commercial banks, and bankruptcy. In principle, Russia could have closed the gap of commercial law development with Western Europe by adopting some of the key economic legislation spreading rapidly throughout the Continent. Japan, for example, leap-frogged to modern capitalism in the dramatic twenty years of radical reforms that followed the Meiji Restoration of 1868. In Russia, debates raged on just such a course of action, particularly during and after the reign of Alexander II, but with few results. Russia continued to mark a kind of geographical barrier to the Eastward diffusion of modern economic laws in the nineteenth century, as was the case in earlier centuries.[1] In every area of reform of economic law that was debated in Russia after the mid-nineteenth century, Russian reforms stopped half-way between its feudal heritage and modern capitalist practices.

This tendency towards stunted reforms was most critical and socially devastating in the question of land ownership. As is well known, the emancipation of the serfs in 1861 was not followed by individual land titling and household farms as in most of Western Europe, but rather by new communal structures (the *obshchina*), which once again deprived millions of rural families economic freedom on the basis of household decision making. The emancipated serfs had to rely on collective decisions of these communal organizations to obtain private land plots or to withdraw from the village itself. The idea of a modern citizenry—individuals exercising rights established in national laws and enjoying the ability to defend those rights in an independent judiciary—eluded mid-nineteenth Russia at the apogee of its Great Reforms. As Blum notes: "The former serfs and state peasants were placed in a peculiar legal category in which they were recognized as free persons, yet were deprived of many of the civil rights that adhered to personal freedom."[2]

The meager base of public and private rule of law that was created in Russia by the early years of the twentieth century—a Duma, semi-independent courts, partially reformed company law, a gold standard as an underpinning of foreign investment—was thoroughly destroyed by the Bolshevik Revolution. All constitutional limitations were cast aside under the Dictatorship of the Proletariat led by the Communist Party. Private property rights, such as they were, were destroyed, together with the brutal suppression or murder of the erstwhile property owners. The Party was, of course, bound by no laws, even those proclaimed by the Party itself. Law, if it had a role of all, was simply an instrument of revolutionary change. The appeal to the rule of law was denounced as a "bourgeois fetish."[3]

What was called "central planning" in the economic sphere was hardly planning at all, or even rule bound, except on paper. The system can be more accurately described as a kind of *ad hoc* bureaucratic negotiation over the allocation of resources among various competing groups within the Party power structure.

Law—as opposed to the almost stupendous number of written decrees and orders that were a major feature of the socialist legal system—began to play a more important role during the period of *perestroika*. In view of the stagnant and declining economy, great hope was placed by the political elite in economic reform legislation that would grant state enterprises more autonomy and provide the basis for limited, non-state economic activities.[4] However, because the pervasive state control over the economy was not abandoned, these reforms remained half measures. Indeed, the only partial liberalization opened the possibility for those in control of economic assets and access to resources and supplies to cash in on their control rights. As a result, partial enterprise reform gave way to "spontaneous privatization" in which future cash flows were redirected to personal accounts of enterprise mánagement, frequently in collusion with state bureaucrats. Still, some important progress was made both in the Soviet Union and in Russia between 1987 and 1991, most importantly with the adoption of joint-venture legislation, an albeit rudimentary regulation on joint stock companies, regulations on securities markets and investment companies, new principles of civil law, and even a law on privatization.

Legal change also took place at the constitutional level. The major reforms included the creation of a federal assembly as one of two houses of the Congress of Peoples' Deputies and the creation of a Presidency both at the Union level and in the Russian Federal Republic. The most important indicator for the greater role attributed to law was the enactment of legislation that provided the basis for challenging the legality of state actions and the creation of a constitutional supervision committee.

However dramatic these changes were at that time, they remained largely cosmetic as the stronghold by the Communist Party over all spheres of life and the economy remained, if diminished in force. Until March 1990 the Party's monopoly over power was still vested in the constitution. When it was finally removed, this was already the prelude for the dismantling of the Soviet Union.

After the failed coup attempt of August 1991, great uncertainty surrounded the fate of the Soviet Union. The newly elected Russian President Boris N. Yeltsin moved quickly to establish Russia's economic sovereignty and requested the Congress of People's Deputies of the RSFSR in November of 1991 to vest him with extraordinary powers to launch economic reform. Surely Yeltsin's championing of economic reform went beyond an interest in the economy per se: his demonstration to the Russian people of forward motion on the economy was part of his *political* strategy to gain the upper hand over the Soviet and communist-era leadership.

When the Soviet Union was formally dissolved and Gorbachev resigned in December 1991, Russia's constitutional and legal order was in disarray. Russia's constitutional order was based on a document premised on Communist Party supremacy. The Constitution had never really been meant to define the actual allocation of powers of different branches of the government, to clearly specify jurisdictions between the center and the constituent parts of the RSFSR, or to provide effective checks and balances. The prerogative of the Communist Party, though removed from the text of the constitution as of 1990, had meant that the supremacy of law was never adhered to nor relied upon.

The demise of the Soviet Union also left a legal vacuum in virtually all other areas of the law. In their quest for independence from the Soviet Union, the signatories of the treaty of the Commonwealth of Independent States obligated their countries to annul all laws of the USSR in existence at that time.[5] This in effect catapulted the former Soviet Union Republics back to earlier stages of legal development, as the most far reaching legal changes were typically enacted first at the Union level before they trickled down to the level of the Union republics.[6] In its ratification decree, the Russian Congress of People's Deputies realized the vacuum the CIS Treaty would create and provided that those laws of the USSR, which were not superseded by Russian legislation *and* did not violate the Russian constitution, would remain in effect.

Russia's Reform Path

Despite the revolutionary change brought about by the demise of the Soviet Union, no attempts were made in 1992 to overhaul the constitutional order. Both the President and the Congress of People's Deputies continued to derive their mandate from a nominal constitution imposed by a one-Party regime that in 1990/1991 had allowed only semi-free elections. The only serious attempt to redefine legal relations was made with respect to the federal order of the new Russia with the adoption of the so-called Federal Treaty in March 1992. As the heightening political crisis between January 1992 and October 1993 demonstrates, the lack of a clear constitutional mandate for the exercise of political power, and the lack of clear constitutional constraints on the exercise of power, had serious repercussions for the reform process.

The reform period can be divided into two phases. Phase one lasted from the introduction of economic reform in January 1992 to the storming of the White House (the Russian Parliament building) in October 1993. The second phase started with the enactment of a new constitution in December 1993 and the concurrent parliamentary elections.

Phase 1: January 1992–October 1993

During this period, economic reforms were launched consisting of three major pillars: price and trade liberalization, stabilization, and privatization. From the very beginning, all of these measures remained incomplete, and some of them indeed failed during this period. The record of stunted reforms is linked to the absence of constitutional order in several ways. First, the Government often lacked the political and constitutional means to implement reforms, especially in the face of entrenched opposition from the communist-era Supreme Soviet. Equally important, the Government lacked constitutional restraints on its own behavior, so that many opportunities for reform were squandered by official abuse and corruption.

The failure of stabilization, for example, can be traced proximately to the behavior of the Russian Central Bank, which issued massive and inflationary credits to the economy. The explosion of credits mainly followed the appointment of Mr. Viktor Gerashchenko, the Communist-era head of Soviet Gosbank, as chairman of the Central Bank in June 1992. This appointment was a deep blow to reforms, and reflected the compromises that President Yeltsin made almost from the start with the old guard, in view of the Government's limited political and constitutional base for reforms. During 1992 and 1993, the Russian Central Bank transferred a very large proportion of national income (perhaps as much as 40 percent of GDP in 1992, and 20 percent of GDP in 1993!) to key pressure groups, political favorites of the Government and the Bank, and various cronies of leading officials, with the transfers being financed by the inflation tax imposed on the society at large. When the Central Bank was subjected to a preliminary audit in the Fall of 1993, the auditors reportedly found the Bank's books to be unauditable, with large flows of untraceable money. No remedial actions were taken, however, in response to the audit. The cost of inflation was paid by the Russian population. Savings were wiped out and current incomes of average households hardly sufficed to meet daily needs.

A similar story of abuse of state power can be found in other areas. International trade was partially liberalized in early 1992. However, in core areas trade quotas were not abolished and their manipulation for the purposes of private enrichment, typically shared between the state bureaucracy and key enterprises, provided an avenue for massive enrichment. Most importantly, Russia maintained quotas on oil exports until 1995. These quotas had the effect of reducing the internal price of oil on Russia's markets relative to world prices. A quota license, therefore, was worth the difference of the domestic price of oil and the world price of oil. Multi-millionaires could be, and were, created overnight by the distribution of quota rights to favored individuals and enterprises. Rough estimates put the market value of these quota distributions at several billion dollars per year, a tempting morsel for the corrupt state apparatus. A related area for massive state corruption came in the allocation of trade credits received from Western Governments in 1992. Russia received commercial credits totaling more than $10 billion, and these credits were distributed in the form of merchandise imports to key constituencies of the Government, virtually for free. In other words, the Russian Government took on more than $10 billion in debt to international creditors during 1992, while transferring the proceeds to key interests inside and outside the government. This massive abuse ended with the drying up of most commercial credits from Western Governments at the end of 1992.

The lack of legal norms and constitutional constraints appears again in the privatization process. Within the formal mass (or "voucher") privatization process, the enterprise insiders, particularly the managers, were able to stake out claims to a very large proportion of enterprise assets, with the implicit, if not explicit, support of the Russian Government. At the core of the privatization process was a political deal that got out of hand: *nomenklatura* support for privatization in return for a large proportion of enterprise assets went to the *nomenklatura* itself. Under the mass privatization scheme, company employees had the option to acquire up to 51 percent of the company's voting stock in a closed subscription. Management typically acquired only small stakes in the privatization process itself. However, the managers succeeded in steering the process to their own benefit. And given the weak control of minority shareholders on managerial behavior, the real power within the enterprises was typically vastly higher than reflected in the formal ownership of shares.

While mass privatization was the locus of much struggle between the President and the Supreme Soviet and received much attention in the West, the prized assets of the Russian state—the natural gas, oil, and minerals deposits—were privatized in opaque ways that lacked even minimum standards of transparency and accountability. These assets had formally been excluded from mass privatization and their transfer to private hands was subject to special decision by the Russian government and/or GKI, the Russian privatization agency. It is no accident that the very first "reform minister" sacked by Yeltsin in 1992 was Vladimir Lopukhin, the Minister of Fuels and Energy. This was simply too lucrative a sector to leave in the hands of young reformers. The energy sector was taken over in August 1992 by the newly appointed deputy prime minister in charge of the fuels and energy complex, Viktor Chernomyrdin, the energy czar of the Soviet Union under Gorbachev.

Special privatization regimes for the oil and gas sectors were carved out as early as August 1992.[7] The oil and gas sectors, for example, were privatized on the basis of a plethora of special Presidential decrees—many of them issued between August and December 1992—that fostered the takeover of a large portion of these prized assets by powerful insiders, including the enterprise managers and politicians linked to them. By January 1993, the monopolistic holding structure Gazprom—which unlike the oil monopoly inherited from the previous regime had not been broken up—had been converted into a joint stock company. Gazprom's centrality in the political firmament was confirmed not only by its vast wealth, but by the promotion of its first Chairman, Viktor Chernomyrdin, as the new Prime Minister in late 1992. Gazprom's privileged position was underscored by the placement of key members of the Government, including deputy heads of the Ministry of Finance and the State Property Committee, on the Board of Directors in January 1993. It seems a cruelly Marxist gloss on Russian politics that Russia's one cash-rich enterprise—with a flood of money to spend on campaigns and clientelism—was quickly able to assert its dominance over the entire political machine!

The common denominator of all these distortions to the reform process was the absence of rule of law in government decision making and executive authority. Procedures were *ad hoc*, non-transparent, and often corrupt. Civil society was too weak to offer important countervailing pressures, so that abuses went largely unchecked. Decision making was not guided by general legal norms evenly applied, but was rather individualized to particular enterprises and pressure groups.

On the constitutional front, continuing struggle accompanied the stunted economic reforms. The political struggle between the President and the Supreme Soviet intensified in the winter of 1992. The extraordinary powers granted to the President in November 1991 expired in December 1992. What followed was a political battle over power between President Yeltsin, the speaker of the Parliament, Khasbulatov, and the chairman of the constitutional court, Zorkin, in which formal constitutionalism was pitched against the continuation of the Yeltsin government. The constitution itself did not provide a way out of this political stalemate—though a series of constitutional amendments increasingly undermined the President's position. In April 1993, a referendum was finally held focusing on the future of economic reforms which supported Yeltsin's reform program. However, the carefully couched wording of the referendum precluded a political, and much less legal, solution to the power struggle, because questions regarding the adoption of a new constitution or early elections for the parliament were not included.

It is therefore not surprising that despite the successful referendum, the power struggle continued mostly over privatization[8] and over the state budget.[9] The President finally reverted to extra-constitutional measures and dissolved the parliament in September 1993. In response, the Russian Parliamentary leaders openly called for insurrection, which culminated in the security forces' storming of the White House on 4 October 1993. In the aftermath of the violent solution of the constitutional crisis, Yeltsin moved quickly to regain control over economic reform and launched a new constitution that was adopted by referendum held together with the elections to the new parliament, the State Duma.[10] The elections themselves, however, brought the reformers a stunning defeat. Yegor Gaidar and Boris Federov both left the government. The only member of the original reform team left was Anatolii Chubais. Viktor Chernomyrdin, the Prime Minister, also remained in place. With the powers of the parliament severely curtailed by the new constitution, the political battles quieted down.

Phase 2: October 1993 to Present

If the first phase of reforms saw the eruption of political power struggles that brought the country to the edge of a civil war, the second phase saw the consolidation of political and economic power by those who had gained the most during the first phase. This consolidation was accompanied by governance of more orderly rules, if not always by formal law. The State Duma operated under the new rules and elections were held as scheduled in December 1995. In addition, presidential elections were held on schedule at the end of Yeltsin's five-year-term.

At the same time, many deep constitutional problems remain.

Struggles over executive power continued in a new though less dramatic guise, between the Government and various parts of the Presidential apparatus. After 1992, the presidential apparatus grew to enormous proportions outside constitutional constraints or public oversight. The president established separate institutions—councils, advisory bodies, commissions—with powers that overlapped those of standing ministries. The President even built a several-thousand-man Presidential Guard independent of the Ministry of Defense.

Also, latent tensions between the federation and Russia's constituencies intensified, breaking out into violent war in the case of Chechnya. After a brief attempt to win the support of Russia's regions in the struggle with the parliament in the summer of 1993 and in response to the wave of declarations of independence adopted mostly in 1993, Yeltsin opted for a strongly centralist constitution. Some regions—Tartarstan, for example—managed to carve out sufficient independence through bilateral treaties with the federal government to avoid an open rift. In Chechnya, however, the tension turned into an open war that cost tens of thousands of lives.[11]

As far as economic reforms are concerned, many of the reform measures introduced in 1992 took hold and some even came to fruition during the second phase. Russia completed voucher privatization in the summer of 1994; most of the remaining licenses, quotas, and price regulations were eliminated; inflation was brought under control in 1995. On the legal front, important progress was made with the adoption of comprehensive legislation in key areas of the law, including civil law, company law, and securities market legislation. Thus, the legal chaos that prevailed during the transition process of often contradictory Presidential decrees and government regulations, which formed the main body of "law," has given way to a more stable legal infrastructure.

At the same time, the new banks, another strong economic group with direct links to the political elite, ascended to power in Russia. Unlike the enterprise *nomenklatura*, which benefited from the compromise reached in mass privatization, or those who secured control rights over future cash flow of the gas giant Gazprom, the most powerful players among the financial institutions were not left-overs of the past regime, but products of the transition process. The best example is Oneksimbank, one of the new private banks that mushroomed in Russia since the early 1990s. Oneksimbank was created by the association of export/import organizations, the successors of the Soviet foreign trade monopolies, and quickly became one of the most financially powerful banks in the country. The bank's chairman, V. Potanin, masterminded the so-called loans-for-shares program launched in the fall of 1995, in which large stakes in Russia's most valuable companies were transferred to a selected group of banks on highly favorable terms. Oneksimbank emerged as the main winner of the loans for shares deal, having acquired controlling stakes in companies, such as Norilsk Nickel, Sidanco and Surgutneftegaz oil companies, the oil trading company Nafta Moskva, and Novolipetsk Metal Works. Oneksimbank's role in the loans for shares deal has been widely criticized for many auctions; the bank operated as the government appointed "auctioneer" and thereby controlled access to the auction process. Prior to the Presidential elections, rumors circulated stating that the government might make use of its contractual rights to take back the shares and return the loans to the banks. However, after the presidential elections, things quickly changed, and it was announced that the program would continue. Indeed, V. Potanin, former chairman of Oneksimbank, was appointed new deputy prime minister in charge of the economy.

Progress, Pitfalls, and Lost Opportunities— An Assessment of Russian Reforms

This overview of the reform process leaves us with many questions. Is Russia today a market economy? Is it a democratic state based on the rule of law? Will the rule of law prevail in the future?

In the most general definition of a market economy, private decisions rather than administrative orders determine the terms and conditions of the exchange of goods and services. According to this definition, Russia today certainly is a market economy. Still, Russia continues to lack many of the underpinning institutions of an *effectively functioning* market economy. Private property rights are weak and their defense often depends on access to political power. Capital markets have been slow to develop. The Russian stock market remains small and illiquid. Neither financial intermediaries (voucher funds) nor companies have been able to raise capital on the domestic market.[12] At the same time the Securities and Exchange Commission claims that Russian households are sitting on vast cash reserves estimated at 20–30 billion U.S. dollars, which they are keeping under their pillow—or out of the country—beyond the reach of financial intermediaries and the state.[13] To this point, mass privatization has not resulted in the development of a liquid capital market. One key institution that was designed to perform the function of a market maker or to develop into active agents of corporate governance, the voucher privatization funds, has failed to evolve as hoped and expected. Of the more than 600 funds registered in 1994, only twenty to thirty active funds remain today. The remaining funds simply ceased to function, leaving the majority of the roughly 25 million voucher investors not only without returns on their investments but also without residual rights. The functioning voucher funds launched a political campaign to ensure their survival after it became evident that policy makers had opted for leaving the voucher funds to their own fate and creating a new set of financial intermediaries, highly regulated unit trust funds.[14] The prospects of voucher funds in Russia had been seriously limited from the outset by the insider domination of privatized firms, illiquid markets, high inflation, and double taxation.[15] The blatant misuse of investors' rights by voucher funds and other financial intermediaries, which mushroomed in the unregulated Russian capital market, undermined the credibility of this market and thereby the prospects of voucher funds to raise additional capital. In fact, many or most funds sold off valuable assets to finance the management fees, thereby depriving the funds of the very basis for their long term survival.

The privatized companies themselves have often been left in a control vacuum.[16] Several of the largest companies have found shelter in financial-industrial groups—vertically integrated structures that link together several, sometimes dozens of companies and financial institutions in a dense cross-ownership network, vaguely reminiscent of Japanese *keiretsu*.[17] The official state register of financial-industrial groups now lists 31 such groups, consisting of over 485 companies in key industry sectors such as metallurgy, car manufacturing, mining, and the chemical industry, which employ over 2.3 million employees.[18] In addition, large holding structures around major banks were created outside the officially registered financial industrial groups.[19] These groups expanded as a result of the loans-for-shares program in which key banks acquired control rights in major industries. This created a tri-partite link between companies, banks as the pledgor of the companies' shares, and the state as the owner of these shares.[20] Finally, some enterprises and some banks found shelter directly with the state. Menatepbank, part of the large Menatep-group, for example, is now owned in part by the state as the result of a share swap, in which Menatepbank acquired stakes in several oil companies and the government in turn acquired shares in the bank.[21]

Another example of re-statization is the recent acquisition by the Moscow City government of a large stake in the giant car manufacturer ZIL with more than 100,000 employees.[22]

Whether rule of law has taken hold in Russia—like the status of Russia's market economy—is a difficult question to answer. The essence of "rule of law" is the constraint by law of governmental behavior and authority. There is no *canon* of the definitive elements of rule of law. However, countries that respect the rule of law usually share the following features: they "divide the powers of government among separate branches; entrench civil liberties (notably, due process of law and equal protection of law) behind constitutional walls; and provide for the orderly transfer of political power through fair elections."[23] The subjection of the sovereign to predetermined legal constraints affects public and private law development in a given country. Where this is the case, arbitrary state interference is minimized, and state action—as a regulator, tax administrator, or contract enforcer—becomes impartial and predictable. Where it is absent, the unpredictability of the state creates uncertainty which directly influences the behavior of economic agents. Rule of law is not necessarily identical with "good" or "efficient" laws. However, the two largely overlap. States committed to the rule of law invest heavily in well-designed laws, which reduce transaction costs, and train their legal personnel to enforce laws, contracts, and property rights in a fair and predictable manner.

Given Russia's long adverse history with respect to the rule of law, one may not expect stellar performance in just five years. It takes time to reform the judicial system, to train and/or to replace its personnel, and to replace existing laws with new ones. Nevertheless, it is important to assess whether the *commitment* to the rule of law, as opposed to personal fiat—however well intentioned—is apparent. Indicators for such a commitment include the division of powers, civil liberties, and the orderly transfer of power.

Before 1991, hardly any of these features were established in Russia. As of 1996, a number of important achievements have come about. A new Constitution is in place, which, despite some doubts about the validity of the procedure by which it was adopted, has apparently found widespread legitimacy. Two parliamentary elections have been held under this constitution. Most importantly, perhaps, Presidential elections have been held and the unsuccessful contender accepted them.

These achievements are significant, indeed remarkable, but we should also note that Russia has not yet experienced an orderly *transfer* of political power, so that the hardest test of the new constitutional order has not yet been made. The composition of the parliament, the State Duma, has changed twice, but this has had only limited effect on the composition of the government. Despite the dismal election results of the party he represents, Chernomyrdin continues as prime minister, an achievement reliant on the fact that the prime minister is primarily answerable to the President. Although the parliament must confirm the appointment, the President may dissolve the parliament if it refuses an appointment three times in a row.

With respect to the Presidential election, it is certainly remarkable that Zyganov and his followers have accepted the outcome of the elections. Despite predictions to the contrary, the country did not collapse into civil war. Still, as the incumbent emerged as the winner, there has not been a transfer of power.

The new constitution acknowledges the separation of powers, but a closer examination reveals the limits of these nominal commitments. In particular, the division of power between the legislature and the executive is blurred. This is most visible in the legislative powers allocated to the President. The President may rule by decree, and decrees are binding as law. The general statement that Presidential decrees may not contradict existing laws or the constitution cannot be equated with an effective separation of powers. First, it is not clear what happens if they do. And second, the decree power gives the President, as the head of the executive, the unconstrained power to establish the legal basis upon which the executive may pursue its policies. Similarly, other parts of the executive, including the government, ministries, and state committees, may pass rules and regulations in all areas where a general law has not been adopted; or if a general law has been adopted, rules may be passed as long as they do not contradict the law. These extensive law-making authorities have given way to an explosion of Presidential decrees, rules, and regulations, which in turn has resulted in a "legal jungle" that lacks transparency. This makes it hard to determine which rules are binding and on what parts of the government; thus, legal claims that challenge the validity of such rules are impossible to support.

Another area that blurs the division of power exists in the relation between the center and the regions. There is some general division of jurisdiction, but with serious flaws. A prime example is the allocation of jurisdiction over taxes. The Constitution states that federal taxes shall be adopted by the federation and other taxes by its constituencies. The key issue is, of course, which taxes shall be "federal" taxes and which ones "regional." The Constitution does not give an answer to this, but delegates this issue to a simple legislation. The core issue of fiscal power is therefore subject to frequently changing majority decisions and constant power struggle.

The failure of the Constitution to establish clearly defined rights and responsibilities between the federation and the regions has resulted in constant bargaining and the conclusion of bilateral treaties between different regions and the center, which has added to the disparity among regions to get the best concessions from the center.

Finally, one may say that the Constitution formally endorses basic rights and civil liberties and that many of these rights are being used in practice to an extent unimaginable only a few years ago. Nevertheless, it is worth noting that most provisions would not hold water if legally contested. The liberal idea that civil rights are natural law rights and shall be used as a defense against the state seems to be alien to the Russian Constitution. In its language, the state grants these rights to its subjects. But what the state grants, it may also take away again. In addition, the Constitution lacks the crucial procedural safeguards to ensure the effectuation of civil liberties, including the equal protection of the law. "Special" laws designed for a particular person or entity as opposed to general laws addressed to an anonymous or only generally defined target group have been rampant in Russia. They provide the legal basis for tax exemptions, special privatization rules, and allocation of rights to those with the best access to the President's decree power. As a result, the state retains ample scope for arbitrariness, which not only creates uncertainty, but also provides a breeding ground for corruption.

We have noted at length that the lack of a clear commitment to the rule of law at the center of state power had a direct impact on the development of the legal framework for a market based economy. Many of the relevant rules promulgated during reforms were *ad hoc* decrees, often poorly drafted and contradictory. During the second phase of reform, considerable progress was made in enacting more comprehensive *general* laws, including but not limited to a new civil code, a company law, and a law on securities—though comprehensive legislation on land ownership is still pending. The quality of these laws differs in terms of clarity and the extent to which they pay tribute to the interests of private economic interests. What is more disturbing from the point of view of rule of law is that they have not prevented the adoption of special laws and regulations designed to exempt individual entities from the force of law. With respect to the company law of January 1996, for example, a special law was passed in May 1996, which extended the period during which already existing companies shall amend their corporate by-laws to comply with the new law from 1 July 1996 to 1 July 1997. As the majority of companies had already re-registered under the new law, this amendment was apparently passed with the companies in mind that had not, which included Gazprom, Norilsk Nickel, and several other companies who were part of the loans-for-shares program, or, in other words, companies with close links to the political elite.[24]

Thus, five years into reforms, Russia has changed dramatically in many ways. Compared to 1991, the country has made considerable progress both with respect to building a market economy and developing a legal system that pays greater tribute to the rule of law. However, it is fair to say that the outcome we currently observe is remarkably different from either the original reform agenda or from what has been achieved in other transition countries.

Would an alternative reform path have produced a superior outcome? Without doubt, stricter attention to the rule of law and constitutionalism by President Yeltsin and his team would have produced a more just and equitable transition to the market economy. And without doubt, most of Russia's leadership paid scant attention to the rule of law in the first few years. Of course, President Yeltsin and his Governments were constantly fighting for sheer political survival, so that constitutional reform might have seemed a luxury compared to the street brawl underway in 1992–1993. Nonetheless, the flagrant abuses of executive authority, the absence of deeper constitutional thinking, the unwillingness of the Executive to subject itself to public scrutiny and transparent rule-making, all are deep historical flaws of the first years of post-Communist rule in Russia. With civil society particularly weak in Russia (compared with Central-Eastern Europe, for example), the importance of leadership was especially great. And here the shortcoming were especially marked, even if explicable in terms of Russia's traditions and inherited political crisis.

Would more gradual reforms have made things better, to give time for the constitutional arrangements to be put in place? In most areas, especially stabilization and liberalization, the answer is almost surely no. While the absence of the rule of law certainly hindered stabilization and liberalization, any deliberate delay in addressing stabilization and liberalization would have made matters even worse than they have turned out (as witnessed by the hyperinflation and more extreme economic collapse in neighboring Ukraine). In the area of privatization, however, delay in privatizing the natural resource industries was certainly called for. The rapid *ad hoc* privatizations of Gazprom and the oil companies in a lawless environment has led to rampant abuse and inequities, with essentially no compensations from improved economic efficiency. And even with respect to mass privatization, it appears in retrospect that a little less speed balanced by more careful lawmaking in front of the process would have been a tradeoff worth making, even taking into account the ugly realities of "spontaneous privatization" and state enterprise collapse that were already underway before mass privatization was even conceived.

Future Scenarios

What are the consequences of Russia's comparative lawlessness for its economic prospects? This is actually a trickier question than it seems, because many rather lawless economies actually grow rather rapidly, at least for a while. This is evident in China after liberalizing reforms in the late 1970s. And even mafia-ridden Palermo has grown over the last 40 years and not just because of drug trafficking but because of the normal processes of economic development.

If we try to marshal the evidence on the future of the rule of law, we can make two points. First, and very importantly, the absence of rule of law in Russia has had a clear and deleterious impact on the distribution of income in Russia since the start of radical reforms, and this inequality is likely to have persisting adverse social, economic, and political effects. The lawlessness of the state was an invitation to high inflation and massive corruption by well-placed officials working in tandem with state enterprise managers. Second, the absence of economic legality has substantially raised the costs of doing business in Russia, and no doubt has severely stifled the emergence of the new private sector. The lack of clarity of company law, the weakness of the judiciary, and the difficulty of enforcing ownership rights in Russia's new private corporations, all have slowed economic recovery and put Russia's medium-term prospects for political and economic stability in continuing question. While we can't easily quantify these effects, there is some evidence of a link between economic growth and progress on legal reform. The index of legal reform established by the EBRD is highly correlated with economic growth rates in 1995: the more progress on legal reform, the higher is the growth of the overall economy. This is admittedly crude, but still interesting evidence on the links of legal reform and the return to economic growth.

Even if one grants that Russia's path to the rule of law has been more tortuous and difficult than in many other post-communist countries, the more important issue involves the *future* trajectory of the rule of law in Russia. Can Russia surmount its adverse historical legacy, and promote the rule of law despite the bleak prior history of law in Russia? Will constitutionalism—a law-bound state—survive or fail in Russia? In the sphere of private law, will Russia gradually create the foundations for a working market economy, based on private property rights and commercial law?

In the long run, a positive outcome cannot be excluded. In the short to medium term, the prospects seem to be more clouded, though not entirely bleak. Even as the Presidential elections of 1996 seemed to strengthen the prospects for the rule of law, Yeltsin's post-election illness cast a pall on Russia's political prospects once again. The results of recent opinion polls, however, give some ground for hope. They suggest that Russians who are typically depicted as advocates of a "strong leader" have come to distrust a strong president and would favor mutual checks and balances and a more powerful parliament.[25] This may eventually provide the basis for a more balanced division of power and a strengthening of the rule of law.

With respect to the development of private law, Russia has made substantial progress in recent years as far as the enactment of new laws is concerned, although much remains to be done. Whether these laws are actually applied and used in practice, is, of course, another matter. There are several new constituencies that demand law and order to protect what they have acquired during transition, among them commercial banks, stake holders in Russia's priced assets, and also small entrepreneurs. However, the demand for law and order cannot be equated with a constituency for rule of law. The exemption of Russia's largest and most valuable companies from the improved investor protection through an amendment of the new company law (described earlier) suggests that it is one thing to protect one's *own* property rights, but quite a different matter to subscribe to the rule of law which vests others with similar rights.

In addition, while private property rights have been created, and while real interests now exist that are intent on defending these rights, even the initial distribution of property is far from settled. The massive corruption of recent years undermined much of the legitimacy of the privatization process and the resulting allocation of wealth. Losers of the first round of the reform process—and there are many that lost in the first round, including large parts of the powerful military-industrial complex—might support an authoritarian pretender to power who vows to "right the wrongs." With low levels of public support for the first phase of reforms, massive inequalities of wealth, and powerful losers, the struggle over the spoils could erupt once again, delaying or even sinking the process of consolidating property rights and financial stability.

Still, there are also reasons for hope. Russia is increasingly participating in the world economy, opening the country for the diffusion of knowledge, institutional change, and internationally accepted standards for commercial transactions. As the enforcement of such standards relies heavily on the domestic legal infrastructure, this may also put pressure on domestic legal and institutional reform.

In earlier centuries, Russia's vast land mass and poor transport effectively cut it off from the trends of the increasingly integrated European market economy. We noted earlier that economic and political institutions diffused only slowly and imperfectly, if at all, from Western Europe to Russia. As a result, Russia developed highly distinctive institutional patterns, and indeed manifested a public ideology of separateness from Europe (which always competed, of course, with ardent proponents of Westernization). Today, the forces of international diffusion of political and economic institutions are vastly more powerful.

Finally, the onset of economic growth may provide the country with the much needed stability for further institutional reform. As of 1994 every country of central Europe has resumed economic growth, and the fast reformers have obtained higher growth than the slow reformers.[26] This may be the most important piece of evidence of all. It shows that simultaneous market reforms and democratization can succeed. It gives hope that Russia too will turn the corner from economic chaos and decline, towards renewed growth and stability under the rule of law. The possibility is clear, and so are the profound risks. The essays in this volume do not offer definitive answers on Russia's future prospects, but they surely will help to illuminate Russia's historical predicament and its future challenges.

Notes

1. See Owen (1991) for a detailed account of the development of corporate law in pre-revolutionary Russia.

2. See Blum (1961), p. 618.

3. W.E. Butler (1988), p. 32.

4. For details, see Gray and Hendley in this volume.

5. See CIS Treaty of 8 December 1991 ratified by the Supreme Soviet of the RSFSR on 12 December.

6. Most importantly, perhaps, the General Principles of Civil Legislation, a condensed Civil Code adopted by the USSR Congress of People's Deputies in May 1991, was left in a void. It was to come into force on 1 January 1992, at a time when the USSR had already ceased to exist. It took Russia over six months to realize this void and to pass a special law which enacted the General Principles as a Russian law.

7. For details, see Pistor in this volume.

8. The Congress of People's Deputies vetoed several times presidential decrees aimed at increasing the percentage of shares to be offered in voucher auctions.

9. In September 1993 the Congress of People's Deputies passed the state budget for 1993, which if implemented would have further fueled inflation and most likely have led to hyperinflation.

10. Whether or not the legal requirements for adopting the constitution in this referendum had been met remains doubtful. However, as all political forces in the country have accepted the new constitution and it has provided the basis for the parliamentary elections of December 1995 and the presidential elections in June/July 1996, this has become mostly a question of historical interest.

11. For details on the political support for the Chechnya war from the center in Moscow, see Waller in this volume.

12. Two major attempts in the summer of 1995 to launch secondary emissions of shares (Krasnaia Oktiabr in Moscow and Khlebnii Dom in St. Petersburg) were supported by massive foreign assistance but failed because of a lack of demand.

13. Russian SEC (KZB) homepage, http//wwwfe.msk.ru/infomarket/enews/law.html.

14. See report of voucher funds in *Kommersant Weekly*, 28 May 1996, p. 52. For a detailed account of the voucher funds post privatization and the emerging unit trust funds, see Pistor and Spicer (1996).

15. See Frydman Pistor and Rapaczynski (1996) on the impact of insider domination on voucher funds. For a discussion of the problems of double taxation see Pistor and Spicer (1996).

16. Saba (1996).

17. The legal basis for financial-industrial groups is Presidential Decree Nr. 2096 of 5 December 1993, which was replaced by a law on financial-industrial groups of 30 November 1995.

18. Karlova (1996), Attachments 1 and 2. This means that on average, each group employs 74,131 workers and each company in a group 4,742. By comparison, the total number of employees in companies privatized through the voucher program amounted to 17.1 million or 1,214 workers per company privatized through mass privatization; see Boycko, Shleifer and Vishny (1995). This suggests that the trend of vertical integration post privatization has affected the larger companies in the country.

19. The most important of these groups are the Alfa Group, Olbi-Group, Menatep-Group, Inkombank, and Rossiskii Kredit. See Karlova, Table 1, p. 34.

20. Beginning in September 1996, the banks were allowed to sell these shares to other parties.

21. These share swaps were acknowledged by the Minister of Economic Affairs Yasin in January 1996, without, however, disclosing the actual stake the government now holds.

22. The privatization of ZIL in the spring of 1993 was hailed as a major success particularly in view of the fact that a large block was acquired by an outside investor. See Boycko, Shleifer, and Vishny (1993), p. 171.

23. *Oxford Companion to Philosophy*, "Rule of Law."

24. *Kommersant Weekly*, 11 July 1996, p. 27. The amendment was passed in May and went into force 13 June 1996. Mandatory provisions of the law shall apply, even where the corporate statutes have not been amended. However, the enforcement of these provisions is likely to be more difficult in cases where companies refuse to adapt their statutes to the new law.

25. Rose and Tikhomirov (1996), Figure II.2 on p. 25.

26. See Sachs (1995a), and Sachs and Warner (1995).

CHAPTER 2

Autocracy and the Rule of Law in Russian Economic History

Thomas C. Owen

What is the relevance of Russian economic history for an understanding of current problems in the post-Soviet economy? The creation of corporations, stock exchanges, banks, and a stable currency in Russia today encounters difficulties; these difficulties are partly inherited from the past and are imposed by the geographical dispersion of natural resources, industrial facilities, and population centers. Economic behavior also reflects the heritage of the political and ideological institutions of Russian autocracy. Current hostility to capitalism and the rule of law, although an axiom of the Marxist-Leninist ideology, has deep roots in the political history of prerevolutionary Russia as well.

Historical research on the Russian economy has stressed the persistence of economic backwardness in contrast to the dynamism of the major European countries. Debate continues on the effectiveness of methods used by the tsarist bureaucracy to combat economic backwardness, especially in comparison to Soviet policies in the 1920s and during the five-year plans.[1] Little attention has been paid, however, to the evolution of capitalist institutions within the bureaucratized system that governed the Russian Empire.[2] Soviet scholarship on the imperial economy reiterated the familiar dogmas of "monopoly capital" and "finance capital" while avoiding investigations of what we call business history, including biographies of capitalist leaders, an essential subdivision of economic history in the West. Recent research on corporate law and the evolution of corporations in the Russian Empire stressed the tsarist government's hostility to capitalist enterprise in the context of the strong ideological traditions of autocracy and xenophobia.[3]

This chapter combines my recent findings with an analysis of the peculiar legal environment of Russian capitalism. The context of this analysis is not only the familiar military and cultural conflicts between Russia and the West but also recurrent confrontations over economic issues, which have received less scrutiny. The enormous momentum of autocratic power over the centuries, from the Muscovite grand princes through Peter the Great to Stalin and his successors, owed much to the impulse to mobilize all available resources for the defense of the state and for

23

its expansion along borders contested by Poles, Swedes, Germans, Turks, and Chinese, among others. The few occasions when autocracy suddenly lost its hold—in the Time of Troubles at the beginning of the seventeenth century, in the collapse of the Russian Empire during World War I, and in the breakup of the Soviet Union after Gorbachev's brief relaxation of autocratic rule in the late 1980s—demonstrated the dependence of the multinational state on the autocratic principle for its existence. Conversely, the weakness of the rule of law in Russian history, specifically the lack of an institutional structure capable of ensuring peaceful evolution under a constitutional system of checks and balances, resulted directly from the repressive force of the autocratic principle.

This chapter is organized as follows. First, it offers brief definitions of autocracy and the rule of law in their historical contexts. This discussion analyzes the persistence of the Russian autocratic tradition over the past several centuries, during which occasional episodes of reform from above alternated with long periods of bureaucratic resistance to reform. Next, it examines two crucial episodes in the late nineteenth century, when major economic reforms based on the rule of law seemed possible: the era of the Great Reforms (1861–1874) and the period of rapid industrial development under Minister of Finance Sergei Iu. Witte (1892–1903). After consideration of why these reforms failed, the discussion concludes with some thoughts on the prospects for the rule of law in the post-Soviet economy.

The Concepts of Autocracy and the Rule of Law

The standard definition of Russian autocracy (*samoderzhavie*) has two components. The primary meaning relates to foreign affairs as a ruler who has no foreign overlord enjoys autocratic power, literally "ruling by oneself." In the absence of internal checks and balances, the term connotes absolute power as well. By the end of Tatar rule, conventionally dated in 1480, the grand principality of Muscovy had made the transition to this system. Over the centuries, in medieval Muscovy, the Russian Empire, and the Soviet Union, the autocratic government required personal service from most if not all of its subjects, issued a host of arbitrary laws, and remained immune from constitutional restraints on its executive power.[4]

A distinction must be drawn between the rule *of* law and rule *through* law. The vast number and complexity of the laws promulgated by Russian autocrats had nothing to do with the defense of human rights or limits on the power of the tsar. The enormous *Polnoe sobranie zakonov* (Complete Collection of Laws, 1649–1913, hereinafter PSZ) and its supplement, the *Sobranie uzakonenii i rasporiazhenii pravitel'stva* (Collection of Governmental Statutes and Decrees, 1863–1917, hereinafter SURP), together with the various codes of laws issued from 1497 onward, indicated the vigor with which tsarist bureaucrats sought to regiment society by means of statutory compulsion and restriction. The law functioned as an administrative device, not as a set of rules to be obeyed by state officials. For example, profiles of all corporations founded in the Russian Empire are contained in the *PSZ* and the *SURP* because every new corporate charter took the form of a law.[5] Under the weak constitution of April 1906, the tsar retained control of the state budget, appointed and dismissed cabinet ministers without the assent of the legislature, enjoyed absolute veto power over all legislation, had sole power to initiate constitutional amendments, and retained the right to rule by temporary decree when the legislature was not in session.

Muscovy, the Russian Empire, and the Soviet Union thus developed a unique system of political organization that I have elsewhere characterized as the "military-autocratic" mode of rule.[6] This analytical term supplements Max Weber's classic trio of the primary modes of political legitimacy: (1) tradition, which Peter the Great and Lenin flouted; (2) charisma, which Nicholas II and Stalin lacked; and (3) legality based on reason and expertise, which tsars and commissars universally despised. For centuries, the Russian state pursued the goal of expanding its dominion over the huge Eurasian plain. To this end, it placed the highest priority on equipping the largest armed force in Europe. Such military strength in turn required the imposition of state service, heavy taxation, state control of key industries, and, above all, the destruction of any countervailing political forces.

To define the rule of law is to clarify how alien it was from these Russian political institutions. The basic legal institutions of European civilization emerged in a specific cultural environment, that of the early Roman Republic. Roman law grew into a complex procedural system administered by trained jurists in the Roman Empire, the Byzantine Empire, and later European monarchies. Because it never imposed constitutional constraints on the executive, it did not ensure the rule of law in the modern sense. Napoleon's famous codes of law and procedure (1804–1811) guaranteed equality before the law and protected private property rights in the tradition of Roman law, but they did not infringe on the prerogatives of the emperor and his spies, censors, and secret police.

The modern European *Rechtsstaat*, or "state based on the rule of law," rested on Roman legal procedures but also grew out of the tradition of checks and balances created by the estates and their representative assemblies in the late medieval period. In the words of Barrington Moore, Jr.,

> The most important aspect was the growth of the notion of the immunity of certain groups and persons from the power of the ruler, along with the conception of the right of resistance to unjust authority. Together with the conception of contract as a mutual engagement freely undertaken by free persons, derived from the feudal relation of vassalage, this complex of ideas and practices constitutes a crucial legacy from European medieval society to modern conceptions of a free society. This complex arose only in Western Europe.[7]

Eventually, elected legislatures in Europe won the power to pass laws that governed the executive authority as well as the population, and governments grew to respect the civil liberties of their subjects.

The Russian translation of *Rechtsstaat*, *pravovoe gosudarstvo*, although common in Russian political discourse in the past decade, scarcely existed in the lexicon of the Russian Empire outside the specialized legal literature.[8] For decades, the concept was vilified by Marxist-Leninist ideologists, who rejected the very concept of legal restrictions on the power of the Soviet state and the Communist Party.[9]

A recent fourfold definition of the rule of law in American legal theory likewise had nothing in common with the Russian autocratic principle. First, laws must embody the principles of "generality, publicity, exclusion of retroactive legislation, clarity, stability, exclusion of legislation requiring the impossible, [and] congruence of official action and declared rule." Second, laws must protect the personal freedom of citizens. Third, laws must govern the actions of the executive power through a constitution and an independent judiciary. Finally, citizens are expected to obey the law even when it conflicts with their own moral beliefs.[10]

The Great Reforms

To what extent did the tsarist government introduce the rule of law into the Russian political system during the Great Reforms? Despite the implication of historical significance in this term, the tsarist bureaucrats who refashioned Russian political institutions in the 1860s and 1870s carefully avoided imposing constitutional restraints on the autocratic state. The reforms thus demonstrated the government's minimal accommodation to the principle of the rule of law. To be sure, the Judicial Reform of 1864 introduced some Western legal norms, such as trial by jury, an independent judiciary, and parallel hierarchies of criminal and civil appellate courts, but these institutions lost much of their effect in the reign of Alexander III (1881–1894). Moreover, little progress toward the rule of law in the Russian economy occurred in the 1860s. Indeed, several major policy decisions, including the retention of communal agriculture after the emancipation of the serfs and the refusal to reform the corporate law of 1836, demonstrated the devotion of Alexander II and his advisers to the military-autocratic tradition.

The most important economic reform from the standpoint of the rule of law was the abolition, in 1863, of the system of liquor tax farming, which had completely corrupted the tsarist bureaucracy. Shortly after this reform, several prominent tax farmers sought new sources of wealth by investing heavily in railroads and industry.[11] The surge of patriotic sentiment in the aftermath of the Crimean War, which had made clear the political costs of economic backwardness, also served to stimulate corporate entrepreneurship. The charters of new banks and steamship companies issued in this period typically contained the names of dozens of founders, so that their average number in new corporations shot up to 7.7 in 1866–1870 and fell only slightly in the following quinquennium to 6.1 before subsiding by 1881–1885 to the usual level of 2.5, where it remained to the end of the tsarist period. Likewise, the flurry of incorporation in railroads, the largest companies in terms of authorized capitalization, drove the annual total of corporate capital to nearly four rubles per capita in 1871, a figure never again equalled, even in the corporate booms of the 1890s and the five years prior to World War I.[12]

These impressive statistics did not, however, signify any weakening of bureaucratic control over the economy. The most important of the Great Reforms—the emancipation of the serfs—contained provisions that limited individual freedom of movement by tying peasants to their communes until such time as they could pay their entire share of the commune's redemption obligation. Because few peasants ever accumulated adequate cash for such payments, an individual farmer class did not develop in Russia. Peasants were free to leave the commune temporarily, so that cities and industrial villages did accumulate a large industrial labor force, but the workers' financial and familial bonds with the village signified more a ruralization of the factory than an industrialization of the countryside.

Few reforms had the effect of freeing commerce and industry from bureaucratic controls. In the words of Richard S. Wortman, the tsarist "government remained averse to the reforms in credit and commercial law necessitated by the new industrial economy. The autocracy thus kept itself apart from the forces of change it had stimulated and, as the Russian economy developed and expanded, ensured its own obsolescence."[13] For example, in 1874, shaken by the economic crisis in Europe and Russia, Reutern abandoned his plan for corporate law reform, which would have introduced the principle of incorporation by registration, adopted by Great Britain in 1844, France in 1867, and the North German Confederation in 1870. Toward the end of his long term as minister of finance (1862–1878), in February 1877, Reutern made clear his fear of the inherent dynamism of corporate capitalism. It was essential for Russia, he warned, to avoid at all costs "the feverish stimulation of industrial and stock-exchange enterprises," as had occurred on the eve of the economic crisis of 1873–1875.[14]

Driven by caution, Reutern pursued a singular strategy, outlined as early as 1866: to balance the imperial budget and stabilize the credit ruble by limiting imports, expanding exports, and curbing the outflow of specie. This program lacked all reference, positive or negative, to legal issues. The only exception to the principle of strict economy came in a series of massive loans from abroad to pay for imported railroad equipment, as the expansion of the rail network appeared to Reutern the best way to stimulate heavy industry and exports of grain, a source of hard currency.[15]

Despite Reutern's high hopes for railroads, however, the subsequent performance of these huge enterprises was marred by extravagance, corruption, and inefficiency. Reutern's laws governing the creation and management of railroad companies proved too crude to ensure economic rationality. On the one hand, Russia lacked a large cadre of experienced corporate managers and investors, so that the government felt obliged to guarantee a firm return on stock and bond capital, usually five percent annually, to make investment attractive. On the other hand, lax monitoring by the government opened the way to all sorts of irregularities, including the granting of absurdly low freight rates to favored customers. Finally, the state lost patience. In 1889, it established a uniform system of freight rates, and it purchased no less than thirty-three railroad companies between 1887 and 1900. In the United States at this time, railroads pioneered the creation of the modern corporate form of organization, but in Russia, the state continued to exercise tutelage and, in frustration, resorted to the familiar pattern of direct administration. On the eve of World War I, three-quarters of the rail network in Russia belonged to the state.[16]

Seen in a comparative context, the Russian state appeared slow to adapt to modern capitalism. It was at this time, in the 1860s and 1870s, that the Japanese government cleared the way for capitalist development, overcoming the much greater cultural gulf that separated it from Europe, the source of new technology and the corporate form of enterprise. Even the Ottoman Empire introduced reforms based on European models: the Code Civil Ottoman (1868–1876); the Constitution of December 1876, issued three decades before its counterpart in Russia; and the first parliament (1877), however weak and ineffective.

The most likely cause of the Russia government's inaction was its fear of political turmoil during the era of the Great Reforms. In keeping with the military-autocratic mode of rule, the Russian government made impressive efforts to assimilate the latest military technology at this time.[17] However, numerous threats, foreign and domestic, heightened the sense of danger: nationalist agitation in the Polish provinces, which erupted in open rebellion in 1863; the war scare of mid-1863; Dmitrii Karakozov's attempted assassination of the tsar in April 1866; the second war scare in 1875–1876 after fighting broke out in the Balkans; the war with the Ottoman Empire in 1877–1878, which delayed for two decades Finance Minister Reutern's plan to introduce the gold standard; and the campaign of terrorism launched by the People's Will in 1878, which culminated in the assassination of Alexander II on March 1, 1881. The conflict with ethnic minorities over Russian rule, not only in Poland but also in the Baltic and western provinces, further threatened stability.[18] These tensions eventually led to breakup of the Russian Empire in the civil war of 1918–1920 and of the USSR in 1991.

The 1890s

In the last decade of the nineteenth century, progress toward the rule of law once again appeared possible. Finance Minister Sergei Iu. Witte, the most energetic and capable of Nicholas II's ministers, expressed his opposition to several forms of bureaucratic tutelage. For example, in his memoirs he criticized one of the counterreforms introduced in the reign of Alexander III: Count Dmitrii A. Tolstoi's appointment, in 1889, of land captains (*zemskie nachal'niki*), often prominent landlords, who exercised broad judicial and administrative power over peasants.

> For a society to be civilized there must be separation of the administrative and judicial branches. The courts at all levels must be completely independent of the administrative branch. Once this separation is breached, [the] rule of law is replaced by arbitrary action. . . . Solid conservatism and order can exist only on the basis of the rule of law. And as long as the entire population does not enjoy the rule of law, one can expect the unexpected.[19]

For this reason, Witte abandoned his early support for the peasant commune, the centerpiece of the Emancipation Statute of 1861.

> The chief cause of the revolution we have experienced [in 1905–1907] is the artificial retardation in our country of the development of the principle of individuality, of private property, of equal civil rights. But life must follow its own course, and as in the case of a badly constructed steam engine there must be an explosion unless the engine is rebuilt.[20]

Witte also saw a logical connection between the appeal of the socialist ideal and the absence of the tradition of Roman law in Russia. In his view, both the bureaucracy and the masses were to blame for the powerful Russian tradition of disrespect for private property.

> Socialism, which rejects the principle of private property as found in Roman law, spread from the West to Russia, where it found a favorable soil in the last fifty years, partly because of the lack of respect shown by the powers-that-be for law in general and for property laws in particular, partly because of the cultural backwardness of the masses. The influence of socialism has been reinforced by the simple belief in the right of "expropriation" and pillage.[21]

Although Witte refused to abandon bureaucratic restraints on free enterprise, he embraced one important principle of the rule of law: high standards of honesty and competence among his subordinates in the Ministry of Finance. In the 1890s, many foreign businessmen continued to pay bribes for the privilege of establishing corporations in Russia, but they wasted their money by making payments to courtiers and journalists who had no real influence, according to Maurice Verstraete, the French financial attaché in St. Petersburg. In fact, "It often cost only several rubles, the price of a few pieces of official paper, and small fees for printing" to obtain a corporate charter. It sufficed "that the founders of new corporations be honorable and serious men."[22] The recently published memoirs of Vladimir I. Kovalevskii, one of Witte's experts, cited several cases in which the minister refused to approve charters of new companies that would have allowed grand dukes and other influential personages to win quick speculative profits on the nascent Russian stock exchange.[23]

In a document of 1893 discovered by Shepelev, Witte criticized the economic policies of his predecessors in the 1860s, 1870s, and 1880s and called for major reforms of the law to facilitate economic development. This document supplemented Witte's secret memorandum of 1899, first published by Theodore H. Von Laue in 1954, in which the minister of finance defended his policy of high tariffs and massive foreign investments to promote Russian industry.[24] Witte apparently chose to camouflage his plan in 1893 because he feared provoking resistance to it in the State Council.[25]

Although he admitted the proliferation of enterprises in the wake of the Emancipation and the railroad boom, Witte complained that existing commercial-industrial legislation, unchanged since the beginning of the century, was hampering industrial development. The rising number of new corporations, the many technical breakthroughs in industrial production, the new devices requiring patent protection, and the expanding trade in commodities and corporate securities on exchanges—all these forms of modern business activity required legislative protection. As a result of outmoded laws, merchants lacked "the kind of strength and stability that is absolutely necessary for today's expanded commercial activities" (page 22). The task of drafting new commercial legislation was further complicated by the lack of a common-law tradition such as that of Western Europe and by the autocratic government's habit of extensive intervention in economic matters in defense of favored individuals, which prevented the growth of precise and impersonal legal norms of commercial practice (page 24). The laws of 1807 and 1836 governing partnerships (*torgovye tovarishchestva*) left unclear a host of issues, such as "mutual relations between participants in the partnership and their plenipotentiaries." These laws allowed no investments except in the form of cash; failed to require a specification of "the share of participation by each partner in profits and losses"; and left unclear the procedures of liquidation. The decisions of commercial courts and the Senate only partially filled the legislative void, to the disadvantage of partnerships and third parties alike (page 25). Witte neglected to observe that in Europe, where centuries of commercial practice had created widely accepted norms of business activity, the law left many details of the structure and functioning of partnerships to the contracting of parties. In Russia, the tiny merchant estate produced few entrepreneurs capable of launching businesses based on European norms. Witte only dimly sensed the central dilemma of Russian capitalism: the vigorous intervention by the state to combat fraud tended at the same time to stultify economic activity.

Especially serious were fetters imposed on corporations, the quintessential institutions of modern capitalism. The corporate law of 1836, left unreformed by Reutern two decades earlier, had "lost all relevance" because its provisions conflicted with the many corporate charters confirmed by the tsars in the preceding half-century (page 25). Thus, each of the 614 corporations in existence in 1892 operated under a separate charter that had the force of law. Because charters of many large corporations granted special privileges in defiance of the law of 1836, no general system of corporate law really existed.[26] Ineffective supervision of corporations by the Ministry of Finance allowed unscrupulous managers to pursue their own financial interests to the detriment of corporations, even to the point of bankruptcy (page 26).

Witte's critiques were well founded, but his program of industrial development appeared excessively bold and optimistic. Despite several favorable references to "private enterprise" (*chastnaia predpriimchivost'*, pages 17, 19, 20, 23), rarely mentioned in tsarist documents, Witte laid out a program for industrial development that depended not only on the reforms that he demanded, few of which the bureaucracy made, but also on a level of flexibility and efficiency within his own ministry that proved impossible to realize. He insisted that the tsarist state, omniscient and all-powerful, should demonstrate a "close and strictly practical concern for the development of every specific sector of our industry and commerce" (page 20). He expressed no doubt that skilled bureaucrats could modify import tariffs to protect infant industries without allowing monopoly pricing to hurt the interests of consumers (pages 17–18). He felt that technical education and commercial-industrial credit facilities also appeared necessary within a comprehensive "national policy" (page 21). He stated that a new tax system based on the profitability of enterprises must replace the current inequitable system (page 23). He pointed out that new consultative institutions composed of government experts and manufacturers were needed to alert the state to the needs of industry on the local level (pages 23–24) and in St. Petersburg (pages 24, 27–29). None of these reforms came into being, and the tsarist bureaucracy never outgrew its notoriously cumbersome mode of behavior.

Witte also failed to fulfill other intentions announced in his memorandum of 1893. The tsar approved in 1901 a minor change in the law regulating the general assemblies and audit commissions of corporations, but no reform of commodity exchanges was ever implemented. The St. Petersburg Stock Exchange, the only such institution in the entire empire, received a special set of rules upon its creation in 1900 as a branch of the commodities exchange at the tip of Vasilii Island, but the tsarist government left unreformed the legislation governing transactions in commodities and securities.[27]

Moreover, despite Witte's emphasis on the need to respect the law, a frankly autocratic spirit animated many of his actions, including the introduction of the gold standard in 1897. Conscious of the overwhelming opposition to monometallism in the State Council, which normally drafted legislation for the emperor's acceptance or rejection, Witte arranged for the reform to be approved by the Finance Committee, a small body of experts, and implemented in the form of an imperial decree. For this imperious action he offered no apology, explaining that the reform "firmly established Russia's credit and placed her on an equal footing in financial relations with the other great European powers. . . . I was able to bring it off despite broad opposition because I enjoyed the Emperor's confidence and support."[28]

Furthermore, Witte cannot be considered a partisan of free capitalist development. He kept the largest construction project in Russia in the nineteenth century, the Trans-Siberian Railroad, firmly in the hands of the state. As Steven G. Marks recently observed, "Witte's policies may have strengthened capitalism and private industry in Russia, but he was not sympathetic to private enterprise or entrepreneurs and the interests he aspired to benefit were not theirs but the state's."[29]

Although Witte pressed for a completely new corporate law, one that would have allowed incorporation by registration instead of by imperial concession, he eventually followed Reutern's example of 1874 and abandoned his own reform at the last minute, in 1899. To be sure, his motives differed from those of his predecessor. Whereas Reutern had feared the economic turmoil that a freely expanding corporate system would permit, Witte sought to protect corporate founders and managers from the intensely nationalistic mood that was beginning to pervade other ministries. By maintaining the concessionary system, he kept in his hands the right to approve corporate charters that contained special provisions, even those that contravened other laws. Specifically, his tailor-made charters routinely exempted Poles, Jews, and foreign citizens from a variety of restrictive laws on landholding in the border regions of the empire that normally affected non-Russians and corporations owned and managed by them. That he abandoned the reform of the corporate law of 1836 after long and painful deliberations, the better to evade other laws, illustrated the complexities of the tsarist legal system, which no one was willing to reform for the sake of capitalist enterprise.[30] In the only mention of corporations in his memoirs, Witte blamed the ministers of interior, especially Viacheslav K. Pleve, for interfering with foreign investment and improvements of legislation regarding incorporation,[31] but he passed over his own abandonment of corporate law reform in silence.

One of the most important economic contributions of the rule of law is to provide a stable institutional environment without which the calculation of risk becomes difficult or impossible. Toward the end of the nineteenth century, the rise of industrial cartels and syndicates, as the sales offices of cartels were called, prompted industrial countries to devise various forms of regulatory legislation. Approaches ranged from the German government's encouragement of cartels in the interest of the rationalization of the market to the invocation of the Sherman Anti-Trust Act of 1890 by Theodore Roosevelt, William Howard Taft, and Woodrow Wilson to break up new industrial combinations in the United States.

Whatever the differences among their policies toward cartels, the major European and North American countries implemented their particular policies through legislation.[32] In the Russian Empire, in contrast, the old law against agreements to fix prices remained in the Code of Laws while the tsarist government gave its informal encouragement to industrial cartels through the chartering of syndicates, notably in beet sugar (1887), iron and iron products (Prodameta, 1902), and coal (Produgol', 1904). This inconsistency persisted to the very end of the tsarist period. Apparently the tsarist bureaucracy appreciated the need for some forms of coordination among manufacturers in the interest of price stability. At the same time, the formal illegality of cartels and syndicates allowed the state, as one liberal jurist put it, to "seize a random victim" from time to time. Whether the ministries of interior, justice, and finance consciously created this perverse legal confusion for the purpose of instilling fear in the corporate elite is not clear. It resulted most likely from the traditional inability of the tsarist bureaucracy to rationalize its own economic law.[33] What is certain is that Witte made no effort to clarify the situation. His memoirs lacked any reference to monopolies, cartels, or syndicates.

The Kadet leader Iosif V. Hessen, who prepared the Russian and German editions of Witte's memoirs for publication in emigration in 1921–1923, referred to Witte both as an architect of "the rule of law," who criticized Prime Minister Petr A. Stolypin for acting in defiance of the Fundamental Law (constitution) of 1906, and as a statesman, whose whole career demonstrated his "loyalty to the principle of autocracy."[34] This characterization captured the contradictory nature of Witte's career. Likewise, Arcadius Kahan considered "the real Witte" less a proponent of state-sponsored industrialization in the tradition that linked Peter the Great with Stalin than a "highly skilled technician in need of a political autocracy (or even a command economy) for the realization of his objectives, a mind inclined toward mechanistic views of social problems, of somewhat limited intellectual capacity and therefore drawn to administrative solutions" instead of liberal democracy and unfettered capitalist development.[35] Witte's accusation, in his memoirs, that the Kadets sought too rapid a political change in 1905 in demanding a cabinet responsible to the State Duma (the lower house of the new legislature) instead of the monarch,[36] revealed the strength of his opposition to a crucial aspect of the rule of law: the accountability of the executive branch to the legislative.

Historical Questions

However fascinating the economic and political drama of the final prerevolutionary decade, the historian of the Russian economy can make a stronger case for the importance of the era of the Great Reforms in setting the Russian Empire on its fatal course toward the October Revolution of 1917. Although the economic recovery that occurred in 1906–1913 called forth an unprecedented flurry of incorporations—an average of 200 new companies per year—only 2,167 corporations, with a total of 8,090 managerial positions, existed at the beginning of 1914, when the population of the Russian Empire stood at approximately 169 million.[37] Even if Prime Minister Petr A. Stolypin had vigorously promoted the development of capitalist institutions in 1906–11, insufficient time remained before World War I shattered the economy and unleashed the largest social revolution in Russian history.

Clearly, however, Stolypin had no such intentions. Witte complained that Stolypin "undermined the rule of law" and made "a mockery of civil rights" by persecuting the press, attacking the autonomy of Finland, and neglecting to punish political murders carried out by right-wing extremists.[38] Despite his endorsement of "a state based on law" in a speech to the State Duma in mid-1906, the prime minister resorted to "formal 'tricks' and blatant illegality" to defend the government's autocratic power.[39] He also refused to institute economic reforms that might have strengthened corporate capitalism. For example, the charter of a railroad company founded by the prominent Polish landowner Count Józef A. Potocki in 1910 empowered the minister of transportation to remove any director from the board without cause.[40] Mechanisms of contract enforcement, crucial to the promotion of rational economic activity, remained correspondingly weak. Only two credit bureaus—agencies that gathered and disseminated information on the financial condition of businesses—were ever chartered under Russian law, both in Moscow, in 1908 and 1912; and only the second of these survived to 1914.[41]

Had the tsarist government implemented in the 1860s the economic reforms that Witte eventually advocated in 1893, and had it established the semi-constitutional form of government that Nicholas II finally accepted in 1906, a vigorous corporate economy might have developed in the five decades that elapsed between the promulgation of the Judicial Reform and the outbreak of the war. Why, then, did the Great Reforms fail to establish a firm foundation for corporate capitalism, a crucial institutional buttress of the rule of law? Three aspects of the economy in this period invite further study: the immaturity of the banking system, the government's failure to create vigorous organizations of local representation for commercial and industrial interests, and the weakness of "Slavophile capitalism" after the Crimean War.

Among the reforms that would have strengthened the rule of law in the economy in the 1860s was the granting of freedom of incorporation, especially to banks, the key institution for the accumulation and investment in this capital-starved economy. Finance Minister Reutern, motivated by a fear of bank failures and the economic chaos that they might precipitate, preferred instead to restrict the number of new banks chartered in the Russian Empire. After the first corporate bank appeared in St. Petersburg in 1864, merchants in other cities, large and small, petitioned for similar charters, so that by the end of 1873 forty-five new banks had come into existence. The tendency of new banks to spring up in the largest cities alarmed Reutern, however. For an entire decade (1872–1882), the Ministry of Finance refused to allow a new bank in any city where one already existed. This cautious policy benefited existing banks by limiting competition in large cities, but it encouraged entrepreneurs to set up banks in small provincial cities. The meager financial opportunities there, coupled with the panic of 1874–1875, had predictable results. Of the twenty-two new banks founded between 1872 and 1879, six (in Kozlov, Rybinsk, Berdichev, Kerch, Kherson, and Kursk) never opened, and three (in Kronstadt, Libau, and Kamenets-Podolsk) failed by 1882. Reutern's policy protected existing banks but contributed to the demise of new banks in small provincial cities.[42]

The Russian Banking Association, which articulated the needs of corporate banks, issued a sharp critique of this restrictive policy after the fall of the tsarist regime. The organization's contention that bureaucratic restrictions on the size of the banking network impeded industrial development for two decades—from the mid-1870s to the mid-1890s[43]—deserves serious consideration in the form of econometric studies.

The second puzzle posed by the Great Reforms was the weakness of consultative organizations. Obviously, bureaucratic intransigence played a major role, but why did Russian manufacturers, traders, and financiers fail to make a persuasive case for unfettered capitalist enterprise for the sake of Russian military power after the Crimean War? A closely related issue was the political impotence of the organizations that represented business interests. Why did none of the business organizations formed in 1860s and 1870s, including the Russian Industrial Society (1867), the Russian Banking Association (1873), and the Association of Southern Coal and Steel Producers (1874), consider it appropriate to challenge the power of the autocratic state in the name of the rule of law? Recent research has revealed the Russian business leaders' preference to address humble petitions to the all-powerful state. By this means they achieved some favorable treatment in the form of tariff protection, moderate levels of taxation, permission to maintain cartels, and other advantages. Still, the situation remained far from ideal, as shown by a host of angry denunciations of "arbitrary action" (*proizvol*) signed by business leaders in the tumult of 1905. Although the tsarist bureaucracy allowed the proliferation of local exchange committees—thirty-nine were created between 1895 and 1904—and several dozen business organizations did come into existence in the last two decades of the tsarist period, the state refused to allow the creation of elective chambers of commerce and industry, under either Witte or his successors.[44] Unfortunately, the study of Russian business organizations has only just begun. The story of the complex relationship between the Russian state and the commercial-industrial elite will not emerge until the most important business organizations in the empire receive the monographic treatment that they deserve.[45]

Third, within the government-sponsored atmosphere of hostility to Western legal norms in the era of the Great Reforms, proponents of what I have called "Slavophile capitalism" sought to mobilize the productive forces of the economy in opposition to the economic threat from the West. They hoped to develop Russian industry without, however, undermining their cherished values: communalism, devotion to autocracy, and Orthodox Christian humility. This group, composed of prominent Moscow merchants and their Slavophile allies in the campaign for tariff protection in the 1850s and 1860s, pursued three main goals. First, they sought to legitimize the new textile factories of the Moscow region by creating a myth of the benevolent factory owner, modeled on the Slavophile myth of the bond of love between the kind landlord and his grateful peasants, the better to distinguish Russian capitalism from the heartless exploitation of labor associated with the European bourgeoisie.

The Slavophile capitalists also turned the long tradition of Russian economic xenophobia against their rivals in the empire, including Jewish textile manufacturers in the Polish provinces, German merchants in the Baltic region, Jewish and Greek merchants in Odessa and other southern ports, and Armenians in the Baku petroleum industry. (The first major pogrom against Jews in Odessa, in 1871, which Russian newspapers excused with allegations of exploitation of non-Jews by Jewish merchants, testified to "the anti-industrialism of the Russian intelligentsia and the use of anticapitalist arguments to justify vandalism against Jews" in the era of the Great Reforms.[46]) The Muscovites' competitors in the world economy also became targets: French railroad concessionaires, German industrialists, Jewish bankers, and, on the eve of World War I, American businessmen.

Finally, partisans of Slavophile capitalism borrowed theoretical arguments in favor of protectionism from the German economic nationalists Friedrich List and Wilhelm Roscher in an effort to refute the old notion of Russia's exclusively agrarian destiny.[47] It remains unclear why this movement failed to create a form of corporate capitalism capable of transforming the Russian economy in the 1860s without the massive foreign investments that Witte considered necessary thirty years later.

Conclusion

This survey of Russian economic history has stressed the extraordinary staying power of the autocratic principle and the concomitant weakness of the rule of law. A respectable tradition of *Rechtsstaat* liberalism did exist in imperial Russia, but its political manifestations remained weak, primarily in the form of *zemstvo* liberalism and the activities of the Kadet Party.[48] Autocratic power, justified largely by the government's fear of the centrifugal forces of minority-group nationalism and mass violence, closed off any significant evolution in the direction of the rule of law in the 1860s and 1890s.

Several implications for the future may be drawn from this general finding. Most significant is the institutional momentum of the centralizing tradition in the Yeltsin era, especially in the Russian government's reliance on arbitrary administrative measures to supply credit to technically bankrupt enterprises and in the lack of adequate legislation conducive to corporate entrepreneurship and the defense of stockholders' interests in privatized enterprises.[49] Also, as the parliamentary elections of 1993 and 1995 showed, hostility toward capitalism in Russia still derives much impetus from the long xenophobic tradition common to peasants, radical intellectuals, and tsarist bureaucrats alike. The identification of corporate capitalism with foreign cultural values remains a serious impediment to the acceptance, by Russians, of the economic implications of the rule of law: free markets, private property, rational procedures for contract enforcement, and a stable currency. Finally, recent legal theory posits the necessity of a moral consensus before the rule of law can function.[50] This suggests future difficulties in light of the deep fissures—along ethnic, regional, and class lines—that currently fragment the societies of the former USSR.

Notes

1. Marks (1991); Davies (1991); Gatrell (1994); Gregory (1994).

2. To my knowledge, only one Soviet historian of the tsarist regime, Leonid E. Shepelev, investigated corporate law, a central feature of any legal system under capitalism. See Shepelev (1973).

3. Owen (1991, 1995).

4. Keenan (1986), p. 132, argued persuasively that the outwardly "monarchic and autocratic" Russian state functioned according to complex "oligarchic and bureaucratic" rules within the walls of the Kremlin.

5. Owen (1992).

6. Owen (1991), pp. 13–14.

7. Moore (1966), p. 415. The contributions of late medieval estates to constitutionalism is stressed in Hintze (1975).

8. Only one tsarist minister consistently endorsed the concept of the *pravovoe gosudarstvo*: Acting Minister of Trade and Industry Mikhail M. Fedorov, who held office for a few months in 1906 but refused to serve as minister of trade and industry under Witte's reactionary successor as prime minister. Witte (1990), p. 560. Fedorov joined the Kadet Party and actively opposed the Bolshevik regime in emigration after 1917.

9. Kartashkin (1991), p. 890, citing an explicit statement to this effect by Lazar M. Kaganovich in 1929. In the same issue, Berman (1991) called attention to the historical precedents of Gorbachev's endorsement of the concept of *pravovoe gosudarstvo* in Russia in the 1860s and in the USSR in the post-Stalin era. For a comprehensive analysis of the evolution of the Soviet regime's attitudes toward the rule of law, see Huskey (1992), esp. pp. 24–33.

10. Gaus (1994), pp. 328–330. The notion of the rule of law does not exhaust the possibilities of democratic government. One recent study criticized the rule of law for requiring "fidelity to law" without due attention to the essentially political issue of "the proper scope and content of legal regulation" and stressed the inherent contradictions in the law between "particularity and predictability" and between "generality and diversity." Flathman (1994), pp. 301, 307. For other critiques, see Wolff (1971), containing essays by Wolff, Howard Zinn, Edgar Z. Friedenberg, Richard Barnet, and others; Shklar (1986); Unger (1986); and Kelman (1987).

11. Christian (1994), pp. 102–114.

12. Owen (1992).

13. Wortman (1976), p. 288.

14. Shepelev (1981), p. 110; Owen (1991), ch. 3; quotation from Shepelev (1981), p. 107.

15. Shepelev (1981), pp. 102–108; Valuev (1961), vol. 2, pp. 471–472.

16. On the new freight rate system, Shepelev (1981), pp. 170–171; on the state's purchases of railroads, Solov'eva (1986), p. 116; on American railroads, Chandler (1962), pp. 23, 32–38. The economic performance of railroads can be measured by several criteria, of which the percentage of a given country's rail network owned by the state is not definitive. According to Girard (1965), 262–264, the federal government of the United States refrained from ownership but regulated railroad companies under the Interstate Commerce Act (1887) and subsequent statutes. Likewise, British railroads remained in corporate hands. In contrast, state ownership of Belgian railroads gathered momentum after 1873, and in the German Empire 94 percent of the railroad network was owned by the imperial government in 1909. In both the U.S. and Germany, railroads operated efficiently despite the different forms of ownership. The financial weakness of many railroad companies in the Russian Empire from the 1880s onward; the shortcomings of the state's Trans-Siberian Railroad, discussed in Marks (1991), ch. 9: "Monument to Bungling"; and the collapse of the entire Russian system in 1917 after three years of war suggest that neither corporate nor state railroads performed well in Russia in comparison to those of other major economic powers in the early twentieth century. This complex issue has yet to be examined rigorously on the basis of available statistics.

17. Kipp (1994), pp. 115–138.

18. See the expressions of profound pessimism in the diary of Petr A. Valuev, the minister of interior from 1861 to 1868, for example, entry of November 13, 1864, Valuev (1961), vol. 1, p. 302.

19. Witte (1990), pp. 143–144.

20. Witte (1990), p. 328.

21. Witte (1990), p. 491.

22. Verstraete (1949), vol. 1, p. 241.

23. Kovalevskii (1991), pp. 66–67.

24. Von Laue (1954).

25. Translated excerpts from this document appeared in print for the first time in Shepelev (1995a). Parenthetical page numbers in the text refer to this translation. The document of 1893 escaped the notice of historians for many decades because it was buried in a blandly written proposal to expand the budget of the Department of Trade and Manufactures. For brief summaries and analyses of the document, see Shepelev (1981), pp. 204–213, and Aer (1995), pp. 134–138, 152.

26. Number from Owen (1992), file FLD1892. On the confusion in corporate law created by the practice of granting charters in the form of laws, see Owen (1991), pp. 26–27.

27. Shepelev (1991), pp.113, 235.

28. Witte (1990), pp. 246–248; quotation from p. 248.

29. Marks (1991), p. 123.

30. Shepelev (1981), pp. 233–235; Owen (1991), ch. 5.

31. Witte (1990), p. 322.

32. Horn and Kocka (1979), eds., with articles on England, France, Germany, and the U.S.A. in German and English.

33. Owen (1991), pp. 132–137; quotation from 136, citing A. I. Kaminka's treatise on business law, published in 1917.

34. Witte (1990), xxv–xxx; quotations from xxvii, xxviii.

35. Kahan (1989), p. 107.

36. Witte (1990), pp. 503–504.

37. Owen (1992). All figures exclude the Duchy of Finland, which had a separate system of corporate law and statistics.

38. Witte's harsh judgment of his political rival (1990), pp. 627–643, 657–658, 679–682, 704; quotations from pp. 657, 679.

39. Ajani (1992), pp. 11, 12.

40. Owen (1991), p. 158.

41. Gorbachev (1910), a manual of corporate management, contains brief sections on lawsuits (pp. 136–139, mostly dealing with questions of determining the place of a court's jurisdiction) and liquidation procedures (pp. 699–701) but no discussion of means of contract enforcement except resort to the courts. On credit bureaus in corporate form, see Owen (1992). According to Gorbachev, 701, procedures for liquidating credit bureaus appeared in the 1903 edition of the commercial code, so such institutions, in the form of unincorporated firms, must have existed at the turn of the century.

42. Shepelev (1981), pp. 111–112; Shepelev (1959), including, pp. 169–174, a chronology of the establishment and demise of Russian commercial banks, incomplete before 1990; Owen (1992).

43. Komitet s'ezdov (1917), pp. 21–28.

44. Shepelev (1981), pp. 215–216; Shepelev (1995b).

45. Besides Shepelev's monographs and articles, some of the most important studies are: Roosa (1967) and her many articles; Rieber (1982); Owen (1985); Hogan (1993); and McCaffray (1996).

46. Zipperstein (1985), p. 125.

47. On the merchant-Slavophile alliance of the 1850s and 1860s, see Owen (1981), chs. 2–3, and Rieber (1982), chs. 4–5. "Slavophile capitalism" is discussed at length in Owen (1995), ch. 5.

48. Walicki (1987).

49. On the spontaneous improvisation of rational-legal procedures of corporate management on the enterprise level at the Saratov Aviation Plant in 1992, see Hendley (1992).

50. Gaus (1994), p. 355.

CHAPTER 3

Russian Legal Tradition and the Rule of Law

Michael Newcity

Russia today gives the appearance of a lawless society. Crime, corruption, and popular distrust of law and legal institutions are pandemic. Introduction of "the rule of law" seems very remote.

The lawlessness that characterizes contemporary Russia has profound implications for efforts to reform the Russian economic and political systems. Laws, legal reforms, and a healthy respect for them provide the rules and framework within which a market economy functions. Without effective legal regulation, Russia's economy will remain predatory and corrupt, reinforcing popular mistrust of market reforms. Similarly, without an effective legal system—and a popular belief both in its effectiveness and in the subjection of political authority to the law—Russian political reform will remain stalled in the personal and authoritarian politics that have characterized it since the collapse of the Soviet Union. The prospects for a transition to genuine democratic governance will remain remote.

The prevalence of criminal behavior in Russia is indicated by a recent study conducted by the Russian Academy of Sciences' Institute of Sociology. According to reports that appeared in the Russian media, the Institute concluded that organized crime and corrupt government officials control over 40 percent of the Russian economy, including approximately two-thirds of all commercial institutions, 35,000 businesses, 400 banks, as many as 47 stock exchanges, and 1,500 government-owned enterprises.[1] In addition, the coordinator of this study, Dr. Olga Kryshchanovskaya, claimed that from 35 to 80 percent of the shares in various national financial institutions were controlled by Russian criminal organizations and that these organizations spend up to 35 percent of their receipts on bribes to government officials.[2]

Statistics from Russian studies such as this one, however, must be regarded with caution. Collecting crime statistics is always difficult, nowhere more so than in Russia. The authors of many Russian studies often fail to define the relevant concepts used in their studies, e.g., what is meant by "organized crime," what constitutes control of banks and other institutions, and so forth. Still, studies such as this one may, at least, indicate the broad magnitude of criminal behavior in Russia today.

The general disrespect for law is also reflected in the way in which widely accepted legal principles are applied in Russia. An example is the immunity of members of the parliament against prosecution. Under the Russian constitution of 1993, members of the State Duma and the Federal Council enjoy virtually complete immunity from criminal investigation and prosecution while they remain in office.[3] Efforts to narrow the scope of this parliamentary immunity have been rejected by the State Duma on several occasions. As a result, a number of individuals who are or have been the subjects of criminal investigations have stood for election to the State Duma. The first and most famous of these individuals was Sergei Mavrodi, the financier who created the MMM investment fund pyramid scheme. In October 1994, when the MMM bubble was bursting and criminal prosecution for tax evasion seemed likely, Mavrodi successfully stood for election to a seat in the State Duma (though he was not re-elected in the December 1995 Duma elections).[4] Others have followed his lead to the extent that, according to the Russian Central Electoral Commission, more than 80 individuals who are or have been the subjects of criminal investigations were standing for election to the State Duma in the December 1994 elections.

Open and notorious lawless behavior by powerful criminals and government officials reinforces popular cynicism and disrespect for the law and its institutions. Evasion of commercial and financial laws, especially tax law, has become a national habit. Russian individuals and businesses routinely evade their taxes; claiming to do otherwise would make it impossible for them to live or remain in business.[5] In 1994, the government collected only 60 percent of projected tax revenues, with the missing 40 percent attributed primarily to tax evasion by individuals and businesses large and small.[6] Copyrights, trademarks, and other intellectual property rights are also universally ignored. The International Intellectual Property Alliance, which represents eight copyright-related trade associations, recently estimated that nearly 100 percent of videos sold in Russia are pirated,[7] and the Software Publishers Association estimates that the rate of piracy of computer software in Russia is 95 percent.[8]

The pervasive evasion of laws like these—and the apparent failure of Russian society to attach any opprobrium to these and many other breaches of the law—reinforces a universal and long-standing popular cynicism about the capacity of legal institutions to regulate commercial and other spheres of activity. This attitude was reflected in the comments of a young Russian film director who recently finished a film in Russia only to see pirated copies of it circulating in Russia's video stores and broadcast on television within weeks of its commercial release. When asked whether he would consider going to court to protect his rights, the director said, "Everything is corrupt and there is nowhere to turn. To go to court is expensive and besides, it just means more bribes."[9]

Apart from this criminal behavior, legal instruments and institutions are often absent or ineffective. Russian legislation and regulations, whether laws adopted by the Federal Assembly, decrees issued by the President, or various kinds of regulations issued by the Council of Ministers and the individual government agencies, are frequently poorly drafted, vague, internally inconsistent, and contradictory of other legislation or regulations. A significant reason behind Russia's fitful economic reforms is that the laws necessary for a modern market economy—contract law, securities regulations, laws governing ownership and security interests in land, bankruptcy, and so forth—have emerged slowly and the laws that have been promulgated are often best—and charitably—described as murky. Once adopted, these laws are often ignored, both by the population at large and by the government officials charged with enforcing them.

The attitudes exhibited by most Russians—ordinary individuals as well as government officials—towards law and legal institutions are hardly respectful. Most Russians seem distrustful of courts and legal processes, regarding them as corrupt and arbitrary. Furthermore, it appears that among many Russians little opprobrium attaches to ignoring the law. This popular disrespect for law and legal institutions is reciprocated by government officials who seem equally disdainful of legal requirements and processes; by bureaucrats, police, and security services who are arbitrary and corrupt; and by a judicial system that is corrupt and distrusted.

In general, the notion that government officials' behavior should be limited by constitutional or statutory provisions has been slow to catch on in Russia. Russia was the last European country to adopt a constitution, and a true commitment to constitutionalism has never fully developed there. For a short period in 1991 and 1992, it seemed that a sense of constitutionalism was developing among Russia's political elite. Yeltsin's attack on the August 1991 coup attempt as "anticonstitutional" suggested that constitutional and legal values were rising to a higher level, at least in Russian political rhetoric, than they had previously occupied. After the coup, the Russian Constitutional Court showed signs that in time it might develop into a significant institution for promoting respect for constitutional and legal values.

These positive developments were overwhelmed in the bitter struggle between President Yeltsin and the Russian Supreme Soviet in the fall of 1993. The shelling of the White House and the December 1993 Yeltsin Constitution, which eviscerated the Constitutional Court, represented major setbacks for the emergence of constitutionalism and the rule of law in Russia.

Reasons for Russia's Apparent Lawlessness

A central issue for anyone interested in Russian economic and political reform must be the parlous state of Russian law and legality, why Russians obey—or don't obey—the law. If the Russian government is ever to exercise the authority necessary to introduce and carry-through important economic reforms, and if Russia is to achieve the degree of social and political stability necessary to implement these reforms, it must foster a more law-abiding atmosphere. How, then, has Russia reached this lawless state?

There are undoubtedly many contributing factors. Political and economic instability, social upheaval, and decades of a cynical communist regime that emphasized the political subordination of legal institutions have all contributed to further weakened legal consciousness in Russia.

Conventional social theory suggests that compliance with the law can be motivated by rewards and punishments.[10] This, of course, was the traditional method for securing compliance with the law in the Soviet Union. At present, however, the ability of the Russian government to secure compliance in this manner, primarily by exercising coercion, is much less effective than it was under the Soviet regime and is hardly desirable. The coercive powers of the state are considerably reduced, the government itself is much less effective in articulating its desires in this regard, and the political and social costs associated with these techniques are substantial. In Russia today, the mechanisms of coercion are inadequate to secure compliance with the law.

Manipulating rewards and punishment, however, is not the only effective method for achieving compliance with the law. As Tom Tyler has demonstrated in the American context, voluntary compliance can also be based on normative considerations, in particular a popular belief in the legitimacy of the law and legal authorities, a sense that "one ought to obey the law."[11] According to Tyler, the strength or weakness of a belief in the legitimacy of legal authority is "strongly connected to judgments of the fairness of the procedures through which authorities make decisions."[12]

Though there is no empirical evidence from Russia to compare with Tyler's study of Americans, we might assume that the possibility of achieving voluntary compliance on these normative bases in Russia is, for the foreseeable future, extremely remote. Intuition and experience tell us that what is dramatically different in the two countries is the strength of the popular belief in the legitimacy of legal authority. Russians as a group do not seem to believe that the procedures through which authorities make decisions are fair and, thus, they do not believe in the legitimacy of the rules that result. In the absence of either effective coercive power by the state, a strongly held moral norm that motivates compliance, or a pervasive sense of legitimacy, Russians often see no particular reason why they ought to obey the law.

The disdain by the Russian population of the law and legal institutions is not surprising. There is little in the Russian experience of the law that would warrant respect or engender a sense of legitimacy. Moreover, there is a circularity in the process by which a sense of legitimacy might be generated. As long as Russia's political leaders and government officials show so little respect for law and its in-

RUSSIAN LEGAL TRADITION AND THE RULE OF LAW   45

stitutions and processes—as long as they continue to show their disdain for law by acting arbitrarily—the positive experience that might begin to engender a sense of legitimacy will not occur.

These are hardly novel observations. Anyone who observes Russia today can comment on the pervasive lawlessness that characterizes that society. What does bear emphasizing is how deeply this disrespect for the law and legal institutions, both on the part of political leaders as well as the general population, is rooted in Russian culture.

In discussing these issues, many American policy makers and advisers seem to assume that Russian disrespect for law is the product of 75 years of communism and the pervasive chaos that characterizes contemporary Russia. By contrast, these attitudes are not new. They long pre-date the Revolution. There is, in fact, a continuity in the Russian legal tradition. Many of the current characteristics of the Russian legal system—overlapping, contradictory, and ambiguous statutes, decrees, and orders; bureaucratic arbitrariness; courts that are often incompetent or corrupt; and a popular disrespect for the law—characterized pre-revolutionary Russia as well. Popular attitudes towards the law and legal institutions were distrustful and cynical then, just as they are today.

These attitudes are deeply rooted in the Russian history and tradition. The Russian legal tradition is fundamentally different from the legal tradition that prevails in Western Europe and North America. Russian culture historically has been predominantly anti-legalistic. For this reason, it is unrealistic to expect that a Western-style respect for law and legal institutions and a commitment to the rule of law will develop in Russia in a short period of time.

Reasons for the Differences in the Russian Legal Tradition

The following discussion compares the Russian legal tradition with the Western legal tradition characteristic of Western Europe, Canada, and the United States. A discussion of legal traditions is not concerned with specific legal rules or doctrines that are in effect in a particular place at a particular time, but rather relates to the concept described by Merryman:

> [A legal tradition] is a set of deeply rooted, historically conditioned attitudes about the nature of law, about the role of law in the society and the polity, about the proper organization and operation of a legal system, and about the way law is or should be made, applied, studied, perfected, and taught. The legal tradition relates the legal system to the culture of which it is a partial expression. It puts the legal system into cultural perspective.[13]

The reasons why the Russian legal tradition is fundamentally different from the Western legal tradition are varied, but the most important are these four:

- The influence of Russian Orthodoxy on the development of Russian legal consciousness;
- A tradition of absolutism that has been virtually uninterrupted since the sixteenth century;
- Delayed economic development in Russia, with the persistence of a traditional peasant culture that emphasized the communal ownership of land well into the twentieth century;
- 75 years of a communist regime that emphasized as a matter of theory that law was superstructure, that as a matter of constitutional principle raised the CPSU above constitutional limitations, and that practiced a highly politicized and increasingly corrupt brand of law.

The Influence of Russian Orthodoxy on the Development of Russian Legal Consciousness

To understand the influence of Russian Orthodoxy on the development of the Russian legal consciousness and tradition, it is first necessary to understand how Western Christianity shaped the Western legal tradition.

Whether there is a distinctive Western legal tradition shared by the nations of Western Europe, the United States, Britain, and the other common law countries, and what its features may be, certainly can be contentious.[14] Harold Berman has argued that the principal characteristics of the Western legal tradition include:

- A sharp distinction between legal institutions and other types of institutions;
- Existence of a legal profession, trained at professional schools;
- Belief in the concept of an integrated, coherent body of law;
- "The coexistence and competition within the same community of diverse jurisdictions and diverse legal systems," which Berman states is the Western legal tradition's "most distinctive characteristic."[15]

Perhaps the most important characteristic of the Western legal tradition as identified by Berman is a belief in the supremacy of law over political authority. According to Berman,

[While] it remained for the American Revolution to contribute the word "constitutionalism," nevertheless, since the twelfth century in all countries of the West, even under absolute monarchies, it has been widely said and often accepted that in some important respects law transcends politics. The monarch, it is argued, may make law, but he may not make it arbitrarily, and until he has remade it—lawfully—he is bound by it.[16]

It is in connection with this last characteristic that the concept of the rule of law is introduced as an integral part of the Western legal tradition. Though there are a number of different definitions of the rule of law, some of which might make the concept applicable exclusively to Britain and other common law countries, the features of this concept that are most important for purposes of this discussion are as follows:

- the supremacy of regular law as opposed to arbitrary, discretionary authority; and
- equality before the law.

The principal influences in shaping the distinctive concepts and beliefs that characterize the Western legal tradition, especially the rule of law concept, have been Roman-inspired legality as transmitted through the Western Christian churches and the notions of reciprocity inherent in Western European feudalism. These influences, and others that have shaped modern notions of the rule of law and legality in Western Europe, however, were missing from Russian culture.

Russian legal development began to follow a substantially different trajectory from comparable developments in Western Europe during the eleventh through thirteenth centuries. The events that were most immediately responsible for starting Russian legal development on this different trajectory were the schism between the Byzantine and Roman churches in the eleventh century and the Mongol invasion in the thirteenth century. These events account for the first two of the reasons why the Russian legal tradition is fundamentally different from the Western legal tradition.

Russia, like Turkey, Japan, Egypt, and many other countries, adopted Romanistic legal forms—principally legal codes—in the eighteenth, nineteenth, and twentieth centuries. The *Svod Zakonov* of the imperial period were not especially good adaptations of Romanistic legal forms, but these codes and other features of Russian legislation of that period reflect a Roman influence. Nevertheless, Russia never developed a legalistic tradition. The reason for this is that it was Christianized by Byzantium instead of by Rome.

Western Europe did not receive Roman legal culture directly. It was transmitted and refracted primarily through the Roman Church, which fostered a legalistic, rather than a mystical, world view drawn from Roman culture. This contrasts sharply with the world view fostered by the Russian Orthodox Church.

One of the basic reasons for the separation of the Roman and Byzantine churches in the eleventh century was a sharp disagreement over the efforts by Rome to establish the Bishop of Rome as the sole head of the church and to separate the clergy from the control of secular rulers. In Western Europe, the Church's efforts to establish itself as an entity with authority and jurisdiction separate from and superior to secular authority sparked a revival of interest in Roman law. Roman constitutional principles were used by Pope Gregory and his supporters to bolster their case for papal supremacy. Thihs led to a systematization of ecclesiastical and secular legal systems. The result, in the West, was a stimulation of legalistic methods of analysis, professionalization of lawyers and judges, and the emergence of law schools. The Church was intent on establishing a universal body of ecclesiastical legal principles that would bind Western Christendom together regardless of secular divisions. The origins of the Western notion of law as an autonomous body of principles to which secular authorities are subject can be traced to this period. The Orthodox church, however, rejected the independence and supremacy of the papacy and remained an integral part of the state. In this way, Russia missed the most important foundations of the Western concept of the rule of law.

As Berman pointed out, one of the most characteristic features of the Western legal tradition was the struggle between different legal systems in a single country. Whether it was the struggle between the ecclesiastical and secular authorities, or, as in the case of England, the struggle between ecclesiastical, mercantile, common law, and equity legal systems, the countries of Western Europe had to resolve these struggles. In doing so, the legal systems of Western Europe learned a great deal about principles of defining and limiting jurisdiction, much of it drawn from Roman law. And in drawing these lines between the different, competing legal systems—by establishing rational, legal principles to define jurisdiction, to determine where legitimate authority begins and ends—Western Europe established the foundation for the rule of law.

In reviving Roman law and refining these concepts of jurisdiction, institutions and techniques were developed that gave Western culture its distinctive legalistic cast. Principal among these were the university law schools, which began to appear in Europe in the twelfth century, and the scholastic method, which developed strongly legalistic intellectual techniques for interpreting and applying authoritative and apparently contradictory texts.

These institutions and influences, of course, were absent from the Orthodox world. Inasmuch as the Orthodox Church was committed to the unity of secular and religious authority, the jurisdictional struggles that contributed to the emergence of the rule of law in Western Europe did not occur.[17] Though there were ecclesiastical courts in medieval Russia, they were chartered by the prince and constituted a complementary, rather than a competing, legal system.[18]

Apart from these institutional and historical features of Orthodoxy that set it apart from the highly legalistic Roman Church, some of the basic characteristics of Russian Orthodox religious beliefs foster an anti-legalistic world view. In Orthodoxy, the emphasis is placed on the personal "religious experience"; the mystical versus the intellectual experience. Orthodox religious ceremonies emphasize the beauty of the liturgy rather than the intellectual force of the homily. The quintessential exercise in religious law-giving—the sermon—which has characterized Western European Christian church services in recent centuries, is absent from Orthodox services. Most Russian churches, in fact, lack a pulpit.

The Roman Church emphasized the importance of promulgating authoritative interpretations of scriptural texts, but the Russian Orthodox religious tradition places little emphasis on either authoritative interpretations or authoritative texts. While the center for medieval Western thought was Church-supported universities, no universities were established in Russia until recent centuries, and then they were established by the state. Moreover, while the Latin language preserved by the Roman Church established a lingua franca and permitted access to the old Roman texts, the use of a national language in the Russian Church permitted access to very little—not even Greek texts that it might otherwise have taken from Byzantium.

To summarize, the different Christian churches fostered very different world views. In Western Europe, the emphasis on competing legal jurisdictions, and a highly rational, scholastic, textual orientation to religion, fostered a very legalistic culture. To Russians, on the other hand, "Christianity always appeared to them not as imposed by authority, but something expressing their own personal relation to God."[19] In Russia, there was none of the regulatory mechanism established by the Roman Church, employing authoritative interpretations of texts and other legalistic devices, to determine the "correct" view.

The writings of Dostoevsky reflect some of the hostility this Orthodox world view held for the Roman-inspired legalistic culture of Western Europe. Andrzej Walicki has written:

> The idea of the Church transforming itself into an omnipotent state, giving bread to the people, indeed, but at the cost of depriving them of their inner freedom, was for Dostoevsky a danger peculiar to the West, inherent in its Roman heritage. Like the Slavophiles, he thought that Roman Catholicism and Western socialism were significantly related to each other, as two variants of "unity without freedom." Russia, in his view, represented a completely different world since the Russian Orthodox Church was not permeated by the pernicious influence of the juridical rationalism of ancient Rome. Because of this, he argued, Russian autocracy should not be regarded as a menace to personal freedom.[20]

In this way, Russian Orthodoxy—the first major element contributing to a distinctive Russian legal tradition—reinforced the second major element: autocracy.

The Russian Autocratic Tradition

In Western feudalism, it was common to characterize the bases for monarchies as contractual, involving reciprocal obligations on the part of both the lord and the vassals. Moreover, Western feudal states were characterized by a high degree of fragmentation of authority, by overlapping jurisdiction and authority. Feudalism as it developed in Russia differed from the West most notably in the absence of reciprocity. While the Russian system of feudalism established under Ivan the Great did exchange land for service, this system was established in the context of a highly centralized state in which the sovereign owed none of the obligations to his vassals that were common in the much more decentralized feudal states of Western Europe.[21]

In the West, the reciprocity inherent to Western feudalism, reinforced by the separation of secular and ecclesiastical jurisdictions, produced monarchies that recognized the limitations imposed on their power, that they were subject to the law. Even absolute monarchs in Western Europe, such as James I in England or Louis XIV in France, acknowledged the implicit constraints of natural law principles on which their power rested.

The same does not apply to the Russian tsars. The models for the Russian monarchy were the Byzantine emperor and the Mongol khan, both of which modeled an absolute, centralized monarchy as compared with the more limited monarchies that characterized Western Europe. This model of absolute authoritarian power has persisted in Russia from medieval time to the present.

Attempts in the nineteenth century to reform and rationalize Russian law by introducing Western-style legal procedures and by granting individuals greater independence and personal authority on economic matters were rescinded when they struck at the heart of Russian autocracy (including the power of the tsar's ministers and bureaucrats). Attempts to reform Russian law to accommodate the emerging capitalist economy conflicted with the desire to maintain autocratic rule. Emphasis on formal justice necessary to cope with this new economy meant greater emphasis on abstractions, legal professionals, and granting greater authority to professionals and individuals. This, of course, challenged the authority of the autocrat and his bureaucracy, a conflict that was resolved in favor of the autocracy.

Delayed Economic Development

Industrialization and economic development in Russia lagged far behind these developments in Western Europe. Modern Western laws, legal institutions, and attitudes toward the state and law that developed during the time of the Industrial Revolution in the late eighteenth century failed to take root in Russia. Instead, peasant society with an emphasis on communal ownership of land and hostile attitudes toward state-authored laws and legal institutions persisted on a large scale up to the 1917 Revolution.

As of 1892, in European Russia, over 90 percent of agricultural land occupied by peasants was in communal ownership. In 1905, 43 percent of all cultivable land in European Russia was under communal control.[22] This meant that though each household had a right to an allotment on an equal basis, ownership was vested in the commune. The commune had the right to repartition the land to reapportion the amount of land in order to equalize the economic opportunities of the households. In this regard, the Russian communes were different from those in Ukraine and White Russia, where communal ownership of land was much less common.[23] Ironically, the abolition of serfdom in 1861 actually strengthened this communal ownership, since the relevant decrees made enclosure and the withdrawal of a peasant from the commune virtually impossible.

The nature of land-holding in the Russian peasant commune, which persisted until relatively recently, provides a partial explanation why the prospects for private ownership of agricultural land have not been enthusiastically received by many Russian farmers. The tradition of small, self-sufficient, single-family farms has never been well-established in much of Russia. Moreover, the nature of Russian peasant society itself may provide reasons why many Russians are hostile to the law.

In Russian peasant communes, most affairs were regulated by customary practices, which were generally regarded as having greater significance than state law. Matters were decided on an ad hoc basis "according to justice" rather than on the basis of carefully spelled-out legal norms.[24] The peasants' attitude toward state-derived law was one of suspicion and, when possible, disobedience. As Boris Mironov wrote:

> The peasant deemed it "immoral" to deceive a neighbor or relative, but to deceive a government official or landlord was quite a different matter—indeed, that was a moral deed worthy of encouragement. . . . The peasants had one morality when dealing with members of their own commune and quite another for outsiders, especially those who were not peasants.[25]

This attitude toward legal obligations, in which individuals apply a high standard to obligations owed to group members and a very low standard to state-generated obligations, should be familiar to anyone who deals in Russia today.

One other aspect of the effect of Russia's economic development on its legal tradition that ought to be mentioned in passing is the effect that the delayed development of capitalism in Russia had on the development of Russian private law. Many of the most important private law innovations in the West—in contract and tort law in particular—occurred concurrently with industrial development in the nineteenth and twentieth centuries. Not only did these developments barely affect Russia, but the behavioral aspects that accompanied them—the movement of legal obligations "from Status to Contract" in Henry Maine's memorable phrase[26]—were not experienced in Russia.

The Communist Legacy

To the degree that a modern legal consciousness akin to the Western legal tradition might ever have developed in Russia, those prospects were dramatically short-circuited by the Bolshevik Revolution. The communists advocated an ideology that emphasized the subordination of law and legality to underlying economic realities. Throughout their rule, they displayed disregard and disdain for legal restraints and the rule of law, building on the existing Russian cynicism about the independence and authority of the law. When the pervasive corruption of the Brezhnev period and the current political and economic chaos is added to this mix, it can hardly be wondered why Russians today are skeptical about "law's majesty." Little in their history or experience persuades them that the law and legal institutions are really worth respecting.

What Is to Be Done?

If it is true that the Russian legal tradition is profoundly different from the Western legal tradition, and that at present there is little inclination to accept the rule of law in Russian political and economic life, what significance do these conclusions have for the prospects of political and economic reform in Russia?

While the discussion above has painted a picture of the central elements of the Russian legal tradition in admittedly broad-brush strokes, it is possible to suggest several conclusions:

Anyone expecting the Russian population to embrace whole-heartedly the rule of law is likely to be disappointed. The rule of law, the notion that political authority should be subject to legal/constitutional limitations and that individuals are entitled to certain fundamental rights including due process, is a concept with little grounding in Russian tradition. That is not to say that tradition is destiny and that Russia could never embrace the rule of law. It does suggest, however, that there is little in Russian culture or experience, and little in contemporary life, that would create the conditions under which a commitment to the rule of law will flourish.

Embracing the rule of law, however, is different from becoming a law-abiding society. The rule of law as used in this analysis is largely a Western cultural construct. There are many countries throughout the world that are law-abiding without a commitment to the rule of law. In this sense, the issue is whether individuals act in accordance with and observe the legal obligations that arise from their private economic and other relationships. Do they abide by their contracts, do they observe the securities laws, do they pay their taxes, and so forth? If the Russian economy is stabilized, if political life becomes less chaotic, it is certainly possible that Russians will begin to act more law-abiding. However, if Tom Tyler's analysis of the reasons why people obey the law is applicable to Russia, a more law-abiding Russia will depend on the emergence of either a stronger and more coercive state or a greater popular belief in the legitimacy of the Russian state and its laws.

Notes

1. *Izvestiia*, September 21, 1995, p. 5.
2. *Izvestiia*, September 21, 1995, p. 5.
3. *Konstitutsiia Rossiiskoi Federatsii* (1993), Art. 98.
4. *Washington Post*, November 1, 1994, p. A17.

5. For the tax burden of Russian entrepreneurs, see also Frye in this volume.

6. *Nezavisimaya gazeta*, May 23, 1995, p. 4.

7. *Washington Times*, February 27, 1995, p. A1.

8. *Computer Dealer News*, March 22, 1995, p. 12.

9. *The New York Times*, February 28, 1994, p. C11.

10. Tom Tyler (1990), pp. 20–21.

11. Tyler (1990), p. 161.

12. Tyler (1990), p. 162.

13. John Henry Merryman (1969), p. 2.

14. Harold J. Berman (1963), p. 1.

15. Berman (1983), pp. 7–10.

16. Berman (1983), p. 9.

17. Berman (1963), p. 199.

18. Daniel H. Kaiser (1980), p. 170.

19. John Meyendorff (1976), p. 316.

20. Andrzej Walicki (1987), p. 78.

21. Harold Berman (1963), p. 197.

22. Francis M. Watters (1968), pp. 146–147, 151.

23. Watters (1968), pp. 134–5.

24. Boris Mironov (1990), p. 12.

25. Mironov, p. 12.

26. Henry Maine (1861), p. 141.

CHAPTER 4

Constitutions and Economic Reform in the Post-Communist Transitions

Joel S. Hellman

An interesting debate has emerged on the role of the constitution—the very foundation of the rule of law—in the process of economic transition. The debate focuses on two questions: Is a stable constitution necessary for successful economic reform? Should the constitution in a transitional political economy be designed primarily to restrain the state from intervening in the economy or to enable the state to implement complex and unpopular economic reforms? The dominant view sees the constitution as a crucial mechanism for establishing the credibility of commitments in the transitional economy.[1] By enhancing the stability of the political system and restraining the discretionary power of the state, the constitution gives economic actors the confidence to enter into contracts and to make long-term investments that are critical for both the initial adoption and ultimate success of economic reform. The dissenting view claims that the adoption of necessary, but inevitably unpopular, economic reforms requires a state with sufficient capacity and flexibility to push through difficult policy choices, to outmaneuver political opponents, and to create the institutional foundation for a new, stable order.[2] In its zeal to prevent the tyranny of the state, an overly rigid constitution can deprive the reformers of the very powers necessary for effective policy-making in the midst of a transition. While one approach advocates the early adoption of a permanent constitution, the other sees advantages in interim constitutions or postponing constitution-making until after the economic transformation. While one supports the idea of *negative constitutionalism,* the other asserts the value of *positive constitutionalism* in the peculiar context of transitions.

So far, the debate has been conducted in largely normative terms. Particular case studies have been used to illustrate arguments, rather than test them. Most of these cases have been drawn from the distant past—England during the Glorious Revolution (see Weingast, 1993 for England), France under the Old Regime (see Root, 1989 for France), the drafting of the U.S. constitution (see Hardin, 1994 for the U.S.)—while the lessons have been applied to the current post-communist transitions. But after more than five years of political and economic transition, the post-communist countries now provide an ideal opportunity to test these competing approaches. The countries already show substantial variation in the extent of economic reform adopted, in the timing of their new constitutions, and in the pattern of political institutions established by those constitutions. Has the early adoption of a constitution facilitated or hindered the process of economic reforms? Do interim constitutions undermine the credibility of commitments necessary for successful reform? Are certain constitutional configurations of political institutions more conducive to reform than others? Rather than suggest what the post-communist countries should do, we can now begin to examine the implications of what they have done to evaluate our general theories of the politics of economic reform.

The chapter begins with a closer review of the theoretical debate about the role of the constitution in the process of economic reform. I attempt to apply the competing approaches to the Russian case, suggesting that this case alone cannot serve as the firm basis for any generalizable claims about the relationship of the constitution and economic reform. Instead, I broaden the focus to conduct a cross-sectional statistical analysis of 25 of the 27 post-communist countries to test systematically for the effects of constitutions on the process of economic reform.

The Debate

Much of the work on the role of the constitution in the economy comes out of the literature often referred to as positive political economy.[3] One important focus of this literature has been the problem of time-inconsistency in the politics of economic policy-making. Simply stated, time-inconsistent policies are those in which policy-makers have an incentive to deviate from previously announced policies after economic actors have already altered their behavior in accordance with those policies. Once actors recognize that policy-makers have such incentives, they will base their response to any proposed policy on the expectation that deviations may occur in the future, leading to suboptimal behavior. If policy-makers could make a binding commitment to a proposed policy from the start—so that the costs of deviating from the policy would be prohibitively high—then time-inconsistency becomes irrelevant. One way for policy-makers to make their commitments credible is to bind themselves by a set of rules that limit their discretionary power. This insight has led to a new recognition of the importance of political institutions in the process of economic policy-making.

Economic reform is also beset by time-inconsistency problems. The implementation of reform requires individuals to make short-term sacrifices in consumption for the promise of future gains. The success of reform also requires individuals to make long-term investments in retraining and restructuring. Yet what prevents the state from reversing reform prior to the achievement of these gains or from confiscating them in the face of fiscal crises or redistributional pressures? Consequently, effective economic reform requires a credible, ex ante commitment on the part of the state not to expropriate the gains from reform ex post. In the absence of such a commitment, individuals will discount the potential gains from reform by the political risk that current policies will be reversed in the future, thus weakening the initial gains for reform and reducing the willingness to invest in the reforming economy. To be successful, economic reform requires more than a well-designed plan, but a state that has the capacity to make a credible commitment to that plan.

The recognition of the time-inconsistency problem in economic reform has focused attention on the role of the constitution in the reform process. As the institution that defines and, thus, constrains the power of the state, the constitution is generally regarded as the primary commitment mechanism in the political system. (For a development view of this argument, see North, 1989 and Weingast, 1993.) By promoting the values of stability and accountability, the constitution enhances the credibility of the state's commitments. It stabilizes expectations about the behavior of the state. It places limits on the discretionary powers of the state. It increases the costs of major shifts in the institutional rules of the game. As a result, political economists have argued that the initiation and ultimate success of economic reform require as much attention to designing an effective constitution as to getting the prices right.

What type of constitution is most conducive to economic reform? If the key problem is the state's threat to expropriate the gains from reform for its own advantage or for that of a particular constituency, then the most effective constitution will be one that maximizes constraints on the state's discretionary power to intervene in the economy. Thus, the credible commitment argument leads not only to an emphasis on the importance of a constitution, but also to a strong preference for negative constitutionalism—the notion that constitutions should be designed primarily to restrain the power of the state.

Paradoxically, it has been a scholar of liberalism—Stephen Holmes—that has raised the strongest objections to the relevance of Western models of a stable and liberal constitution for the post-communist transitions. Though he agrees that such a constitution should be the ultimate goal of these societies, he questions whether it is appropriate for the particular challenges and opportunities of the transition period (see Holmes, 1995). Indeed, he fears that the rush to adopt a Western-style constitution in the midst of the transition could ultimately undermine efforts to create a stable and liberal constitutional order in the long run.

Holmes's approach to the role of the constitution in the politics of economic reform is rooted in an analysis of the particular dynamics of transition periods.[4] He argues that the sheer magnitude of the tasks associated with simultaneous political and economic reform in a period of unprecedented social change places a premium on centralized executive power and institutional flexibility. Reforms, even those designed to establish a liberal democratic order, cannot necessarily be implemented through liberal-democratic means. The politics of reform, in his view, consists of ad hoc decision-making, technocratic skills, and strategic maneuvering to strike bargains among competing social groups. Compact executives with concentrated power are more likely to succeed than contentious legislatures or broad-based political coalitions. Moreover, such executives require the capacity to adjust quickly to changing constraints and opportunities. Institutions that place rigid restrictions on executive power deprive reformers of the flexibility necessary for effective policy-making in a highly fluid and uncertain context.

In contrast to the view that the role of the constitution in the process of economic reform is to disable the state's capacity to intervene in the economy, Holmes argues that it should enable the state to meet the complex and contentious challenges of reform. Transitional systems have a "crying need" for strong executives that can combine effectiveness and legitimacy in a context of rapid social change.[5] However, he recognizes that high levels of state discretionary power and institutional flexibility would not be desirable in a long-term constitutional order. Consequently, Holmes argues that interim constitutions—or what he calls "stopgap constitutionalism" (see Holmes, 1995)—might be more appropriate for transitional systems or, alternatively, that the process of constitution-making be postponed until after major economic reforms have been implemented.[6]

While the credible commitments argument stresses the importance of stability and predictability established by a constitution, Holmes emphasizes the virtues of ambiguity in interim constitutions (see Holmes, 1993b, p. 39). By leaving the distribution of political power incompletely defined, interim constitutions create some flexibility for executives to maneuver around the inevitable opposition to economic reform from legislatures and existing state bureaucracies. Politicians need to be able to renegotiate the rules of the game while they are playing the game to insure their capacity to re-adjust to changing circumstances. By leaving some ambiguity in the rules of the game, stopgap constitutionalism creates room for executives to build state capacity.

Two sharply diverging views on the role of constitutions in the process of economic reform have emerged. Both sides share the goals of establishing a liberal democratic constitution and a market economy, but differ on the best path to achieve them. The dominant view in the debate, so far, reflects the increasing prominence of credible commitments arguments in the broader political economy literature. Constitutions—or, more specifically, liberal constitutions that restrain the discretionary power of the state to intervene in the economy—are seen as political commitment mechanisms critical to the adoption and success of economic reform. Holmes presents a strong challenge to this view based on a recognition of the particular dynamics of political systems in transition. Evaluating these competing views against the evidence from the post-communist cases promises not only to shed light on our understanding of the role of the constitution in the process of economic reform, but also to bring some preliminary empirical evidence to bear on two different theoretical approaches to the political economy of reform.

The Case of Russia

The case of Russia can be used as a benchmark by both sides of the debate. On the one hand, battles over the constitutional division of powers can be blamed for undermining economic reform, suggesting the importance of a constitutional agreement for creating the political stability and credibility necessary for reform. On the other hand, the extreme concentration of presidential power following the violent conflict with parliament, encoded in what many see as a temporary, strategic constitution, is often credited with advancing the process of economic reform after December 1993. Different interpretations of the politics of economic reform in Russia support different poles of the debate over the role of the constitution in the economic reform process.

One issue is beyond dispute: economic reform in Russia quickly became enmeshed in conflicts over the distribution of political power—primarily between the president and the legislature—that were played out in constitutional politics.[7] These conflicts had a debilitating effect on economic reform.[8] As early as April 1992, less than four months after the introduction of a comprehensive price liberalization and macroeconomic stabilization program, parliamentary opponents of reform began a strategy of attacking the powers of the president. At the Sixth Congress of People's Deputies,[9] opponents of reform threatened to curtail the president's power over government appointments. Yeltsin responded by calling for a referendum on a new constitution that threatened the very existence of the Congress as a legislative institution.

At the Seventh Congress of People's Deputies in December 1992, opponents of economic reform blocked Yeltsin's attempts to extend his control over ministerial appointments and threatened to withhold approval for an extension of the president's decree-making powers. In response, Yeltsin explicitly argued that economic reform required a clarification of the separation of powers among Russian political institutions. Once again, he used the threat of a constitutional referendum to extract concessions from the Congress. Yet at an extraordinary session of the Congress in March 1993, Yeltsin's decree powers were sharply curtailed, leading him to threaten to declare an extraordinary presidential regime to advance the process of economic reforms.

After scoring an important victory in an April 1993 popular referendum on his leadership, Yeltsin moved quickly to try to seize control over the constitution-making process by creating his own constitutional convention. He also attempted to dilute the power of the Congress of People's Deputies and the Supreme Soviet by creating a Federation Council, a consultative body composed of representatives of Russia's regions. These moves led the Supreme Soviet to adopt a series of economic measures designed to cripple the president and reverse the process of economic reform. In July 1993, the Supreme Soviet approved a state budget of 22.5 trillion rubles that doubled the deficit forecast by the Yeltsin government and disqualified Russia for disbursements of Western aid. The parliament suspended a presidential decree that accelerated the pace of privatization and curtailed the powers of the State Committee on the Management of State Property (GKI) to manage state enterprises slated for privatization. The Supreme Soviet also tightened its control over the Central Bank as a prelude to a new, massive infusion of cheap credits into the Russian economy.

The Supreme Soviet's unrelenting obstruction of the government's economic reform program was the pretext for a military offensive against the parliament in early October. Following the violent destruction of the legislature, the Yeltsin government moved quickly to implement several hundred administrative decrees designed to accelerate the pace of economic reform. The chairman of the Central Bank was placed under government authority. Macroeconomic policy was tightened with the implementation of greater controls over credits and subsidies. There was a lifting of many remaining price controls, primarily on energy and bread, and a further liberalization of foreign trade. Yeltsin also moved to strengthen his control over the regions by disbanding regional legislatures (soviets) and passing administrative power to his own appointed regional representatives.

Yeltsin consolidated his victory shortly thereafter with the approval by referendum of a new constitution. The constitution creates what Holmes calls a "super-presidentialist system" (see Holmes, 1994). The president is granted nearly unconstrained decree power. Presidential vetoes can only be over-ridden by a two-thirds majority of both houses of the new legislature, allowing the president to govern with the support of only one-third of the deputies. Legislative votes of no confidence in the government are virtually meaningless, since the first vote can be ignored and the second gives the president the option to call new parliamentary elections. In adopting a constitution to prevent the political instability of the previous period and to promote economic reform, Russia moved not to disable the state, but to concentrate and expand executive powers in an effort to enable the state.

An assessment of the adoption of the constitution and the consolidation of presidential power on the process of economic reform depends upon an assessment of economic performance after the parliamentary elections and constitutional referendum in December 1993. Unfortunately, the economic reform picture has been mixed.[10] Several prominent economic reformers left the government (Yegor Gaidar and Boris Fedorov), while others were promoted (Anatolii Chubais). Inflation fell sharply during the first half of 1994, but then began a steep rise reaching 18 percent per month by January 1995 before falling again. Privatization proceeded at a breakneck speed through the end of June 1994, but slowed considerably as the voucher phase of privatization ended and investment tenders began. Agricultural privatization has remained stalled. The ruble began a steep fall in late September 1994, beginning to stabilize in mid-1995. With this mixed record, it is difficult to make any clear assessments of the role of the constitution and the consolidation of presidential power on the course of economic reform.[11]

The case of Russia raises more questions than it answers about the constitution and economic reform. Does the Russian experience highlight the dangers of embarking on economic reform without a stable constitutional division of powers or the problems that constitution-making itself raises for the adoption of economic reform? Did the adoption of a constitution—albeit a superpresidential constitution—provide the stability and predictability to enhance the prospects of economic reform? Indeed, should the Russian constitution itself, crafted strategically for a particular individual, be considered a permanent constitution or merely an interim constitution passed to meet the challenges of economic reform? Was the consolidation of presidential power necessary to continue economic reform or was it a trade-off that ultimately hindered the process of reform?

With competing theories about the role of the constitution in economic reform and different views of the course of reform in Russia, there is no foundation for a definitive interpretation of this relationship in the Russian case. Moreover, Russia cannot serve as the basis for any generalizable claims about the constitution and economic reform. An alternative approach is to broaden the focus to include a larger set of post-communist transitions in an effort to find patterns across cases of the relationship between constitutions and economic reform.

Constitutions and Economic Reform

Does the adoption of a constitution enhance the prospects for economic reform in the course of simultaneous political and economic transitions? Does economic reform require the consolidation of a stable set of political institutions and rules represented by agreement on a new constitution?

One approach to these questions is to examine those cases that have introduced comprehensive economic reform plans. Table 4.1 lists those countries that have adopted, though not necessarily sustained, an IMF-approved economic reform or stabilization program. The date of implementation of the reform is compared to the date of ratification of the country's constitution. Of the 16 cases listed, only four—Croatia, Estonia, Macedonia, and Romania—initiated economic reform plans prior to or at the same time of the adoption of their constitutions. While Croatia, Estonia, and Macedonia have all implemented comprehensive reform programs, Romania has adopted a much more limited macroeconomic stabilization plan and is generally ranked among the least successful reformers in Eastern Europe. The remaining 12 cases—including the most often cited success stories of the Czech Republic, Hungary, Poland, and Slovenia—initiated their reform programs without agreement on a stable constitution. Poland and Hungary both eventually adopted interim constitutions, though these were explicitly temporary

TABLE 4.1   Constitutions and the Introduction of Comprehensive Reform Programs

Country	Reform Date	Date of Constitution Ratification
Albania	4/92	Interim
Bulgaria	3/91	After (7/91)
Croatia	12/91	Before (12/90)
Czech	1/91	After (12/92)
Estonia	6/92	Simultaneously (6/92)
Hungary	From 1988 on	Interim (10/89)
Kyrgyzstan	7/92	After (5/93)
Latvia	7/92	After (7/93)
Lithuania	6/92	After (10/92)
Macedonia	4/92	Before (11/91)
Moldova	3/93	After (8/94)
Poland	12/89	Interim (12/92)
Romania	12/93	Before (12/91)
Russia	1/92	After (12/93)
Slovenia	10/91	After (12/91)
Ukraine	10/94	Interim

and, consequently, did not necessarily provide the long-term stability and predictability normally associated with constitutions. The other countries passed their constitutions after the implementation of economic reform programs, with the exception of Albania and Ukraine which have yet to reach agreements on their constitutions.

One possible argument to explain this trend is that these countries did not face substantial disagreements over the eventual shape of their political institutions. As a result, the delay in adopting their constitutions need not reflect any unpredictability about the future configuration of political institutions, but the inevitably lengthy period necessary to draft and approve such an important and complex document. Yet the experience of most of these countries suggests otherwise. In Albania, Kyrgyzstan, Lithuania, Poland, Russia, and Ukraine, delays in the adoption of a new constitution were or continue to be caused by an impasse between the president and parliament over the distribution of political power.[12] Comprehensive economic reform plans tended to be launched in the midst of these intense conflicts over new political institutions, often leading to an exacerbation of tensions. In several of these cases, the introduction of economic reforms appeared to be part of the president's strategy to strengthen his powers in relation to parliament. Sali Berisha in Albania, Askar Akaev in Kyrgyzstan, Boris Yeltsin in Russia, and Leonid Kuchma in Ukraine all used economic reforms to demand increased presidential powers.[13]

The case of Czechoslovakia is a particularly interesting example. Generally considered to be one of the most successful cases of post-communist reform, Czechoslovakia nevertheless introduced its reform program in the midst of substantial uncertainty about the distribution of political power.[14] In August 1990, negotiations began between the federal and republican governments over an extensive amendment to the existing 1968 constitution that would determine the distribution of power over economic policy-making. The negotiations resulted in a stalemate. Constitutional amendments required approval by a majority of both republican caucuses of the upper chamber of parliament, a majority of the lower chamber, and majorities in both republican parliaments. Consequently, a small group of deputies had veto power over any decisions. After months of failure, President Vaclav Havel proposed a new round of constitutional amendments to increase the emergency powers of the president in an effort to break what he called the "paralysis" of government. A provisional agreement was reached in January 1991, just as the comprehensive economic reform was initiated. Yet the agreement was reached at the price of postponing many of the most difficult institutional questions about the powers of the federal and republican governments, as well as the powers of different actors within each level of government. Indeed, the issues were so intractable that they eventually led to the break-up of Czechoslovakia. Nevertheless, despite this political uncertainty over fundamental constitutional issues, a comprehensive economic reform program was adopted and successfully implemented.

The limited evidence in Table 4.1 already suggests some interesting implications. Clearly, in the post-communist context, agreement on a stable constitution is not a precondition for the adoption of economic reform. Conflicts over the distribution of power among political institutions and the political uncertainty associated with them do not necessarily hinder the economic reform process. In addition, interim constitutions or the postponement altogether of constitution-making need not prevent the adoption of reform. In contrast to the importance placed on constitutions in the credible commitments approach, some of the most successful cases of reform appear to have occurred without the stability and predictability encoded by a constitutional agreement. Moreover, the adoption of economic reform does not require a resolution of the distributional conflicts that can lead to stalemate in the realm of constitutional politics.[15]

The evidence in Table 4.1 serves only to raise questions about the claims of the credible commitments approach; it does not constitute a conclusive test of the competing theories of the role of the constitution in the economic reform process. To provide a more systematic test of the competing theories, I have conducted a cross-sectional statistical analysis with data from 25 of the 27 post-communist countries.

The first challenge is to construct or identify an adequate measure of the dependent variable—the extent of economic reform adopted—in each case. One approach is to use basic indicators of economic performance—growth rates, inflation rates, fiscal balances, etc.—as proxies for economic reform on the assumption that reform will directly improve economic performance. Yet especially in the short term, this can be a very misleading measure of the extent of reforms adopted. Countries that introduce comprehensive reform programs may experience much sharper deteriorations of economic performance in the short term than those that choose to maintain the status quo. Therefore, the concern here is with economic policies, not performance.

To measure the extent of economic reform policies, I rely on a set of indicators devised by the European Bank for Reconstruction and Development (EBRD). Comprehensive market-oriented reform is divided into six equally weighted categories: large-scale privatization, small-scale privatization, enterprise restructuring (corporate governance and the hardness of budget constraints), price liberalization and competition, trade and foreign exchange liberalization, and financial sector reform. Based on a survey of EBRD analysts, each country is given a rating from 1 (little or no reform) to 4 (comprehensive reform) in each category, representing the cumulative progress achieved on the path towards a free market economy by September 1994.[16] The indicators do not measure the pace of change,[17] nor are they meant to reflect short-term economic performance. Instead, they are qualitative indicators intended to provide a basis for systematic comparison of the course of market-oriented reform among the post-communist countries. Since the ratings in all six categories are uniformly highly correlated with each other, a cumulative reform score for each country can be created by taking the mean of the six ratings. The component ratings and the cumulative reform scores, as well as a more detailed explanation of the ratings criteria, are reproduced in Table 4.2.

I test to determine the effects of two different elements of constitution-making on the progress of economic reform. The first independent variable (*constitution*) measures the timing of the adoption of a new, post-communist constitution. It consists of the number of months since the first free elections in the East European cases or the formal recognition of independence in the former Soviet and former Yugoslav cases to the ratification of a post-communist constitution.[18] It is designed to test whether the pace of constitution-making has any effects on the progress of economic reform. The second independent variable (*constitution dummy*) simply measures whether a new constitution was adopted at any time during the economic reform process through September 1994. It is a dummy variable which gives each country a score of 1 if a constitution was ratified prior to that date or 0 if it was not. It is designed to test whether having a new, post-communist constitution advances or hinders reform in a comparative context, regardless of the timing of its adoption.

A set of baseline control variables is also included in the regression. *Time* measures the number of months from the first free elections or formal recognition of independence through September 1994. This measure accounts for differences in the length of time each country has been engaged in the process of economic reform. *Agriculture* measures the share of agriculture in GDP in 1992 to account for structural differences in the post-communist economies. *GDP85* measures the per capita GDP of each country in 1985 to account for different levels of eco-

TABLE 4.2 EBRD Economic Reform Ratings

	Large scale Privat.	Small scale Privat.	Enterprise Restruct.	Price Lib.	Trade Lib.	Finan. Reform	Mean Score
Czech Rep.	4	4	3	3	4	3	3.50
Estonia	3	4	3	3	4	3	3.33
Hungary	3	4	3	3	4	3	3.33
Poland	3	4	3	3	4	3	3.33
Slovak Rep.	3	4	3	3	4	3	3.33
Croatia	3	4	2	3	4	3	3.17
Slovenia	2	4	3	3	4	3	3.17
Lithuania	3	4	2	3	4	2	3.00
Kyrgyzstan	3	4	2	3	3	2	2.83
Latvia	2	3	2	3	4	3	2.83
Macedonia	2	4	2	3	4	2	2.83
Romania	2	3	2	3	4	2	2.67
Russia	3	3	2	3	3	2	2.67
Albania	1	3	2	3	4	2	2.50
Bulgaria	2	2	2	3	4	2	2.50
Moldova	2	2	2	3	2	2	2.17
Uzbekistan	2	3	1	3	2	1	2.00
Armenia	1	3	1	3	2	1	1.83
Belarus	2	2	2	2	1	1	1.67
Kazakhstan	2	2	1	2	2	1	1.67
Tajikistan	2	2	1	3	1	1	1.67
Azerbaijan	1	1	1	3	1	1	1.33
Georgia	1	2	1	2	1	1	1.33
Ukraine	1	2	1	2	1	1	1.33
Turkmenistan	1	1	1	2	1	1	1.17

SOURCE: EBRD, Transition Report, October 1994 (London, 1994). Classification system described in Box 4.1.

nomic and social development on the eve of the transition. *Communists* measures the average percentage of parliamentary seats held by the communist party or its direct successor in each country during the transition. It is often asserted that the strongest political obstacle to economic reform is the continued influence of the communist party. Though this is certainly not an exhaustive list of potential control variables, it does take into account some basic political and economic differences among the post-communist countries. Summary statistics on all the variables are listed in the data appendix.

Before presenting the results of the multivariate regressions, it is useful to examine graphically the bivariate relationship between the pace of constitution-making and economic reform. Figure 4.1 presents a scatterplot diagram with the EBRD reform scores on the vertical axis and the number of months till ratification of a post-communist constitution on the horizontal axis. The scatterplot re-

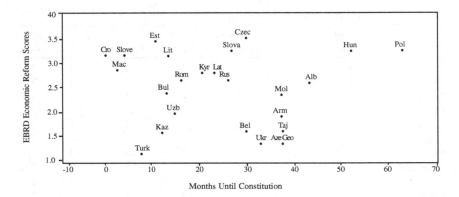

FIGURE 4.1   Constitution-Making and Economic Reform

veals no direct, linear relationship between the two variables. The early constitution-makers run the gamut of the reform continuum from virtually no reform (Turkmenistan) to the most comprehensive economic reform (Estonia). Interestingly, the range of variation among the post-communist counties on the pace of constitution-making is greatest at the highest levels of economic reform. Among those countries with a reform score of 3.0 or higher are those that have moved fastest to ratify a new constitution (Croatia, Estonia, and Slovenia), as well as those that have postponed constitution-making the longest, relying instead on an interim constitution (Poland and Hungary).

The results of the multivariate regressions are presented in Table 4.3. If the credible commitments approach to the role of the constitution in the process of economic reform is correct, the *constitution* variable should have a negative sign indicating that delays in constitution-making are correlated with lower levels of economic reform. If Holmes's theory of the benefits of postponing constitution-making is correct, the *constitution* variable should have a positive sign. In Equation 1, the *constitution* variable is tested against the EBRD reform scores along with the baseline control variables. Though the sign of the variable is negative, its coefficient is close to zero (−0.007) and it is statistically insignificant. The share of seats held in parliament by the communist party or its successor is, as expected, negatively correlated with economic reform. The share of agriculture in GDP is also negatively correlated with economic reform. Those countries that began their transitions earlier, as measured by the *time* variable, have higher economic reform scores. The level of economic development going into the transition, as measured in *GDP85* variable, is only borderline significant. The results suggest that neither the early adoption of a new, post-communist constitution nor the postponement of constitution-making have any significant effects on the extent of economic reform adopted across the entire set of post-communist countries.

TABLE 4.3. Constitutions and Economic Reform

	Equations		
	(1)	(2)	(3)
No. of observations	25	25	25
Constant	3.233*	3.497*	2.284*
	(3.46)	(2.63)	(2.43)
Variables			
Agriculture	−2.661*	−2.672*	−1.971*
	(3.00)	(2.61)	(2.33)
Communists	−1.265*	−1.172*	−0.994*
	(3.62)	(2.42)	(2.49)
GDP85	−9.18E-05	−8.89E-05	−9.93E-05*
	(1.46)	(1.37)	(1.77)
Time	0.027*	0.022	0.027*
	(1.81)	(1.25)	(2.38)
Constitution	−0.007	−0.015	
	(1.06)	(1.09)	
Democracy		−0.138	0.328
		(0.24)	(1.34)
Interaction term (Constitution ×		0.011	
Democracy)		(0.62)	
Constitution Dummy			0.479*
			(2.57)
Adj-R^2	0.704	0.684	0.762
S.E.E.	0.416	0.429	0.373

NOTE: Dependent variable is the mean EBRD economic reform score, ranging from 1 (minimal reform) to 4 (comprehensive reform); absolute values of t statistics in parentheses.

*Significant at the 0.05 level.

One potential objection to the analysis so far is that constitutions imposed by authoritarian regimes are treated the same as constitutions ratified through the democratic process. Surely constitutions have different effects under different political regimes. Constitutions imposed by authoritarian rulers may not provide a secure foundation for credible commitments, since authoritarian rulers cannot be held accountable to constitutional constraints (see North, 1989; Root, 1989; Weingast, 1993). As a result, the credible commitments approach would suggest that constitutions in authoritarian systems should not necessarily facilitate economic reform as they would in democratic systems. Holmes argues that postponing constitution-making should have a greater positive impact on economic reform in more competitive and fragmented political systems than in political systems with a greater consolidation of political power (see Holmes, 1995). In competitive democratic systems, economic reforms are more likely to be delayed by conflicts over the constitution among competing interest groups and institutions. As a result, the virtues of postponing the constitution for economic reform should be more apparent in democratic systems than in authoritarian systems.

To test these competing theories of the effects of constitutions on economic reform in democratic systems, I add an interaction term into the regression. A new interaction term is formed by multiplying the variable, *constitution,* by a dummy variable, *democracy,* indicating whether or not the case can be classified as a democracy. Countries that score an average rating of 3.5 or lower on the 7-point Freedom House index of political and civil liberties for the period 1991–1994 are classified as democratic regimes and given a score of 1; countries with a rating higher than 3.5 are classified as non-democratic regimes and given a score of 0.[19] The interaction will allow us to distinguish the particular effects of the timing of new constitutions among democratic regimes only. As before, the credible commitments approach would predict a negative relationship between the *interaction term* and economic reform; Holmes's theory suggests a positive relationship.

Equation 2 presents the results of the regression with the interaction term. The effects of the timing of the constitution on economic reform among democratic regimes are determined by adding the coefficients of the variables *constitution* and the *interaction term.*[20] Once again, this coefficient is negative, but very close to zero (–0.004). Moreover, both variables are statistically insignificant. The coefficients of the baseline control variables are stable. The results of Equation 2 suggest that differences in the pace of constitution-making among democratic systems do not appear to have any systematic influence on progress in economic reform.

A different, though somewhat weaker, test of the competing approaches is to focus not on the timing of the adoption of a new constitution, but simply on whether a new constitution was adopted at any time during the period examined. This eliminates some interesting variation among the cases, since it does not allow us to detect the effects of any differences in the timing of constitution-making among those countries that do have new, post-communist constitutions. Nevertheless, such a test should determine whether the adoption of a new constitution has any effect at all on the economic reform process.

In Equation 3, the *constitution* variable is replaced with the dummy variable, *constitution dummy,* which has a value of 1 if a new constitution was passed prior to September 1994 and 0 if a country was still operating under some form of interim or amended communist-era constitution. In contrast to the results for the timing of constitutions, the coefficient of *constitution dummy* is positive and statistically significant. Adopting a new, post-communist constitution produces a 0.48 increase on the 4 point EBRD economic reform scale. Though these results support the argument of the credible commitments approach that the adoption of a permanent constitution enhances the prospects for economic reform, they do not have any specific implications for the timing of constitution-making and its relationship to the economic reform process. In addition, the results should be interpreted with some caution, since they could be biased by "endogeneity" effects, namely, the possibility that higher levels of economic reform have a reverse effect by influencing the likelihood of adopting a constitution.[21]

Taken together, these simple tests do suggest some preliminary conclusions. Postponing the adoption of new constitutions does not appear to advance the process of economic reform both in the entire set of post-communist cases and in the narrower set of post-communist democracies. There is no evidence to suggest that, in the comparative context, post-communist constitutions have been an obstacle to economic reform. Instead, the adoption of a new constitution does appear to have some positive effect on the process of economic reform, though such a constitution is hardly a precondition for the adoption of economic reform.

Executive Power and Economic Reform

Since the use of a constitution dummy variable is not a particularly precise or convincing test of the competing approaches, it might be useful to test more specifically other elements of the "causal chain" of the different arguments linking constitutions and economic reforms. In both approaches, the relevance of the constitution for the process of economic reform is determined by its effects on constraining state and executive power in economic policy-making. The credible commitments approach values the constitution because it restrains politicians and other state actors from intervening in the economy to expropriate the gains to individuals from their investments in economic reform. Holmes's argument for postponing the constitution is centered on his fears that an overly rigid constitution will rob the executive of the capacity and flexibility that are temporarily necessary for initiating unpopular economic reforms against strong vested interests.

These approaches have different implications for the relationship between executive power and the process of economic reform. The credible commitments would suggest that successful economic reform should be correlated with restraints on executive powers. Holmes's argument implies the opposite: successful economic reforms should be associated with strong executives with substantial policy-making powers.

The first step in testing these competing arguments is to develop a measure of executive powers across the post-communist cases. I focus exclusively on presidential powers as a proxy variable for the extent of executive powers, since all of the post-communist countries do have presidencies with widely varying powers.[22] Though this eliminates important variation in prime ministerial powers across the parliamentary systems, it still provides one comparative indicator of the extent of executive powers in these systems.

An index of formal presidential powers is constructed on the pattern of previous efforts by Shugart and Carey (1992), Geddes (1994) and McGregor (1994).[23] The index is based on the allocation of standard specific appointment and legislative powers. For each power, a number is assigned on the basis of whether that power is explicitly granted to the president exclusively, to the president with

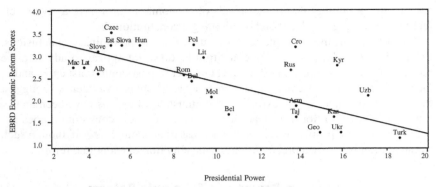

FIGURE 4.2   Presidential Power and Economic Reform

qualifications, or not granted to the president at all.[24] Furthermore, the numbers are weighted for systems with direct as opposed to indirect elections for the presidency.[25] The logic behind this system is that presidential powers have different weights within different institutional structures. When the president is elected by parliament, all of his/her powers are circumscribed, to some extent, by the parliament's capacity to deny reelection. Directly elected presidents are less constrained, but the extent of their powers differs on the basis of the structural division between presidential and semi-presidential systems. The scores on all the powers are summed to determine an overall indicator of the formal presidential powers for each country. Summary statistics on the presidential powers index are listed in Table 4.5.[26]

Figure 4.2 displays a scatterplot with *presidential power* on the vertical axis and the EBRD scores on the horizontal axis. The scatterplot shows a negative, linear relationship between the concentration of formal presidential powers and the extent of economic reform adopted. The bivariate correlation is relatively high at $r = -71$.

Table 4.4 presents the results of the multivariate regressions. In Equation 1, *presidential power* is tested against the EBRD economic reform scores with the same baseline control variables as in the previous regressions. The coefficient on *presidential power* is negative and statistically significant indicating that higher concentrations of presidential power are associated with lower levels of economic reform across the post-communist countries. A shift from Macedonia with the weakest formal presidential powers (3.25) to Turkmenistan with the highest (18.5) leads to a substantial 0.63 decrease in the four point EBRD reform scale.

It is possible that the concentration of presidential powers is serving as a proxy for the distinction between democratic and authoritarian systems. In Equation 2, the democracy dummy variable, *democracy,* is added to control for differences in regime type. The coefficient of the *presidential power* variable remains very sta-

TABLE 4.4   Presidential Power and Economic Reform

	Equations		
	(1)	(2)	(3)
No. of observations	24	24	24
Constant	3.948*	4.535*	5.309*
	(4.64)	(7.14)	(11.13)
Variables			
Agriculture	−2.714*	−2.957*	−3.002*
	(3.36)	(3.70)	(4.94)
Communists	−0.842*	−0.766	−0.999*
	(2.11)	(1.65)	(3.09)
GDP85	−8.65E-05	−9.73E-05	−7.51E-05
	(1.46)	(1.63)	(1.57)
Time	0.011		
	(0.98)		
Presidential Power	−0.041*	−0.046*	−0.123*
	(1.70)	(1.91)	(4.16)
Democracy		0.057	
		(0.22)	
Constitution Dummy			−1.106*
			(2.67)
Interaction Term (Presidential			0.116*
Power × Constitution Dummy)			(3.36)
Adj-R^2	0.718	0.704	0.822
S.E.E.	0.394	0.404	0.314

NOTE: Dependent variable is the mean EBRD economic reform score, ranging from 1 (minimal reform) to 4 (comprehensive reform); absolute values of t statistics in parentheses.

*Significant at the 0.05 level.

ble and significant. The *democracy* variable is not significant and its addition reduces the adjusted-R^2 of the model. When controlling for the effects of regime type, greater concentrations of presidential power are still correlated with lower levels of economic reform.

Though interesting, these results do not relate directly to the effects of constitutions on the economic reform process. To examine the relationship between constitutions, executive powers, and economic reform, an interaction term was added to the regression. Equation 3 includes a dummy variable (*constitution dummy*) representing those countries with a new, post-communist constitution prior to September 1994 and an *interaction term* derived by multiplying the variable *presidential power* by *constitution dummy*. The results are surprising. The coefficient of the variable PRESPOW represents the effects of the concentration of presidential powers on economic reform in only those countries without a new, post-communist constitution (i.e., when the value of *constitution dummy* is zero). The coefficient of *presidential power* jumps nearly three times from −0.046 in Equation 2 to −0.123 in Equation 3 and is highly significant suggesting that the negative effects of higher levels of formal presidential powers are much greater in countries without new constitutions than in the entire sample of post-communist countries.

To obtain the relationship between presidential powers and economic reform in those countries with new constitutions, the coefficient of *presidential power* is added to the coefficient of the *interaction term*. This new coefficient, 0.008, is close to zero suggesting that increases in presidential powers in those countries with new constitutions have almost no effect on the progress of economic reform. The coefficient on the variable *constitution dummy* (−1.106) in Equation 3 of Table 4.4 has the opposite effect and increases substantially in magnitude in comparison with its value in Equation 3 of Table 4.3 (0.479). With the inclusion of the interaction effects, the coefficient of *constitution dummy* represents the effects of a constitution on economic reform when *presidential power* is set to zero. This suggests that the overall positive effects of having a constitution for the adoption of economic reform revealed in the first set of regressions was largely a function of the positive effects of the constitution in those countries with powerful political executives. In those countries in which executive power is already highly constrained, the adoption of a constitution no longer has a positive effect on the adoption of economic reform.

The effects of this interaction among presidential powers, constitutions, and economic reform are even clearer when the relationships are expressed graphically. In Figure 4.3, a scatterplot diagram of the level of presidential powers (on the horizontal axis) and the EBRD economic reform scores (on the vertical axis) is depicted with each case belonging to a subgroup of countries defined by whether they have adopted a post-communist constitution. Regression lines are fitted for each subgroup (dotted line for those countries with a constitution; solid line for those countries without a constitution). By comparing the slope of the regression lines between the subgroups, it is clear that the negative effects of increased presidential powers on economic reform are substantially greater in countries that have postponed constitution-making (*constitution dummy*=0) than in those that have adopted new constitutions (*constitution dummy*=1).

The rationale for "stopgap constitutionalism" is that the restriction of executive powers in the midst of an economic transition limits the capacity and flexibility of the executive to win the contentious battles over the introduction of economic reform. Postponing the constitution allows for the granting of temporary powers to the executive that are crucial in the early stages of the reform process, though not necessarily desirable to encode in the political system over the long term. Yet the results of this preliminary analysis suggest not only that higher levels of executive power are negatively correlated with the success of the economic

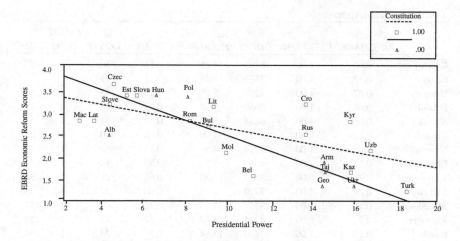

FIGURE 4.3   Presidential Power and Constitutions

reform process, but that the negative effects of executive power are worse pre-cisely in those countries that do postpone their constitutions. As a result, the strat-egy of postponing constitution-making to grant executives increased powers (if only temporarily) to reform the economy does not appear to advance the reform process when considered against the experiences of the entire set of post-commu-nist countries.[27]

Conclusion

This effort to test an ongoing debate within the politics of economic reform against the experiences of the post-communist countries has yielded some inter-esting, preliminary results. While not a precondition for the adoption of eco-nomic reforms, constitutions do appear to contribute to the success of the eco-nomic reform process. From a comparative context, stopgap constitutionalism or simply postponing the constitution-making process has no discernibly positive effects on economic reform even among contentious democracies, though the quick adoption of a new constitution has no clear advantages for reform either. If the consequences of the constitution in the course of economic reform are based upon its restraining role on executive power, then this analysis suggests that stronger executives are associated with less economic reform and that under stopgap constitutions the consequences of strong executive powers are even worse for economic reform. Stable constitutions that place constraints on execu-tive, and hence state, power appear to have a positive effect on the process of economic reform, even in this still early stage of the post-communist transitions.

TABLE 4.5   Data Appendix

	ARGSHARE	FREEDOM	GDP85	PREPOW	COMMU	CONST	CONST DUM	TIME
Czech Rep.	0.06	1.00	8105	5.25	0.18	30	1	53
Estonia	0.13	1.00	7163	5.25	0.18	11	1	38
Hungary	0.07	1.00	7259	6.25	0.15	53	0	55
Poland	0.083	1.00	5630	9.00	0.52	63	0	65
Slovak Rep.	0.06	1.00	6888	5.50	0.19	27	1	53
Croatia	0.12	0.00	6382	14.00	0.06	0	1	37
Slovenia	0.05	1.00	10724	4.50	0.15	3	1	37
Lithuania	0.28	1.00	6663	9.50	0.39	14	1	38
Krygyzstan	0.28	0.00	3512	15.50	0.60	21	1	38
Latvia	0.24	1.00	7720	3.75	0.00	23	1	38
Macedonia	0.12	1.00	3254	3.25	0.26	2	1	37
Romania	0.2	0.00	4735	8.63	0.42	17	1	53
Russia	0.13	1.00	7804	13.64	0.26	24	1	34
Albania	0.56	1.00	2509	4.75	0.38	42	0	43
Bulgaria	0.16	1.00	7122	9.00	0.38	12	1	53
Moldova	0.33	0.00	5314	10.00	0.41	36	1	38
Uzbekistan	0.39	0.00	3523	17.00	0.86	16	1	38
Armenia	0.41	0.00	5822	14.00	0.10	36	0	38
Belarus	0.24	0.00	7388	10.58	0.84	30	1	38
Kazakhstan	0.38	0.00	4776	15.50	0.79	13	1	35
Tajikistan	0.33	0.00	3096	14.00	0.94	36	0	38
Azerbaijan	0.29	0.00	5170		0.84	36	0	38
Georgia	0.48	0.00	6391	15.00	0.18	36	0	38
Ukraine	0.23	1.00	5853	16.00	0.62	34	0	35
Turkmenistan	0.48	0.00	4070	18.50	0.90	8	1	36

If the concentration of executive power actually impedes economic reform, then the advantages of stopgap constitutionalism are no longer so clear. Since even the proponents of this view recognize that there is a risk that the extraordinary executive powers of a stopgap constitution could be encoded permanently in the political system, the political risk would appear to exceed the potential payoff of the stopgap approach.

Though this analysis must still be considered tentative given some of the caveats mentioned with respect to measurements of the political variables and the possibility of endogeneity bias in the regressions, it does bring some systematic evidence to a debate largely carried out in normative terms or on the basis of prominent individual cases. It suggests that the 27 countries that have arisen from the disintegration of the former Soviet bloc can provide fertile ground for testing competing theories about the politics of economic reform, as well as a wide range of other issues.

BOX 4.1   CLASSIFICATION SYSTEM FOR EBRD ECONOMIC REFORM SCORES

Large-Scale Privatization

4 More than 50 percent of state-owned assets privatized in a scheme that reflects support for corporate governance.

3 More than 25 percent of state-owned assets privatized or in the process of being sold but with major unresolved issues regarding corporate governance.

2 Advanced comprehensive scheme almost ready to be implemented; some sales completed.

1 Little done.

Small-Scale Privatization

4 Comprehensive and well-designed program implemented.

3 Nearly comprehensive program implemented, but design or lack of central supervision leaves important issues unresolved.

2 Substantial share privatized.

1 Little done.

Enterprise Restructuring

4 Restructuring program which substantially improves corporate governance in operation; strong financial discipline at the enterprise level; large conglomerates broken up.

3 Structure created (e.g., through privatization combined with tight credit and subsidy policies and/or enforcement of bankruptcy legislation) to promote corporate governance; or strong action taken to break up conglomerates.

2 Moderately tight credit and subsidy policy; weak enforcement of bankruptcy legislation; little action to break up large conglomerates.

1 Lax credit and subsidy policies weakening financial discipline at the enterprise level; few other reforms to promote corporate governance.

Price Liberalization and Competition

4 Comprehensive price liberalization and price competition; anti-trust legislation in place.

3 Comprehensive price liberalization and price competition.

2 Price controls remain for several important product categories.

1 Most prices remain formally controlled by the government.

Trade and Foreign Exchange System

4 Few import or export quotas; insignificant direct involvement in exports and imports by ministries and state-owned former trading monopolies; almost full current account convertibility at unified exchange rate; no major non-uniformity of customs duties.

3 Few import quotas; almost full current account convertibility at unified exchange rate.

2 Few import quotas; almost full current account convertibility in principle but with a foreign exchange regime which is not fully transparent (possibly with multiple exchange rates).

BOX 4.1 (continued)

1 Widespread import controls or very limited legitimate access to foreign exchange.

Financial Sector Reform

4 Well functioning bank competition and prudential supervision.

3 Substantial progress on bank recapitalization, bank auditing, and establishment of a functioning prudential supervisory system; significant presence of private banks; full interest rate liberalization with little preferential access to cheap refinancing.

2 Interest rates significantly influencing the allocation of credit.

1 Little progress beyond establishment of two-tier system.

Notes

1. This argument is primarily associated with Jon Elster (1993; 1994a; 1994b), Russell Hardin (1989; 1994), Douglass North (1989; 1990; 1993), and Barry Weingast (1992; 1993).

2. This view has been most forcefully articulated by Stephen Holmes, the Editor-in-Chief of the quarterly journal *East European Constitutional Review*. His views are presented in a series of articles in that journal (Holmes, 1993a; 1993b; 1994). His approach to the politics of economic reform has much in common with a recent work by Stephan Haggard and Robert Kaufman (1995).

3. Many of the key contributions to this literature have been brought in a two volume collection edited by Persson and Tabellini (1994).

4. In this respect, his work draws from the lessons of the study of transitions by O'Donnell and Schmitter (1986).

5. Such a concentration of executive power is possible in parliamentary systems, if the party system is sufficiently developed and consolidated. In the absence of a stream-lined party system, Holmes advocates some form of presidential or semi-presidential system (Holmes, 1993b).

6. Holmes also claims that constitutions written during the transition period are unlikely to become "sacralized" since "myopic political bargains made under turbulent circumstances are unlikely to be treated as beyond the reach of political recasting," see Holmes (1993a) p. 22. As a result, postponing the constitution should not only improve the outlook for economic reform, but will enhance the legitimacy of the document once it is approved. In the post-communist context, in particular, Holmes believes that constitutions written early in the transition are likely to overemphasize negative constitutionalism, as the problem of tyranny looms a lot larger in the minds of constitution writers than the threat of anarchy. Over time, drafters are more likely to strike a balance between the enabling and disabling functions of the constitution as they have more experience with the threat of anarchy.

7. For a good review of these conflicts, see the reports in the *East European Constitutional Review* (EECR 1993; 1994).

8. For an excellent account of the struggles over economic reform through the end of 1994, see Åslund (1995).

9. At the time, Russia maintained a two-tiered legislature. The Congress of Peoples' Deputies was the "parent" legislature which met periodically to approve the general direction of the smaller, permanent legislative body, known as the Supreme Soviet.

10. Government data on Russian economic performance are available in Russian Federation (1995).

11. Nevertheless, the destructive and costly war in Chechnya, as well as Yeltsin's increasingly erratic behavior, has raised awareness of the potential costs of unconstrained executive power.

12. Details of these conflicts are summarized in the "Constitution Watch" section of the *East European Constitutional Review.*

13. This corresponds with the findings of a recent set of case studies of the political economy of reform in several developing countries. In summarizing the cases, Bates and Krueger (1993) find that economic reforms tend to strengthen the powers of the executive branch even as they limit the powers of the state to intervene in the economy.

14. For accounts of the politics of economic reform in Czechoslovakia, see Adam (1993), Olson (1993; 1994), and Wolchik (1991; 1993).

15. This finding also has interesting implications for another literature. One of the most frequently cited models of the politics of economic reform is the "war of attrition" model proposed by Alesina and Drazen (1991). They claim that reforms can be delayed as rival groups try to wait each other out in an effort to shift the costs of reform on to their opponents. In this model, reform occurs once one group wins a decisive victory over its opponents and can therefore impose its preferred distribution of the costs of reform. Conflicts over the distribution of power are predicted to delay reform, which is most likely to be implemented after the resolution of such conflicts. Yet in the post-communist context, the adoption of economic reform programs has tended to occur in the midst of such conflicts, raising questions as to the applicability of the war of attrition dynamic.

16. Obviously, there are significant disagreements on what constitutes the end point of this path. The EBRD indicators try to measure the extent to which the state has withdrawn from ownership and regulation recognizing that zero ownership and zero regulation are not the intended ideals EBRD (1994) p. 9.

17. The ratings include progress made on this path prior to the downfall of the communist regimes. So, for example, a country that had already privatized small-scale business prior to the transition would receive a 4 in this category even though no comprehensive small-scale privatization program was introduced during the transition.

18. Since the EBRD ratings measure economic reform through the end of September 1994, the cut-off point for the constitution measure is also September 1994. Countries that did not adopt a new post-communist constitution prior to September 1994 were coded on the basis of the number of months from the date of independence or free elections to September 1994.

19. The Freedom House scale ranges from 1 (highly free) to 7 (unfree), see Freedom House (1994).

20. The coefficient for the *constitution* variable represents the effects of the constitution common to both groups, while the coefficient for the interaction term represents the additional effects specific to the group of democracies. Thus, the combination of the two coefficients yields the full effects of the timing of the constitution on economic reform among democratic regimes.

21. One of the standard methods for correcting for endogeneity bias—two-stage least squares—cannot be used in this analysis, since its results are only valid for comparisons of a large number of cases.

22. Since these transitions have produced both presidential and parliamentary systems, it would be preferable to compare the powers of presidents and prime ministers on the same scale. However, there is no existing common scale to compare them. At this stage, data to compare the powers of prime ministers is not readily available. In many cases, these powers are based on legislative acts or decrees that are not widely available for many of the post-communist countries.

23. The index was developed jointly with Timothy Frye.

24. In presidential systems, a score of 1 is given for an exclusive power, .5 for a qualified power, and 0 if the power is not granted to the president at all.

25. In parliamentary systems with direct elections for the presidency, the scores are .75, .375, and 0, respectively. In parliamentary systems with indirect elections for the presidency, the scores are .5, .25, and 0, respectively.

26. Of course, de facto presidential powers consist of more than the formal powers granted by the constitution. Yet this study is explicitly designed to examine the effects of the particular content of the constitution or interim laws on executive powers and, consequently, focuses exclusively on formal powers. Since, in many cases, sitting presidents in the post-communist countries have presided over the drafting of constitutions and interim constitutions, the formal powers encoded in those documents should be a good reflection of their de facto powers, given the strong incentives to institutionalize those powers.

27. The argument that increased executive powers are necessary for economic reform, or at least for the initial introduction of economic reform, is also quite common in the broader political economy literature. For examples, see Geddes (1994), Haggard and Kaufman (1995), Nelson (1993), and several of the contributions to Williamson (1994). The results presented here raise broader questions about the relationship between the concentration of executive power and economic reform beyond the post-communist context.

CHAPTER 5

Economic Causes of Crime in Russia

Anders Åslund

Crime has become a major popular concern in the Russian transition from a communist state to a market economy and democracy.[1] Since 1993, inflation and crime have been the two top public concerns. In a representative opinion poll in February 1995, 58 percent of the respondents said that the increase in crime was their greatest concern, only superseded by inflation, which 83 percent considered their main concern.[2]

While the crime rate in Russia has risen substantially, this rise and its significance tend to be exaggerated and misinterpreted. A typical view is: "Organized crime has penetrated all governmental levels of the former Soviet Union. . . . Organized crime is limiting civil society, hindering free elections, and compromising a free press. . . . Therefore, the collapse of communism in the former Soviet region may not lead to democratization and the transition to a competitive market economy."[3] This paper will focus on four views on Russian crime and try to dispel or moderate them. It focuses on aspects of crime related to the economy.

First, the rise in crime in Russia is frequently connected with the introduction of a market economy. This is only partly true. Crime rose during the collapse of communism and only during the very initial stage of the introduction of a market economy. The crime rate stagnated and started to fall as soon as the main distortions of the burgeoning market economy were eliminated.

Second, it is frequently argued that the rise in Russian crime is uniquely great, and that it has reached an extraordinarily high level. In reality, according to official data, Russian crime has risen approximately as in other post-communist countries, and the Russian level of crime in general is not uniquely high. However, Russia differs from other post-communist countries with respect to the remarkably high murder rate.

Third, a common perception has evolved that Russia has developed into a country of organized crime dominated by racketeering and corruption that is unlikely to abate, rendering Russia a uniquely criminalized country. In particular, the privatization process is pinpointed as a major cause of lasting corruption. My argument is on the contrary that the main sources of corrupt revenues are distor-

TABLE 5.1   Registered Crimes in Russia, 1985–1995

Year	Total number of registered crimes (thousands)	Annual change (percent)	Index 1985 = 100
1985	1,417	1.0	100.0
1986	1,338	–5.5	94.7
1987	1,186	–11.4	83.5
1988	1,220	2.9	86.6
1989	1,619	32.7	114.2
1990	1,839	13.6	129.8
1991	2,173	18.1	153.0
1992	2,761	27.0	194.3
1993	2,800	1.4	197.5
1994	2,633	–6.0	185.8
1995	2,756	4.7	194.5

SOURCE: Inga B. Mikhailovskaya, "Crime and Statistics: Do the Figures Reflect the Real Situation?" *Demokratizatsiya,* vol. 2, no. 3 (Summer 1994), p. 413; Goskomstat Rossii, *Sotsial'no-ekonomicheskoe polozhenie Rossii 1994 g.,* Moscow, 1995, p. 168 and *Sotsial'no-ekonomicheskoe polozhenie Rossii 1995 g.,* Moscow, 1996, p. 289.

tions of government regulations, and since most gross distortions have been abolished, the criminalization of Russian society may very well abate.

Fourth, a widely made argument is that Russian organized crime is growing "exponentially."[4] The overall crime rate, however, has stagnated since 1993, and there are so many reasons to assume that crime will be checked that it would be very surprising if Russia does not eventually experience a long period of declining crime rates, as Britain did from the great liberalization in 1846 until 1939.

When Did the Crime Rate Rise in Russia?

A popular view has evolved both inside and outside Russia that the sharp rise in crime is connected with the liberalization of the economy and privatization. This is not borne out by the official statistics. Confusingly, the Russian crime rate fell from 1985 to 1988, but this decrease was artificial and not tenable. It was caused by Mikhail Gorbachev's anti-alcohol campaign, which temporarily brought down official alcohol sales by half.[5] Indeed, it is widely argued that this campaign laid the foundation of much of organized crime. Therefore, 1985, the starting year of the campaign, is preferable as a standard for the old crime level. As we can see in Table 5.1, the Russian crime rate approximately doubled from 1988 to 1992. The years of the greatest rise were 1989 and 1992 with growths of 32.7 and 27.3 percent, respectively.

1989 marked the breakthrough of the full freedom of speech and Russians felt freer than ever before, but it was also a year of accelerating shortages and market imbalances. Together with the Law on Cooperatives, which had been adopted in May 1988, this allowed many to exploit these market distortions to their own benefit. In addition, the anti-alcohol campaign collapse in 1989, and increasing alcohol consumption boosted the crime level. The ensuing years, 1990 and 1991, showed ever greater market imbalances but not all that much greater freedom. The monetary overhang peaked in December 1991, when there were virtually no goods left in state shops, which caused abundant opportunities for arbitrage between fixed state prices and free—mostly black market—prices. Many "cooperatives" created on the basis of the 1988 law freely exploited the opportunities of this distorted market.

1992 was the year of the great price liberalization. It was also the year of the greatest rent-seeking. This was the result of market distortions, because the liberalization of prices and trade did not go far enough. Moreover, inflation peaked in 1992, because of massive rent-seeking through subsidized credits.

In short, we can characterize the four years 1988–1992 as a time of massive market distortions and market imbalances, connected first with a gross monetary overhang and later with extreme inflation. To the extent that the state of the economy contributed to crime, we would expect such conditions to be conducive to a high and rising crime rate.

A little noted fact is that after a steep rise between 1988 and 1992, the Russian crime rate stagnated in 1993, with an increase of only 1.4 percent, and it fell sharply by 6.0 percent in 1994, though it rose again by 4.7 percent in 1995 indicating a relative stabilization (see Table 5.1). As market distortions were being alleviated, and inflation was falling, opportunities for rent-seeking (legal or illegal) diminished. It would be surprising if such substantial changes would not have a significant impact on the overall crime rate. It thus appears that we are facing a very ordinary development of a rise in crime during a short period of interregnum between two economic and social systems, characterized by disorderly and inconsistent state regulation. As soon as the new social and economic system will be installed, we should expect greater order.

But can Russian crime statistics be trusted? All the official crime statistics are provided by the Russian Ministry of Interior. They are published by the Russian State Committee for Statistics (*Goskomstat Rossii*). The same statistics are used in public appearances by representatives of the Security Council and the successors of the KGB. The Soviet Union did not publish any crime statistics at all after 1933. The first comprehensive publication occurred in the late 1980s.[6] In general, what is not published tends to be poorly measured. According to official data, the Russian crime level is surprisingly low, and the share of solved crimes high. Moreover, the traditional suspicion of authority is great, making it plausible that fewer crimes are reported and registered in Russia than elsewhere.

It could be argued that rather than the crime rate itself, the share of registered to actually committed crimes had fallen, because people avoid reporting crimes to the police which is perceived to be corrupt, passive and ineffective. However,

TABLE 5.2   Registered Crimes in Russia by Kind, 1991–1994 (annual increase in percent)

	1991	1992	1993	1994	1995
Total	18.1	27.0	1.4	−6.0	4.7
Homicides	4	42	27	11	−2
Theft	23	62	12	−19	−5
Burglary	36	33	−4	−17	4
Hooliganism	−0.5	13	31	20	0.2
Drug crimes	19	54	79	41	7

SOURCE: Goskomstat Rossii, *Sotsial'no-ekonomicheskoe polozhenie Rossii 1994 g.,* Moscow, 1995, p. 168. Goskomstat Rossii, *Sotsial'no-ekonomicheskoe polozhenie Rossii*

also before, many crimes were still committed by the police, and people may have seen no point in reporting them. After communism, people have less reason to be afraid of the police, which could lead to higher reporting rates. The very fact that crime statistics are now being published alerts people to report crimes. Moreover, the major annual variations make sense. In particular, the reported annual swings have been so great that changes in reporting alone cannot explain them.

The Development of Various Types of Crime

When probing into the subcategories of the Russian crime statistics, a clear pattern emerges with four major categories of crimes (see Table 5.2): (1) property crimes; (2) homicide; (3) petty street crime (hooliganism); and (4) drug crimes.

First, with the introduction of a market economy, property crimes—thefts, burglaries and robberies—surged sharply. Marketization and monetization had multiple effects. The liberalization of both domestic and foreign trade broadened the market. Anything could be sold on the new market. As a result, transaction costs fell and many assets assumed a market value. Monetization further reduced transaction costs. It also led to greater anonymity, thereby providing a shield for thieves and fraudsters. Traditionally, Russian homes had miserable locks and no other form of security. This made them easy victims of theft. Hence, it was natural that property crimes rose drastically.

However, people could do a great deal to protect themselves against property crimes. Suddenly, all apartments with valuable possessions appear to have steel-doors, provided at a price of $150.00 from otherwise idle producers of armor and installed professionally at a price of $4.00.[7] In shops and on exposed ground-floor windows, iron bars have quickly been installed. Shops, banks and important people acquired private security guards. At the same time, people have become much more cautious when and where they walk. Thus, it is equally natural that property crimes started falling sharply in 1994. Thefts and burglaries fell by 19 and 17 percent, respectively.

The second major feature in the emerging pattern of crimes is the development of homicide rates. The number of registered homicides rose less sharply than property crimes in 1992. A surge of 42 percent in 1992 was shocking enough. The number of murders increased moderately in 1993 and 1994 and finally fell slightly in 1995. Behind the rise in murders we detect hard organized crime that requires more resolute measures than steel-doors and iron bars, though even with respect to these cases a stagnation is apparent.

Petty street crime, or hooliganism, represents a third major feature. It has expanded continuously at a relatively high rate, though little of hooliganism is reported, as these are minor crimes that the police tends to disregard, rendering the statistics particularly uncertain. The development of petty street crime is hardly related to economic causes. A better explanation seems to be that fewer efforts are made by the police to fight this type of crime in the transitional disorder. The solution here would be a strengthening of the state in general.

Fourth, drug crimes are skyrocketing under market conditions, as has been the case in the West. Starting from a low level, reported drug crimes grew by 41–79 percent a year from 1992 to 1994, and they are becoming a serious social burden. Obviously, drug trade evolves more easily with open borders, a less regulated economy and monetization. This is an evident cost of a market economy, and it is also a reflection of organized crime. Serious police efforts will be required to cap drug crimes, but they will hardly be more successful than in the West.

To summarize, today, Russians are well aware of crime and take a great deal of private precautions, which helps to reduce property and other less severe crimes. The law enforcement organs appear to improve their work and sensibly seem to focus on the most serious types of crime, notably murders, which explains the decline in homicide rates. However, as of now the police have not managed to get a grasp on hard organized crime, as indicated by the fast expansion of drug crimes. Moreover, the police forces have no time for minor misdemeanors. The natural focus for our investigation becomes ruthless organized crime with economic motivations.

How Does Russia's Crime Development Compare with Other Countries'?

In order to put Russian crime in an international perspective we need to answer the following question: is the Russian crime rate and its development extraordinary by international standards?

A first test is a comparison of the total crime rate per capita. According to official data from a variety of countries, the number of all registered crimes per 100,000 Russians in 1992 was 1,856, while in 1990 the corresponding ratio was 5,820 in the US, 6,169 in France, 7,031 in Germany, 7,956 in the UK and 1,834 in Japan.[8] At this level of generalization, Russia appears to be as extremely law-abiding as Japan. However, as definitions and registration of crime vary across

TABLE 5.3   Homicides per 100,000 Inhabitants in Various Countries

Country	Homicide Frequency	Year
Russia	21.8	1994
Russia	10.9	1991
Colombia	74.4	1990
Mexico	16.8	1990
Brazil	16.3	1987
Venezuela	12.1	1989
USA	9.1	1989
Argentina	5.9	1989
Poland	2.9	1991
Hungary	4.0	1991
Czechoslovakia	2.0	1990
Italy	2.2	1989
France	1.1	1990
Germany	1.0	1990
Japan	0.6	1991
England and Wales	0.5	1991

SOURCE: Goskomstat Rossii, *Sotsial'no-ekonomicheskoe polozhenie Rossii 1994 g.,* Moscow, 1995, p. 168; United Nations, *Demographic Yearbook 1992,* New York, 1994, pp. 691–705.

countries, we may content ourselves with observing that the gross registered crime rate in Russia even at its peak is not particularly high.

For an international comparison of crime levels, we are better served by looking at specific crimes. Homicides are reasonably easily defined and well recorded in most places. The number of homicides per 100,000 inhabitants in a variety of countries is presented in Table 5.3. A first observation is that Russia with 22 murders per 100,000 inhabitants in 1994 has a very high rate. The data also reveal that homicide rates vary greatly among countries, and Russia has currently a rate which is about twice as high as in the US and slightly higher than in several large Latin American countries, which are known for their high incidence of violent crimes, such as Mexico and Brazil. Still, Colombia's homicide rate is three to four times higher than Russia's.

The Russian murder rate has been very high for a long time. Already in 1985, based on official Russian statistics published later, it equaled the homicide rate in the US at 8 per 100,000 inhabitants.[9] However, as it was not reported at the time, this was completely unknown.

In fact, it seems that the differences among countries are far greater than changes in Russia over time. Thus, in Western Europe and Japan, the murder rate is 0.5–2 per 100,000 inhabitants, and 2 to 4 in transition countries of Eastern

TABLE 5.4   Development of Crime in Russia, Poland and Hungary, 1989–1993 (annual increase in percent)

		1989	1990	1991	1992	1993
Russia		32.7	13.6	17.9	27.3	1.4
Poland		15.2	61.3	-2.2	2.0	-3.2
Hungary		21.6	51.3	29.1	1.6	-10.3
	1988*	1989	1990	1991	1992	1993
Russia	100.0	132.7	150.7	177.6	226.2	229.4
Poland	100.0	115.2	185.9	181.8	185.4	179.4
Hungary	100.0	121.6	184.0	237.6	241.3	216.3

*Index 1988=100

SOURCE: Glowny Urzad Statystyczny, *Rocznik Statystyczny 1991,* Warsaw, 1991, p. 74; Glowny Urzad Statystyczny, *Rocznik Statystyczny 1994,* Warsaw, 1994, p. 92; Hungarian Central Statistical Office, *Statistical Yearbook 1989–1990,* Budapest, 1991, p. 374; Központi Statisztikai Hivatal, *Magyar statisztikai évkönyv 1992,* Budapest, 1993, p. 314; Központi Statisztikai Hivatal, *Magyar statisztikai évkönyv 1993,* Budapest, 1994, p. 339.

Europe (Poland, Czechoslovakia, and Hungary). Moreover, in Soviet times Russian crimes were not very conspicuous as they were not concentrated in large cities, but remote regions. In 1989, the homicide rate in Siberia and the Far East was even twice as high as in the rest of Russia, as these areas were populated by many deported criminals.[10]

By comparison, other violent crimes do not appear to be higher in Russia than in other countries. If we compare selected crime rates of violent crimes in Moscow and New York in 1994, we find, for example, that the number of reported assaults is 13.1 times higher in New York than in Moscow.[11]

Another useful international comparison is the development of crime in the most advanced post-communist countries in East-Central Europe and in other former Soviet republics. For a comparison with Poland and Hungary, which offer the best and most comparable crime statistics, see Table 5.4.[12] The most surprising observation is how similar the development of crime has been in all three countries—far more so than any economic variable. In all these countries, the crime rate approximately doubled from 1988 to 1992. The Russian peculiarity is that the crime rate has risen more gradually with a maximum annual rise of only 33 percent in one year to compare with rises of 51 and 61 percent in Hungary and Poland, respectively.

After a big increase that ended in 1990 in Poland and in 1991 in Hungary, these two countries have experienced slight reductions in their crime rates. A tentative explanation for this development is that a more radical economic reform strategy appears to produce steeper increases in crime rates in the short term, while the total increase over time may be lower than in countries that pursue

TABLE 5.5   Increase in Crime in Some Former Soviet Republics from 1988 to 1992

Country	Increase in percent
Radical reformers	
Russia	126.2
Kyrgyzstan	129.1
Half-hearted reformers	
Belarus	98.8
Ukraine	97.6
Kazakhstan	89.4
Azerbaijan	60.2 (in war)
Moldova	51.9
Conservatives	
Tajikistan	89.4 (civil war)
Turkmenistan	38.8
Uzbekistan	33.6

NOTE: The war-ridden countries of Armenia and Georgia have been excluded for lack of comparable statistics.

SOURCE: Adapted from Inga B. Mikhailovskaya, "Crime and Statistics: Do the Figures Reflect the Real Situation?" *Demokratizatsiya,* vol. 2, no. 3 (Summer 1994), p. 414.

more gradual economic reform. The Russian crime development is more akin to Hungary's than to Poland's, with relatively large increases in crime during several years, that presumably is related to the more gradual reforms than in Poland. In comparison with these Central European countries, the Russian crime development is less dramatic.[13]

If this interpretation is correct, we would expect to see an early peak in the rise of crime in the most radical reformers among the former socialist countries. The half-hearted reformers would presumably see a more gradual increase in crime over a longer time, while the conservatives might experience these traumas much later.

In order to test this hypothesis, we take ten of the former Soviet republics for which data on the development of crime rates are available for the period from 1988 to 1992 and divide these ten countries into three groups: first, comparatively radical reformers, second, half-hearted reformers and third conservative reformers—countries which are pursuing only a minimum of reform.

The pattern we find supports our hypothesis (see Table 5.5). The most radical reformers (Russia and Kyrgyzstan), which were the only former Soviet republics to avoid hyperinflation, experienced the greatest rise in crime from 1988 to 1992. The half-hearted reformers form an intermediary category. The most conservative countries (Turkmenistan and Uzbekistan) saw little increase in crime with the exception of Tajikistan which was caught in civil war, which boosted its crime rate.[14] In light of this comparative evidence, the development of crime rates in Russia is not extraordinary. The close correlation between reform strategy and development of crime rates as reported in official statistics also lends credibility to this data.

We can conclude that the Russian crime rate is low by international comparison with the exception of the Russian homicide rate, which is considerably higher than in the US, Western Europe, or Japan. However, it does not exceed the murder rate in some of the Latin American countries. There are several tentative explanations for Russia's higher murder rate, although more research is certainly warranted. First, murder rates have been high traditionally. And second, a certain share of these murders is caused by organized crime.

With respect to other crimes, in comparison with the development in Eastern Europe, Russia's experience does not appear to be unusual. The same is true when we compare Russia with other former Soviet Union republics. Until 1992, crime increased faster in Russia than in most other former Soviet republics (with the exception of Kyrgyzstan). As has been pointed out, this appears to be related to the pace of economic reforms with a steeper rise in crime early on, which is likely to be followed by a leveling off of crime rates relatively soon after the introduction of reforms.

Several causes of crime are economic. From this initial review of the development of crime in post-communist countries, the suspicion arises, that the transition to a market economy is characterized by three broad processes with relevance for crime. First, a market economy does open new opportunities for crime. Second, during transition, sources of illicit private revenues are plentiful. This boosts the crime rate both directly and indirectly. Third, once the pillars of a market economy have been properly built and most property has been privatized, many sources of illicit rents dry up, and a new discipline is gradually imposed. This is likely to lead to a subsequent decline in the crime rate.

How a Burgeoning Market Initially Stimulates Crime

The introduction of a market economy gives people and enterprises opportunities to undertake many more transactions and lowers transaction costs. The Soviet economy was monetized only to a very limited extent. Therefore, a thief found it difficult to sell his booty, and he might have been forced into barter, which reduced the benefits of the theft. The limited availability of markets made it less attractive to steal both commodities and money. Monetization raised the value of the loot and reduced the risk of detection. The opening of the borders means that contraband can be imported and exported, raising the price of valuable goods, such as antiques and art. Moreover, emerging markets typically breed a large number of rich capitalists, offering criminals more attractive targets than the Soviet poverty provided.

While the market emerged, little was done to discipline it. If a date should be chosen for when the old Soviet repression ended, it would probably be 1989, when the First USSR Congress of People's Deputies in May and June signified the breakthrough of the freedom of speech. Hence, old-style repression ended before the market had been established. New market-conforming legislation, however, evolved only several years later. This resulted in a legal vacuum or a war of laws, as old laws were too absurd to be taken seriously, but new laws were not yet in place. There was little the police and courts cared to do—all the more since they had become viewed as public enemies. The funding of the police was badly neglected in the midst of the financial crisis, and the police had low wages and little equipment. Nor were the courts in any shape to take contention, as the old judges had been used to pass judgments without allowing any defense.

Another reason for the burgeoning crime rates in Russia and much of Eastern Europe during the early days of reform is that the supply of potential criminals may have increased. Court sentences grew milder, and the prison population fell sharply as a result of various amnesties. In the Czech Republic, much of the rise in the crime rate can be explained by the prison population falling from 16,000 to 6,000 through an amnesty in early 1990. Many hard criminals came out of the camps, exploiting the new opportunities. Yet, it would be an exaggeration to say that the social order broke down. The state was only temporarily weakened.

A peculiarity of Russia in comparison with Eastern Europe is that organized crime evidently became important from the outset. This is an interesting issue that may be explained in various ways—historically, ethnically or economically. One explanation is that the Russian crime world has long been well-organized.[15] Another historical reason is that the Communist Party was so corrupt that it really comprised a Mafia.[16] Third, the war in Afghanistan left Russia with tens of thousands of well-trained killers with no other occupation. A fourth explanation is the dominance of many ethnically organized gangs with tight personal relationships based on clan membership.[17] A fifth explanation ventured by Nikolai Shmelev is that they emerged from the semi-prohibition of Gorbachev's anti-alcohol campaign, similar to the rise in organized crime in the US during the period of prohibition.[18] Finally, there is some anecdotal evidence that Russian criminals often kill rather than leaving witnesses, as the penalty for minor crimes is so intimidating that criminals prefer to diminish the risk of detection, even though they may risk more severe sentence. Finally, the decaying military left Russia with plenty of cheap arms. As a consequence, the real cost of a contract murder fell, and their share of the total has long increased, while domestic homicides fell from 41 percent of the total in 1988 to 25 percent of the total number of homicides in 1992.[19]

Market Distortions Causing
Large Illicit Revenues

As noted above, the peculiarities of Russian crime are a high homicide rate and strong organized crime. Organized crime is typically run as a profit-oriented enterprise. Because of its economic nature, we need to seek its economic roots.

Typical causes of organized crime are gross market distortions, such as restrictions on trade and price regulations.[20] In the wake of the systemic change, a large number of ways for more or less legal enrichment arose. Even if they were formally legal at the source, they were so distorted and offered such blatant enrichment that they gave rise to criminality. For instance, subsidized credits might be given legally, but traded illegally at huge premiums. Three major sources of concentrated wealth were at hand during the early stages of the Russian transition to capitalism.[21]

As early as 1988, one important source of privileged wealth opened up. Well-connected traders could purchase oil and metals domestically at very low state-controlled prices and sell them abroad at the world market price. These exports, that accounted for about two thirds of Russia's exports, were regulated through quotas and licenses. Therefore, they involved either privilege or bribery. In the spring of 1992, the price of Russian oil was only one percent of the world market price, and even in January 1995, the Russian oil price was only one third of the world price.[22] In 1992, the gross amount of such effectively subsidized exports was at least US $24 billion, that is, over 30 percent of the GDP that year. Total Russian exports outside of the CIS were officially US $42.4 billion in 1992. Of these exports about two thirds were subject to export quotas and licenses and the average domestic price of these goods—primarily oil, gas, and metals—were not more than one tenth of the world market prices. From this amount the total actually paid in export tariffs amounted to roughly US $2 billion. Note also that GDP in 1992 was only US $80 billion.[23] A full liberalization of all exports would do away with this source of illicit revenues.

A second major source of illicit rents was similar but related to imports. Russia had special exchange rates for so-called critical imports until 1993. As a result, Russian importers of grain paid only one percent of the world market price of grain they imported, while they sold the bread products at ordinary domestic prices. These huge import subsidies, which amounted to $12.5 billion in 1992 or 15 percent of GDP,[24] were pocketed by Russian foreign traders and gave rise to substantial bribery in the foreign trade organization. Moreover, the wholesale trade network for food has become heavily involved in organized crime. Fortunately, this source of illicit income was abolished by Minister of Finance Boris Fedorov in 1993.

A third vast source of illicit incomes has been subsidized state credits, issued by the Central Bank of Russia (CBR). In 1992, the CBR issued huge subsidized credits at an interest rate of either 10 or 25 percent per annum, while the inflation amounted to 2,500 percent. In 1992, this volume was in the order of 30 percent of GDP. Thus, these subsidized credits were sheer gifts from the state to various middlemen. As a consequence, the banking sector was impregnated with crime. The subsidized credits were stopped by Boris Fedorov in September 1993. Although some were issued to agriculture in 1994, both the volume and the degree of subsidization are much less.

In total, these three sources of rents amounted to no less than 75 percent of GDP in 1992 or $60 billion (as these are gross numbers, they can add up to several times the GDP).

As of 1995, one of these sources of rent unfortunately remains. That is the export controls for oil and natural gas. Total exports of oil and oil products outside of the former Soviet Union amount to about $15 billion a year, and exports of natural gas to some $7 billion. Together they composed 45 percent of Russian exports in 1994.[25] At a maximum, illicit revenues from the energy sector might have amounted to half the exports, that is, $11 billion or 4 percent of GDP, which is significantly lower than in 1992 but still a lot of money. The Russian capital flight in 1994, conservatively estimated at $5 billion, is widely considered to pertain primarily to the energy sector. Thus, the oil and gas sector, that is controlled by a dozen men, executives of big companies and ministers, has net assets of several billion dollars freely available abroad that they can use as they please. These assets can be put into anybody's bank account abroad as a bribe or be used for personal enrichment. The gas industry is legally exempt from taxes, and the export controls are designed to benefit oil executives who trade limited volumes of oil on their own account. Therefore, these privatized energy revenues are no better than tax evasion.

These illicit revenues dwarf racketeering, which is the most renowned crime. In general, Russian traders state in interviews that they pay 15–20 percent of their turnover to racketeers. However, not all pay and everybody has an interest in exaggerating such burdens to provoke action. Therefore, it appears more plausible that about 10 percent of the retail sales is paid to racketeers. Since total retail sales corresponded to one third of GDP in 1994, that would be 3.3 percent of GDP or about $10 billion.[26] Our figure is an estimate of gross illicit revenues from racketeering, and that is a far more labor intensive activity than oil trading. Without venturing too far into guesstimates, total net rents in the oil and gas industry are most likely greater than total net revenues from racketeering in Russia.

These findings present a very different perspective on organized crime in Russia from the conventional attitude. The main problem of organized crime is not racketeering, prostitution, drug trade or trade in nuclear materials, but the exploitation of the state treasury for the benefit of well-placed vested interests.

A second conclusion is that the problem with this kind of organized crime has dwindled sharply—from gross revenues of some $60 billion in 1992 to about $11 billion in 1994 or from 75 percent of GDP to 4 percent of GDP.

A third conclusion is that the main target today should be to eliminate the illicit energy rents that go to a small number of individuals who use their position in the government and at the top of public enterprises for their illegitimate personal enrichment. Technically, this is easy: it is enough to effectively liberalize oil and gas exports and impose ordinary taxes on these industries. Politically, the number of direct beneficiaries is too small for their own good, though they can pay others.

To fight entrenched racketeering is far more difficult, but some steps are obvious. The freedom of enterprise has not been fully established in Russia, as local licensing is required for most enterprises. As a consequence, local authorities limit competition and subject enterprises to pressure. This lack of legal certainty facilitates racketeering.

Why Crime in Russia Is Likely to Fall

Based on the findings presented in this paper, we may conclude that there are many reasons why we should expect crime to fall in Russia. Overwhelmingly, the most important economic roots of crime have dwindled—price controls, export controls, subsidized credits and multiple exchange rates. In addition, the whole Russian society is mobilizing against crime. It would be surprising if such an onslaught would not reduce crime for a long time.

There are several reasons why we should expect the Russian crime rate to fall in the future. First, liberalization and stabilization have removed most of the mechanisms of rent-seeking and corruption. Liberalization has eliminated import subsidies. Since most regulations have abated, formally or informally, the Russian market has achieved a significant saturation and regional price disparities have fallen in 1995. Hence, also racketeers are being squeezed and find it increasingly difficult to extract their protection payments, as there is less monopoly rent for them to tax. Export restrictions have been eliminated for almost all products but oil and natural gas, and these export restrictions now compose the greatest remaining source of rent-seeking. Thanks to the abolition of subsidized credits, and the reduction of inflation, a great deal of rent-seeking has been abolished.

Second, far-reaching privatization has transferred most state property to the private sector. Therefore, corrupt officials have less "public" property from which they can extract illicit rents. While privatization might involve once-for-all bribes, the leasing of state property implies persistent flows of bribes, as is unfortunately the case in Moscow, which has not gone through the standard privatization procedure. Moreover, the new property owners demand that the government protect their newly won property, and they will be the main source of financing for political campaigns.

Third, step by step, the Russian legislation is being improved. A constitution was adopted in December 1993. Gradually, socialist legislation is being abandoned and market economic legislation is being adopted. A market-oriented civil code was passed in early 1995; a company law was enacted in January 1996; a new criminal code has now been enacted and "speculation" is no longer a crime. Thus, Russian legislation is improving, even if more sophisticated laws against racketeering, corruption and white-collar crimes are still missing.[27]

Fourth, in communist times, crime was barely reported in the media. Today, the Russian media report professionally and extensively on crime. This has many effects, and they are all the greater as Russian criminals tend to target the upper middle class rather than poor people. Russians think crime has risen more than it has. Hence, they demand that the authorities intensify their fight against crime, exerting a strong political pressure. An additional consequence is that the public adjust their habits and undertake various security measures that diminish their personal risk of being harmed by crime.

Fifth, government allocations to law enforcement have risen considerably, and are internationally at a very high level, almost 2 percent of GDP. The Russian police have received plenty of new equipment: fast western cars, bullet-proof vests, submachine guns, and mobile telephones, even if they are still short of computers. Russian police salaries have risen sharply and are now substantially higher than the average wage. The police force and the number of judges are expanding.

Sixth, during the last years of communism, the number of prisoners fell rapidly. Many convicted criminals, who were let out, soon committed new crimes, which is an important reason for the rising crime rate. Now, on the contrary, the number of prisoners is increasing fast. In 1994, the number of sentenced criminals kept in camps and prisons rose by 65,000 to 676,400—proportionately a slightly higher figure than for the US with 950,000 convicts in prison.[28]

Seventh, after the momentous changes of the last years of communism and the introduction of a new economic and political system, social order is improving.

Eighth, Russian lawyers have a wonderful labor market, as new commercial enterprises need lawyers for a variety of purposes, and they pay well. Hence, the legal education has become very prestigious and attractive. Over time, this should boost the number and quality of lawyers.

Finally, the Russian market is gaining strength, but crime implies high transaction costs, which impede the effective functioning of the market. Millions of Russian entrepreneurs have eminent incentives to undertake a large number of small acts to reduce transaction costs. Hence, they will naturally endeavor to reduce crime, and for instance the Association of Russian Bankers persistently demands that the government takes firmer actions to combat organized crime, while the banks themselves have developed extraordinary security measures to salvage themselves from being harmed by crime. It is inconceivable that the many new entrepreneurs would accept to pay large fees to an unreliable and dangerous Mafia. Moreover, the Mafia is not all that sophisticated. In its racketeering, it appears to limit itself to cash transactions.[29]

Against all these reasons why crime should decline, there are few grounds for suggesting the opposite development. It is frequently argued that organized crime will become—or has become—so well entrenched and developed that it will become insurmountable.[30] A danger does exist, but countervailing forces are many, as discussed. The new international openness of Russia does provide new opportunities for crimes. Notably drug crime is serious and will provide a long-term ground for crime. The possible trade in nuclear materials poses unique dangers. Yet, in the overall picture, these phenomena appear of limited significance.

To put the current hysteria over Russian crime both in Russia and the West in an appropriate perspective, a historical parallel is useful. Contrary to what many believe, the world has seen the creation of capitalism before, and comparative empirical evidence is at hand. In the 1840s, Western Europe went through one of the greatest liberalizations of all times. Suddenly, stifling feudal regulations were abandoned for *laissez-faire*. All kinds of free markets opened up, both domestically and internationally. The economy started booming, but a public outcry raged over rising crime as the old patriarchal order was abandoned. Legislation was minimal; police and new independent courts barely existed.

However, very soon the crime rate started falling. Laws were gradually promulgated; the courts gained strength; the police developed. All kinds of crime statistics show a drastic decline in the frequency of crimes in Britain and France, the two best studied countries, from around 1850 until World War II. Curiously, this had minimal impact on the public debate, although the quality of the reporting increased all the time. Until the end of the 19th century the discussion on the right as well as the left was dominated by a discussion about rising crime, for which there was no statistical evidence. Since reality did not fit the perceptions of major political groups, the falling crime rate was disregarded.[31]

A multitude of different political groups opposed the new order and insinuated that it caused more crime. Socialists argued that a growing gap between rich and poor and the crisis of capitalism caused crime. Conservatives thought that industrialization and urbanization brought about a decline in traditional values, social control and religion, and thus prompted more crimes. Few paid attention to reality, and those who did were largely neglected.

Clearly, the Russian situation today is similar. Those on the left and many Sovietologists attack shock therapy and liberalization as evil. Russian communists and conservatives romanticize traditional values or repression. Free and independent media bring out all the terrible events in society in the open as was the case in the second half of the 19th century in Western Europe. Journalists find that sensational stories about the criminalized Russia sell well. Some Sovietologists, journalists and Russians who want to emphasize the unique nature of Russia argue that Russia is becoming a unique Mafia-dominated country.[32] Under such circumstances, reality becomes victim to prejudice.

Notes

1. Melissa Meeker has assisted me with tracing materials for this paper.
2. *OMRI Daily Digest*, February 15, 1995.
3. Louise I. Shelley (1995), p. 56.
4. Seymour M. Hersch (1994), p. 62.
5. Anders Åslund (1991).
6. Sheila Marnie and Albert Motivan (1993), p. 80.

7. Personal experience when getting a steel-door installed at my apartment in Moscow in the fall of 1993.

8. Inga B. Mikhailovskaya (1994), p. 412.

9. Marnie and Motivan (1993), p. 81.

10. Marnie and Motivan (1993), p. 82.

11. Steven Erlanger (1995), p. A10.

12. The Czech statistics are not fully comparable, but the crime rate in the Czech Republic appears to have risen more than even in Hungary but from a very low level. Jiri Pehe (1994), pp. 43–44.

13. The striking similarities in the development of crime in Russia and Central Europe may also be seen as a verification of Russian crime statistics. If Russian crime develops approximately as we would have expected from our knowledge of crime development in Central Europe, Russian crime statistics are probably not too bad.

14. Inga B. Mikhailovskaya (1994), pp. 414–415.

15. Arkady Vaksberg (1991); Stephen Handelman (1995); "Vory v zakone zanimayut ofisy" (Izvestiya, October 19, 1994), p. 5.

16. Ilja Zemtsov (1982).

17. "Grafa national 'nost' v ankete bandy." (Izvestiya, October 21, 1994) p. 5; Vadim Belykh, "Gruzinsky sled rossiiskoi mafii" (Izvestiya, November 9, 1994), p. 1.

18. Nikolai Shmelev (1987), pp. 142–158.

19. "Ubiistvo po preiskurantu" (Izvestiya, October 20, 1994), p. 5.

20. See Åslund (1995).

21. Data in this section come from Anders Åslund (1995).

22. OMRI Daily Digest, February 14, 1995.

23. Åslund (1995), pp. 156–161, 197, 281.

24. International Monetary Fund (1993), pp. 132–133, 140.

25. Goskomstat Rossii (1995), pp. 73–74.

26. Rossii (1995), p. 3.

27. Louise I. Shelley (1995), p. 57.

28. "Results of the Work of the Internal Affairs Organs and the Internal Troops in 1994" (Segodnya, February 23, 1995), p. 7.

29. Personal interviews with various business people in Moscow from 1993 to 1995.

30. Sterling (1994); Hersch (1994), pp. 61–86; Handelman (1994), pp. 83–96; Handelman (1995); Marshall I. Goldman (1995), p. C2.

31. Lynn McDonald (1982), pp. 404–420.

32. Sterling (1994); Hersch (1994), pp. 61–86; Handelman (1994), pp. 83–96; Handelman (1995); Goldman (1995), p. C2.

CHAPTER 6

Police, Secret Police, and Civil Authority

J. Michael Waller

Rule of law depends on the effective and universal enforcement of laws in independent courts. Despite the West's assistance in legal reforms, virtually nothing has been devoted to transcending the Soviet legacy of the police and secret police, and their corrosive effect on civil authority. Not enough recognition has been given to the need to transform the law enforcement administration from its corrupt and totalitarian legacy and to promote civil controls by elected officials, impartial courts, and independent public oversight. This has had detrimental effects on markets, political development, human rights, international business and investment, as well as international security.

While many laws and much of the criminal code have been developing for the better, the changes in law enforcement since the Soviet era have been minimal. Law enforcement is selective, often motivated by political, business, or criminal factors. After 1994, Russian authorities resumed arresting and imprisoning citizens for their political views. In addition, federal law enforcement leaders were among the prime initiators and executors of the war in Chechnya, which claimed tens of thousands of lives. Many of the casualties were inflicted by the combat troops of the federal police, which made up half of Chechnya's fighting force of mechanized units, armor, and artillery.

The Chechnya war sapped the federal police budget to pay decent salaries to officers, upgrade transportation, communications, and criminological technology, improve training and analysis, and rebuild the crumbling physical structure of police stations across the country. Yet the commander of the murderous internal troops in Chechnya, Anatoly Kulikov, was promoted in 1996 to become Russia's top law enforcement officer.

This chapter gives an overview of the history and transition of the Soviet security forces since the introduction of *perestroika* reforms in the mid-1980s. It traces the common roots of the KGB and the MVD in the *chekist* culture of the early days of the Soviet regime and provides evidence on how this culture has infiltrated civil state administration in the post-Soviet period. The chapter argues that the roots of organized crime and corruption in present day Russia lie in these unreformed structures. They were able to trade their political power for far reaching economic power, while still preserving sufficient influence on the new political elite to prevent any serious restructuring attempts of these forces. The post 1991 reform governments have proven incapable or unwilling to overcome this resistance to reform. As a result, a crucial opportunity for providing the basis for the development of a civil society and for a state based on the rule of law accountable to its citizens and constrained by checks and balances has been foregone.

Russia's Inheritance

The Russian Federation's legal, investigative, and judicial system are direct holdovers of the late Soviet regime. The government of President Boris Yeltsin inherited the structures and personnel of the USSR Ministry of Internal Affairs (MVD) on its territory and subordinated it to the Russian Federation MVD as the national *militsiya*–police force. The Soviet and Russian state procuracies,[1] who were responsible for investigating and prosecuting a range of crimes and for reviewing all MVD activity, were also merged. The Yeltsin administration absorbed and divided the function of the main pillar of government coercive power, the Committee for State Security (KGB).

In a single organization, the KGB performed foreign espionage and intelligence, internal security, military and police counterintelligence, transportation security, ideological enforcement (including political and religious repression), eavesdropping, prison administration, electronic intelligence and counterintelligence, cryptography, construction and administration of nuclear bunkers and other strategic sites, security of nuclear weapons, personal security of the political leadership, border security and coastal patrol, and an array of other functions, ranging from criminal investigations of certain major economic crimes and crimes against the state to law "enforcement," obtaining banned goods from abroad for Party officials, and conducting political assassinations at home and overseas. With some of the Soviet Union's brightest minds and most ruthless thugs, the KGB was an armed bureaucracy of more than 500,000 officers, 240,000 troops, tens of thousands of support staff, and millions of agents and informers. KGB cadres were regimented in a vertical structure commanded from the center and extending to all levels of society. The KGB's most potent weapons were the ability to procure information and unchecked power to intimidate and coerce. The organization collected, synthesized, and safeguarded the secrets not only of the party and the state, but of the individual—his beliefs and associates, habits and indiscretions. As the single most important information source for Kremlin leaders, the KGB influenced what decision-makers thought and what they decided, and officers often carried out the orders they had originally helped to design.[2]

The KGB always dominated the MVD. Second in the law enforcement hierarchy, the MVD's responsibility was to fight crimes against the individual such as armed robbery, assault, pederasty, evasion of child support; offenses termed "state crimes" such as prostitution and pornography, black market trading and theft or damage of state property, trade and natural resource violations, theft or forgery of documents; and vehicular, firearms, and drug violations.[3] The MVD also maintained standing armies of special riot forces and internal troops to put down not only civil disturbances but to wage domestic military operations, such as the war in Chechnya.

Chekist Culture

As the enforcement mechanisms of totalitarian rule, the KGB and its post-Soviet successors, MVD and State Procuracy, shared bureaucratic cultures rooted in the hard core of Bolshevism, the Extraordinary Commission for Combating Counterrevolution and Sabotage, known by its acronym VChK or "Cheka." Established under V. I. Lenin and headed by Feliks Dzerzhinsky, the Cheka waged a campaign of systematic repression, mass theft, and mass murder to impose Bolshevik control over the territories that became the Soviet Union. To mobilize individuals capable of committing such crimes, the Bolsheviks recruited directly from fanatical party cells and also enlisted common criminals in tsarist prisons. The procuracy and MVD fully served as KGB accomplices. The Cheka, with the MVD as its surrogate, acted with such impunity from the start that even under Lenin it was an open question as to whether the party controlled its own enforcers. In July 1918, a Bolshevik commissar of justice pointed to the lack of controls and warned that unless the Party limited the Cheka's powers, "We shall have a state within a state."[4] Ironically that was what Vadim Bakatin, the last chairman of the USSR KGB, called the Cheka's successor three-quarters of a century later.[5]

From the beginning chekist cadres, the *chekisti*, developed a distinct sense of superiority over society and over the *militsiya*, enjoying almost unlimited power. An individual officer could deal with ordinary citizens at whim. The elite world of chekism came to bear many of the hallmarks of a cult: a closed group, an existence on the outskirts of society, secret internal rites, and a fanatical devotion to its leader or founder. Stalin developed a Dzerzhinsky cult of personality alongside that of the late Lenin, until he dwarfed both with his own. De-Stalinization under Khrushchev restored the Lenin and Dzerzhinsky personality cults. After becoming KGB chairman in 1967, Yuri Andropov painstakingly refined the idealization of Dzerzhinsky, both within KGB bureaucratic culture and among the Soviet public.

What does this all have to do with Russian law enforcement and security today? The continuum is unbroken. The *chekisti* and *militsiya* have outlived the Communist Party. Eighty years after the Bolshevik Revolution, most of the Cheka archives remain sealed, and the iconography of the Cheka and Dzerzhinsky has been preserved. The security and intelligence services, the MVD and the State Procuracy, traded the hammer-and-sickle for the double-headed eagle, but all maintain the sword and shield of the Cheka as their institutional coats of arms. After Russian President Boris Yeltsin's anti-communist campaign, which even sullied the greatness of Lenin, Dzerzhinsky emerged as the only Bolshevik leader free of official taint. To this day, the MVD's most elite unit bears the name of the Cheka founder.[6]

Roots of Organized Crime in the Russian Federation Today

With their near-absolute powers given by the party to monitor, arrest, prosecute or persecute Soviet citizens (*nomenklatura* excepted), their joint supervision with the procuracy over the *militsiya*, and the all-too-willing collaboration of the courts, the *chekisti* effectively controlled law enforcement. This raises the question about the levels crime and competition have reached under the eyes of the seemingly ever-present police and secret police. Particularly during *perestroika*, when politicians freely called for the KGB to be abolished, the *chekisti* scrambled to find new *raisons d'être* to win public support; they could have redeemed themselves by employing resources and authority for the common good.

In fact, since the mid-1980s, the KGB had become increasingly involved in fighting crime. *Perestroika* image-making campaigns cast the KGB as the hero in the war against naked graft and gangsterism that broke the surface under glasnost.[7] After radical democrats, allied with Andrei Sakharov in the newly opened political system, publicly demanded that the KGB's vast domestic spying networks be dissolved, the *chekisti* credibly cast themselves as crime fighters and upholders of the law. Russia's MVD chief remarked in late 1991, "Why . . . did the KGB get involved in [fighting crime] at all? Its leaders simply felt that sooner or later they would be asked for concrete results, for something real done in the state's interests . . . and so [fighting] crime was needed."[8]

This implies that the KGB's anti-crime crusade was a tactical and cynical move to curry political legitimacy, but had little impact on impeding the actual development of crime. In a one-party regime that controlled all legal economic activity, natural market forces went underground: petty theft of state resources, small-time bribery for bureaucratic favors, protection payments to keep the authorities at bay—these became standard and unofficially accepted means of survival. Organized corruption and, on a grander scale, organized crime flourished by feeding off the massive state administrative command system. In a kind of symbiotic parasitism, much of the bureaucracy prospered by abusing power and demanding bribes and other payoffs from legitimate and illegitimate businesses.[9]

Midway through the *perestroika* period, sociologist Tatyana Zaslavskaya described the situation of crime, law enforcement, and justice. To her, the "mafia" was not the underworld but the state:

The first element of the mafia is corrupt party and government officials. The second part is the workers and employees of the retail trade, at every level, who are obliged to pay money to the chain that kicks back the apparat. It is impossible to work within this branch if you don't go along with the program. You will be disposed of very cruelly . . . But there's a third element of the mafia, without which it could not operate. The *militsiya*, prosecutors, courts, judges—all the law enforcement people are bought by the trade people. So it is quite impossible to get social justice by appealing to the courts.[10]

Such corruption had been endemic for years. During the Brezhnev era, the KGB leadership recognized the problem but the party would not allow it to act. Viewing corruption of law enforcement as a greater security threat than organized crime, KGB Chairman Yuri Andropov, who succeeded Brezhnev as Communist Party General Secretary in 1982, soon ordered the KGB to impose direct control over the MVD. For reasons not entirely clear—perhaps due to the depth and breadth of corruption within the *militsiya*, procuracy, and courts—the KGB sought not to build legal cases for trials against suspect officials, but to enter the fray of power struggle and corruption.

According to Georgy Podlesskikh and Andrei Tereshonok, two former KGB officers who wrote an important book on the Russian *mafiya* based on internal state security documents, the KGB renewed the Cheka's practice of "relying on criminals in combat" against "enemies of the people." This time, the enemies were not dissidents but corrupt bureaucrats, party functionaries, and MVD officers. The KGB recruited gangsters marginalized from Soviet society—the so-called *vory v zakone* or "thieves-in-law"—and provided them with material support, intelligence, and direction to terrorize corrupt targets in Soviet officialdom.[11]

Podlesskikh and Tereshonok cite specific cases showing that the practice continued well into the *perestroika* period. KGB protection, tradecraft, and information transformed the *vory* substrata into a much more influential force at a time when *perestroika* began to open the economy with limited, partial privatization and early joint ventures with Western firms.[12] Soon, however, the temptations that long before had corrupted the *militsiya* through its personal contact with the criminal underworld began to influence the *chekisti*. The state security organs were able to misuse the new opportunities offered by *perestroika* reforms to further their own interests. When the economy began to open under party direction, the CPSU leadership assigned the KGB the task of devising means to set up front companies and other organizations to handle the disposal of state properties and raw materials abroad, and to assist with moving the money accrued from illicit activities.

At the same time, the party granted the KGB broader crime-fighting authority, in addition to its standing authority, to investigate economic crimes and theft of state property.[13] The *chekisti* were at a crossroads: the regime was undergoing a radical power shift, whereby functionaries with mere administrative authority could now officially control and own wealth. In a time of extreme uncertainty, everyone seemed to be scurrying for a piece of this new power base. Soviet-era laws rapidly became obsolete as the enforcement of socialist statutes no longer served a practical purpose. In such an environment, the KGB was not only duty bound to investigate, monitor and pursue lawbreakers; it was empowered to help move large amounts of money illicitly and protect officials flagrantly engaged in criminal activity. It could perform both contradictory roles free of checks and balances.

Perestroika Transition: Corruption of Reform

In order to understand why Mikhail Gorbachev received near-unanimous support from the party Central Committee to abolish the CPSU's monopoly on political power in 1990, let us review the exchange of political for economic power that took place in this period. This transition ensured that the economic reform legislation of 1987 began a process that allowed the *nomenklatura*, including state enterprise directors and bureaucrats, to own legally what they had until then merely administered.

The ruling class—Party, Komsomol, military-industrial complex (VPK), fuel and energy complex (TEK), state bureaucracy, elements of the armed forces, and the KGB—took full advantage of economic and political reform processes under *perestroika*. Enjoying simultaneous control over the state distribution system, the groups in power were able to allocate assets among their members without competition from private entrepreneurs. The Central Committee assigned the KGB the task of developing the mechanisms for these transactions. As controls over economic assets were decentralized, KGB officers participated with the transfer of cash, strategic materials, weapons, and other marketable products under their control. In this process, they became a major part of the emerging private sector. This early privatization was dubbed *prikhvatizatsiya*, a pun on the verb *prikhvatit*, meaning to grab.[14]

The first joint ventures with foreign firms were subject to state controls that ensured that only authorized officials could run and profit from business with foreigners. The Party ran many of the early joint ventures; others were run by the KGB frequently in conjunction with cooperatives using private and state capital. A key role in forming and running joint ventures was played by go-betweens affiliated with the Communist Party. They were officially banned for ideological reasons in 1989, but they remained a crucial element in the transitional economy. An example of the extent of the Party's involvement in joint venture activities and a symptom of internal party struggles over *prikhvatizatsiya* was the ANT venture founded in 1987. Involving a reported twenty KGB officers with support of Soviet Prime Minister Nikolai Ryzhkov, ANT imported Western goods for the *nomenklatura*. It was exposed in 1990 by rival factions.[15]

The KGB set up similar enterprises outside party channels. Colonel Viktor Kichikhin witnessed the process from his post in the KGB Fifth Chief Directorate. "In 1989–1990, most of the Soviet-Western joint venture enterprises were created by our directorate, except those which were established directly by the Central Committee of the CPSU," Kichikhin recalls.[16] Banks and holding companies that sprang up during this period, either as party or KGB creations or as independent enterprises that relied on official backing, came to dominate the emerging post-socialist economy. The leadership of the Fifth Chief Directorate was in charge of the informant networks, compilation of dossiers, and supervision of cadres in journalism, education, economics, and the rest of society—and could use a variety of means to secure the cooperation of budding businessmen—and also took care of members by securing them in key corporate positions.[17]

Some prominent Russian businessmen who saw the KGB take over their own enterprises have described the process. One of the few to speak on the record is Konstantin Borovoi, who founded the Russian Commodities and Raw Materials Exchange in 1989. Based on his own experience and conversations with other entrepreneurs, Borovoi explained that when it saw a potentially profitable business, the KGB operated as a "racket," placing strong pressure on the enterprise, which was then coming forward with "a KGB proposal to help." In exchange for "help," the entrepreneur would appoint "KGB officers into the top leadership of the company, or the leadership of the company [would get] in close contact with the KGB." Either way, said Borovoi, "the company ceased to exist as an independent commercial organization." Borovoi continued, "As a rule, at first these companies run into some economic difficulties, and then such a commercial organization suddenly begins to receive absolutely fantastic benefits or licenses—for aluminum, zinc, copper, or tomato paste—and begins a strong development. . . . The insiders immediately know that this organization has become a part of the financial structure of the KGB."[18]

To Borovoi and others, the KGB itself was an "organized crime" operation and, like the mafias of the West, attached itself parasitically to legitimate enterprises. As Zaslavskaya had found in her scholarly work during *perestroika*, Borovoi observed "a very close interaction between criminal groups and law enforcement agencies."[19]

In addition to the KGB control of selected companies, the government leadership launched several larger scale enterprises. A Russian Supreme Soviet investigative commission concluded that in the final few years of the Gorbachev regime,

. . . realizing as irrevocable the loss of then-authoritative and ideological priorities in society, the Politburo of the CPSU CC made several secret resolutions directed toward direct concealment in commercial structures of property and monetary resources actually accumulated at the expense of the nation. Based on this, at all levels of the party hierarchy, there was a mass founding of party banks, joint enterprises, and joint stock companies in 1990 and 1991.[20]

Most information on these activities remains secret, but some key documents have become public. A Central Committee resolution, titled "On Emergency Measures to Organize Commercial and Foreign Economic Activity of the Party" and passed on 23 August 1990, shows how the party, with KGB assistance, camouflaged its holdings in the emerging market system. The resolution, authored by Central Committee Administrator Nikolai E. Kruchina, called for the "preparation of proposals to create some new 'interim' economic structures . . . with minimum 'visible' ties to the Central Committee, which could become focal points of the 'invisible' party economy." It also sought to devise "plans for using anonymous organizations to mask direct links to the party when launching commercial and foreign economic party activity," to consider "merging with already functioning joint ventures, international consortiums, etc., through capital investment." The resolution envisioned the creation of a controlled bank for "hard currency operations" and investments abroad of "the party's hard currency reserves in international firms controlled by friends of the party."[21]

Though this particular resolution describes a plan and not an operation, it offers insight into the thinking of the party leadership in the late *perestroika* period. Other plans, as well as operations, demonstrably moved the party-controlled money abroad. The Central Committee leadership had placed Nikolai Kruchina, responsible for the CPSU financial and economic records, in charge of key offshore operations. A Politburo directive transferred KGB foreign intelligence personnel to Kruchina's office. In the words of one Russian report, the officers were assigned "to coordinate the business activity of the Party's economic structures in a changing situation."[22] One of the officers, Colonel Leonid Veselovsky, recommended arrangements to establish joint-stock companies in countries such as Switzerland with soft tax systems. He laid out a long-range plan to include the creation of a "multi-profile joint-stock company" as a partnership between the Swiss-Canadian Seabeco Group and the Union of Afghan War Veterans. The plan envisioned a "banking system, an airline, an international trading house, a privatization fund,[23] and a network of holding companies all over the country."[24]

Evidence suggests that these and similar directives were successfully implemented. Selected party officials signed "personal obligation" statements in July 1991, to be entrusted with hiding party funds.[25] With Central Committee documents ordering officials to "hide it," procuracy investigators opened criminal cases in late 1991, but little political will existed to pursue the suspects, and efforts to recover the funds and bring perpetrators to justice evaporated.[26]

Specific cases ultimately surfaced over time. The Seabeco firm, subject of Veselovsky's intrigues in 1990, became the focus of a major scandal in 1994 when the Russian press published reports that the wife of state security chief

Viktor Barannikov went on a six-figure shopping spree in Switzerland courtesy of the joint venture. This and other corruption allegations, which surfaced after Barannikov had had a severe disagreement with the president, prompted Yeltsin to relieve his security minister from his post.

Russian investigators and journalists, as well as Western intelligence services, have probed several large Russian firms established in the late 1980s and early 1990s to launder Communist Party–controlled funds in conjunction with the KGB. The most prolific case is Nordex, a Vienna-based company linked to Prime Minister Viktor Chernomyrdin and other high officials. A classified German BND intelligence report characterizes Nordex as a spy asset established "to earn hard currency for the KGB."[27]

While that view is not universally shared, it is clear that Nordex is one of many large firms that emerged during *perestroika* to become prominent in the post-Soviet economy, and that it allegedly conducted large-scale money laundering, commodities smuggling, and other trafficking with direct participation and support of high-level Soviet and Russian officials.[28] Far from being part of an anarchistic "Wild West," these robber barons are part of the political and economic establishment.

Impediments to Reform

Post-Soviet society thus emerged with a distinct disadvantage in overcoming corruption and organized crime. The security organs, though divided along functional lines after the 1991 putsch, posed a strong political threat to the civilian government of the Russian Federation. President Yeltsin reversed earlier insistences that the KGB be broken apart. Once the security organs were in his hands, he sought to co-opt them for his own purposes.

Russia's standing national police force remains the *militsiya* of the MVD.[29] The *chekisti* of the former KGB are now divided into five major components but reorganizations and name changes are frequent.[30] The Federal Security Service (*Federalnaya Sluzhba Bezopasnosti*, FSB) contains most of the KGB's old internal security apparatus, archives, and personnel. The External Intelligence Service (*Sluzhba Vneshnei Razvedki*, SVR) is the former KGB First Chief Directorate, whose domestic operational functions include recruiting foreigners within the Commonwealth of Independent States. Secure communications and electronic intelligence are performed by the Federal Agency for Government Communication and Information (*Federal'noe Agentsvo Pravitelstvennoy Sviazi i Informatsiy,* FAPSI), most of which is the former KGB Eighth Chief Directorate and 16th Directorate. The Federal Border Service, approximately 180,000 strong, conducts the same frontier guard and coastal duties as when it was the KGB Border Guards Chief Directorate. The Main Guard Directorate (*Glavnoye Upravleniye Okhrany*, GUO) operates security in government buildings, and from it was spun the Presidential Guards Service. A new Department of Tax

Police of the State Tax Committee was established after late 1991 and staffed with KGB personnel.

Elements of the security, intelligence and law enforcement organs, as well as the procuracy, have been strong proponents of across-the-board crackdowns on crime and corruption. They contain serious, dedicated personnel who do their best despite diminished prestige, low pay, and poor working conditions. Many have been maimed or killed in the line of duty. Some of the most famous crime-fighters—talented, incorruptible and dedicated public servants who unmasked major organized criminal activities among government officials only to find the government unwilling to prosecute—quit in frustration.[31] A combination of poor pay that understandably tempts rank-and-file officers, and high-level corruption at the top and in the government, has rotted the corps. Few officers are truly versed in liberal concepts of law, civil rights, *habeas corpus*, and due process.

Absence of Civil Controls

Five years after the introduction of political and economic reforms and in spite of the fact that a new post-Soviet constitution was enacted in late 1993, the state security forces remain without effective oversight or control. Most importantly, they are answerable only to the executive and have not been made accountable to the legislature. Under the current constitution, the security services report to the president directly and indirectly through the Security Council of the presidential apparatus; the Ministry of Internal Affairs reports directly to the procuracy and the president. It is not subject to direct Security Council control.[32]

President Yeltsin took a byzantine view on checks and balances. He did not introduce new institutional controls. Instead of installing strong leaders to root out corrupt and criminal elements inside the security bureaucracy, to safeguard against further corruption, and build entirely new services free of the chekist stigma, Yeltsin entrusted internal security and law enforcement to cronies whose greatest attributes were their personal loyalties to him. He initially tried to concentrate the *chekisti* power, not reduce it, under MVD control by merging the largest former KGB internal units with the *militsiya* in an immense but short-lived Ministry of Security and Internal Affairs. In late 1991 and early 1992, the Supreme Soviet and Constitutional Court successfully challenged his KGB-MVD merger, forcing him to retreat. Yeltsin dissolved both. He used military force to settle the conflict with the Parliament and subsequently authored a new constitution that left the legislative and judiciary branches as weak complements to a powerful executive.

Meanwhile, Yeltsin kept the internal security services in a constant state of conflict by splintering them, creating new and diverse organizations, and re-naming and reorganizing them. The central chekist internal security organs underwent five such changes under six chiefs between 1991 and 1996. As his personal watchdog against the *chekisti*, Yeltsin formed a 25,000-strong praetorian guard, loyal to him personally and endowed with its own powers of political patronage and the right to generate its own hard currency.[33] The Presidential Guards Service was created by decree, with no regulations or legal definition of its duties.[34] Yeltsin's closest civilian aides feared that the service had bugged their telephones and offices, finding themselves unable to conduct affairs normally.[35]

Despite the fact that laws enacted by the Russian Supreme Soviet and the fourth and fifth State Dumas specifically provided for parliamentary oversight, the parliament performs almost no oversight functions at all. It has so little authority to monitor state security and law enforcement that members of the Committee on Security of the State Duma and the Committee on Defense and Security of the upper house, the Federation Council, have requested information about the MVD from American authorities.[36] The Procurator General, which has strong supervisory authority over the *militsiya*, in 1994 scrapped its central department for supervising the *chekisti*.[37]

With no effective legal constraints, such as conflict of interest rules and ethics codes, officers have used their powers in such a way that it is next to impossible for civilian authorities to determine what activities are being conducted by the security forces in the interests of the country, or what activities simply amount to corrupt or criminal freelancing by individual officers. In other words, the distinction between national security, private business, and organized crime are blurred.[38] External sources of funding of the security organs ensures that their budgets are not subject to control by either president or parliament. Indeed, internal security chief Barannikov supervised the authorship of the 1992 Law on Security that specifically permitted the security organs to be financed by "extra-budgetary funds."[39] Furthermore, journalistic or scholarly reports of alleged wrongdoing within the security services is potentially a crime if the information is deemed to be a "state secret" or is "insulting the honor and integrity" of *chekisti* and their family members.[40]

Law Enforcement as a Political and Economic Tool

Law enforcement can be selective and subject to manipulation for political, economic, and extralegal reasons. Many of those who persecuted Soviet dissidents under the old regime remained in office as security and police officers.[41] Cases of continued persecution include dissident chemical weapons scientist Vil Mirzayanov, former Army Major Vladimir Petrenko, and former Navy Officer Aleksandr Nikitin. Those accused did not break any laws, but their statements and revelations antagonized the military, and as a result they were jailed or persecuted.[42]

State security hounded former Soviet dissident Sergei Grigoryants when he began pressing for the exposure of KGB crimes in 1993. They disrupted his conferences, ransacked his offices, and assaulted him as well as members of his family. Evidence strongly suggests that security forces murdered his son, Timofei, in January 1995.[43] When he and Glasnost Defense Foundation leader Alexei Simonov organized a campaign for an international tribunal on Chechnya war crimes in 1995, authorities confiscated their documents, including materials from the Soldiers' Mothers organization. Among the confiscated documents were a Memorial report on a March 1995 army massacre of civilians and a letter from human rights figure Yelena Bonner.[44] In the first eighteen months of the Chechnya war, state security and the MVD arrested hundreds of journalists and confiscated notes, tapes, film, and equipment.[45] Human Rights Watch/Helsinki and others reported that after a brief blossoming of civil liberties after the Soviet collapse, human rights violations have "soared" since the end of 1993.[46]

Former KGB officers who became strong critics of the system also found themselves persecuted. The most notable case is the "revenge" prosecution of Viktor Orekhov, a former KGB Fifth Chief Directorate captain who had served seven years in a Soviet labor camp for having warned dissidents, including Sakharov, of their impending arrests.[47]

Top officials who sought to investigate wrongdoing in President Yeltsin's inner circle quickly found themselves without jobs. Yeltsin fired his own security and anti-corruption chiefs who probed or reported alleged graft on the part of his political allies. The first casualty was Yeltsin's personal state security chairman, Gen. Viktor Ivanenko, a professional KGB officer who in late 1991 informed the president of high-level corruption and alleged that Interior Minister Barannikov was part of the problem. Yeltsin fired Ivanenko and named Barannikov to replace him.[48] A second casualty was Yeltsin's state inspector, Yuri Boldyrev, whose March 1992 appointment to fight government corruption lasted only a year because, according to Boldyrev, his probes led him to the president's inner circle.[49]

In late 1992, President Yeltsin established an interbranch commission headed by Vice President Aleksandr Rutskoi to coordinate a new anticorruption campaign. Commission staff included 50 senior officials from the SVR, Ministry of Security, MVD, and Ministry of Defense.[50] The commission was empowered to investigate any official suspected of corrupt activity. However, just as the commission began to function, Yeltsin fired Boldyrev and replaced him with Andrei Ilyushenko, who switched the focus to the president's political opponents. By early 1993, those opponents included Barannikov and Deputy Interior Minister Andrei Dunayev—about whom the hapless Ivanenko had complained to Yeltsin—and the increasingly reactionary Rutskoi. Ilyushenko promptly investigated the three, this time without incurring the president's wrath.[51] All were soon removed from office but not criminally charged. Yeltsin sacked Ilyushenko after the official had become a political liability amid allegations of corruption.

Anti-corruption fighters within the law enforcement structures were also purged or felt compelled to resign, from street-level detectives and city prosecutors to police generals.[52] MVD Major General Aleksandr Gurov, who created and headed the MVD Administration for Combatting Organized Crime, found himself squeezed out of the Interior Ministry. He was transferred to the chekist Federal Security Service (FSB), only to be forced to retire. The reason for his removal, he says with irony, was that his attitude toward organized crime "hampered economic reforms." He authored a well regarded book detailing the structure of the Russian criminal world and its penetration into law enforcement agencies, concluding that the police are part of the problem.[53]

Continued Penetration of Society

The Russian security forces and their members continue to penetrate society, including the government bureaucracy, parliament and the courts, law enforcement and the procuracy, the military, academia, journalism, business, and even religious life. This authority, once vested in secret CPSU decrees, is now enshrined in law. The organs use three major human means in addition to electronic spying: "active reserve" or "operational reserve," "reliables," and "secret helpers."[54]

Active reservists are full state security officers who operate, usually under cover, in the civilian sector. According to journalist Yevgenia Albats, they occupy cover positions such as "deputy directors of scientific research institutes and deans responsible for foreigners in academic institutions," but they may also appear as "translators, doormen at hotels that serve foreigners, telephone engineers, and journalists."[55]

After being officially "disbanded" in 1991 (the officers remained in place on "special assignments"), the active reserve was formally reinstated the following year by presidential decree. At the same time, thousands of KGB officers left active duty to go into politics and business, or were transferred directly to positions in the civil state administration. Thus, the active reserve allowed the security organs to continue to function secretly within the emerging political and business sectors and throughout the government bureaucracy.[56] The impact of this infiltration is not immediately tangible. However the presence of these forces undermines confidence in the independence of civil institutions.

"Reliables" and "secret helpers" are civilians covertly recruited to perform certain tasks. Reliables are considered "probably the largest group in the KGB's shadow staff," according to Albats, and are mostly found in executive and management positions: "mass media executives, plant directors, deans of academic institutions, party officials, editors of publishing houses, telephone operators, garment workshop employees, telegraph workers, and housing office staff."[57] The secret helpers are mostly informers or *stukachi*. Stukach networks originally were established by the Cheka to consolidate and expand political control. Not all secret helpers are informers; some are used as agents of influence to persuade or manipulate the behavior of other state security targets.[58]

Although it is unlikely that *stukachi* still operate on the massive scale of the Soviet period, it would be a mistake to conclude that the secret helpers simply stopped their activity. There are no effective controls to ensure that they will not be reactivated; their identities are permanently protected by a law making it a crime to identify current or former *stukachi*.[59] A reorganization of internal security in 1994 prompted some to anticipate the discontinuation of the secret helper networks. However, before long then–internal security chief Sergei Stepashin publicly stated that the old KGB informant networks "most certainly" would be preserved, the identities of past KGB collaborators protected, and that the special services would continue domestic spying operations against individuals based on their political views.[60]

In contrast to Russia, the Czech Republic, Hungary, Lithuania, and Poland enacted laws on *lustration*, not as a punitive measure, but as an attempt to screen officials and their staff in public service, economic and financial structures, and educational institutions, to ensure that the new society would not be manipulated by the communist-era security networks.[61] In the former German Democratic Republic, Stasi secret police files on individuals were opened, and a de-stasification program sought to uproot the secret police legacy.[62] Poland's reversal of its *lustration* laws permitted the accession to power of a prime minister who had to resign amid official allegations that he was a Russian intelligence agent, plunging the country into a political crisis and diminishing Western confidence in the country's reliability as a potential NATO ally.[63]

The issue of KGB collaboration remains a major obstacle to effective, objective law enforcement and development of true civil society. Beyond a brief flash sparked by former dissidents in the early 1990s, Russia spared itself the political agonies of several Central and East European countries over the collaboration issue. Here lies the danger of the continued existence of old informant networks and various reserve statuses of cadres of unaccounted agents and officers throughout government and civic life. Questions remain about the security forces' continued ability to exploit or manipulate political parties or politicians. The embarrassing records remain in the former KGB's hands; no individual has the right to view his own file. Parliamentary investigators discovered the existence of intact personal dossiers following the 1991 putsch, but were unable to secure them for safeguarding documentation to be used in legal recourse, or to allow the release of this information for ethical reasons.[64] It has been alleged that extremists such as Vladimir Zhirinovsky received assistance and funding from the KGB to launch their political movements.[65] The KGB itself considered Communist Party members already co-opted.[66] Thus it appears that the two largest blocs both in the fourth and in the fifth State Duma are quite compromised. Evidence suggests that the KGB also recruited democratic politicians as agents, informers, or provocateurs, though the political sensitivity of the subject permits nothing substantive to be offered for the record. However, revelations in Lithuania suggests the possible extent of KGB infiltration in present day Russia. During a lengthy screening effort in 1991, Lithuanian leaders found that some of their top democratic, anti-Soviet friends and allies—including a prominent human rights activist and member of the Sajudis movement that led the country to independence in 1991, and the prime minister during the transition—were KGB operatives.[67] In Moscow, leaders of the Democratic Russia party attempted to pass a law to disqualify former KGB collaborators from holding high office, but without success.[68] The political elite in post-1991 Russia did not see the need to screen public officials for past or continued collaboration with the secret police. As a result, much remains as it had been during the times of the Soviet Union.

Lack of Training to Function in a Democratic Market Environment

Security and law enforcement officials seem to believe that if only they had the proper technology and material resources and the training to go with them, their problems would be solved. Western aid providers seem to share that view, focusing efforts on simply changing laws, criminal codes and regulations, and training judges and prosecutors. While these programs may make a contribution to reform, they are practically useless without effective law enforcement. Commitment and professionalism of many officers notwithstanding, the *chekisti* and *militsiya* lack the fundamental training and institutional culture to fight financial crime and crimes against legitimate businesses. Belated micro-training and cooperation programs initiated by the FBI, while potentially valuable, are on a scale which is too small to make a real difference.

During the initial post-Soviet rearrangement of the security organs a parliamentary investigator found the old chekist ways entrenched: "Meetings and conversations with KGB leaders of various ranks clearly highlight one detail. They have no understanding in their minds that they are serving the constitution or the law, they have no reverence for the rule of law and citizens' rights."[69] Nor did Russia's political leadership express a will for such understanding. The Supreme Soviet commission to investigate the circumstances of the August 1991 coup attempt was met with stiff resistance not only from the former KGB, but also from the *nomenklatura* which was still in power. Commission Chairman Lev Ponomarev observed early in 1992, "We are facing a confrontation of interests, a struggle over power structures, primarily in the struggle over secret services. No one will talk here about making them civilized or democratic."[70]

During the KGB reorganization following the 1991 putsch, a disgusted officer cautioned, "Decent people will simply not be able to work in the KGB if we don't get rid of our legacy and the fear that everything will continue as before." New recruits, he said, "get a crippled mentality because they have seen abuses and impunity."[71] Little has changed since. Large-scale departures of professional officers prompted their replacement by inexperienced new recruits. Paradoxically, professionalism is reported to have declined as KGB veterans left the service.[72] A 1995 Federal Border Service internal report said that 60 percent of its personnel were too unstable for the job and were unfit to carry a weapon.[73]

Little evidence indicates that personnel training now differs substantially from the Soviet period. Instead of creating a unit to recruit and train new officers with a more liberal world view, the main internal security service preserved the old KGB Cadres Directorate and appointed as its head a veteran of the Fifth Chief Directorate, the Soviet KGB's dissident-hunting division.[74] Instead of naming reformers or proven honest cops to head the Federal Customs Service and the new Department of Tax Police, President Yeltsin appointed KGB generals and staffed the Tax Police with former Fifth Chief Directorate officers.[75] Nowhere is the contrast between the optimistic time of 1991 and Yeltsin's reelection in 1996 more vivid than in the state security headquarters for the city of Moscow. During the birth of the Russian Federation, the head of the Moscow KGB was a civilian, Yevgeny Savostyanov, who had been allied with dissident Andrei Sakharov. He was replaced by Anatoly V. Trofimov, a Fifth Chief Directorate veteran who had spied on and persecuted Sakharov's fellow dissidents including Sergei Kovalev.[76] Little appears to have changed in the former KGB service academies. As long as old mentalities are not anathematized as they were in postwar Germany or post-apartheid South Africa, little genuine reform can be expected from the training academies.

Poor Discipline in Leadership and Ranks

Corruption within the ranks and in the government has poisoned the atmosphere for young officers less burdened by the ideological baggage of the past. Until top-level personnel shakeups in 1995 and 1996, both the chekist and MVD leadership included known organized crime figures in their social circles. One of the most visible was Otari Kvantrishvili, a leading Moscow *mafiya* chief who was assassinated in early 1994. He had positioned himself so well that, in the words of *Moscow News*, he "could successfully settle conflicts between Moscow officials, financiers, and representatives of the underworld. Therefore, many criminal authorities were among his pals, as were top officials in the *militsiya*, actors, sportsmen [and] politicians." Kvantrishvili even appeared regularly at state security and MVD social gatherings.[77] Investigative journalist Yuri Shchekochikhin reported that the gangster was "surrounded by people close to the president, famous writers, actors and police generals."[78]

MVD pay is low and working conditions are poor. The result is demoralization and cynicism, and a new generation of bad cops—or often initially good cops forced by circumstances to break the law just to make ends meet. As stated before, this does not mean that there are not many officers with good intentions to carry out their duties and stay despite the greatest adversity. As late as 1995, the MVD leadership admitted it was "not working hard enough to combat corruption within our own forces."[79]

On taking office in 1995, Interior Minister Anatoly Kulikov launched *Operation Clean Hands* to illustrate how corrupt the federal police had become. As part of a sting, Kulikov sent a contraband-laden truck from southern Russia toward Moscow to see how many police checkpoints the drivers could pass with simple bribes. The truck passed all but two checkpoints. In spite of this evidence, the MVD leadership failed to provide the needed resources to upgrade facilities and vehicles, procure computers and other technologies, and pay decent salaries to its personnel, or develop a training program consistent with the rule of law.

The war in Chechnya, fought largely by the MVD's Internal Troops (which Kulikov commanded on the ground in the early part of the conflict), deprived the *militsiya* of most of its expected crime-fighting resources.[80] The MVD and state security organs seem so compromised that some of Yeltsin's advisers argued for creating entirely new law enforcement agencies to wage war on crime.[81]

Police and procuracy investigators motivated to carry out that effort are not in short supply. The problems are mainly the federal government's lack of political will and the concomitant reluctance or refusal of the federal procuracy to act objectively, and increasing corruption of the judicial system. A Russian Criminological Association study presented evidence showing that fewer and fewer criminal cases are being brought to trial, and that by 1995 more than half of all initiated cases never made it to court. Women and juveniles faced trial in disproportionate numbers to men, suggesting that petty criminals lacking a "roof" are punished, while organized crime manipulates the criminal justice system.[82]

Legislation Is Inadequate—and Sometimes Irrelevant

Legislation likewise continues to reflect a mentality forged by more than seven decades of communist rule. The core post-Soviet law governing the security services is based on the 1991 Law on State Security Organs of the USSR. This law was drafted by the KGB based on eight Soviet laws and more than 800 secret decrees that had provided the legal base for the secret police since their creation,[83] and was presented personally to parliament by KGB Chairman Vladimir Kryuchkov.[84] The 1992 Russian Federation Law on Security and subsequent legislation bear many of the same provisions. Despite clauses that pay lip service to civil liberties, the laws fail to protect basic rights, while granting law enforcement officers wide discretion. For example, no judge has authority to issue warrants. Searches and seizures, break-ins, and wiretaps are authorized by the procuracy, and the law does not require prior approval by a judge. Nor does the law define the conditions under which such far-reaching measures can be applied.[85] It took nearly five years after independence for a new criminal code to be adopted, and even that was a compromise package enacted by a communist-dominated parliament. Although laws (as in most Western countries) have not kept up with increased sophistication of crime, or the technological and economic advances of society, they allow the former KGB to expand its power accordingly. The Law on Security gave the secret services authority over industry, transport and agriculture, as well as "services ensuring the security of means of communication and information, customs services, nature conservation organs, public health organs," and other areas.[86] Other basic laws enshrined old KGB powers to penetrate any and all private institutions, including newspapers, churches, non-violent political groups, and human rights organizations.[87] Many lawmakers recognized the severity of the flaws in the legislation they voted for, but went along for fear of retaliation from the secret services.[88]

Delays in passing the needed laws and guidelines are not solely the responsibility of the parliament. President Yeltsin waited nearly three years after 1991 to issue decrees to authorize the police and security services to fight organized crime and corruption.[89]

The scope of violation of these new laws by federal officials, particularly since late 1994, raises the legitimate question of whether the laws that govern the security services and police even matter at all. Commenting in late 1995 on widespread and flagrant violations of laws governing the security services and police, former USSR Supreme Soviet Constitutional Committee Chairman Sergei Alexeev concluded, "despite a number of democratic innovations in Russian law . . . our legal reality in Russia preserved unwritten principles based on a communist legal consciousness."[90]

The violations were laid out at a series of roundtables and conferences in Moscow and Stockholm on the legal accountability for the war in Chechnya. The war, which was seemingly restricted to a remote and backward region of the federation, had strong ramifications on police, state security, and civil society at large. The *chekisti* provoked the war through illegally created special units whose existence was explicitly forbidden under law.[91] Throughout the conflict the authorities in Moscow carried out activities that flagrantly violated constitutional guarantees and limits of presidential power. Thus, Chechnya set a dangerous precedent for law enforcement and civil society.

The MVD provided half the combat troops and much of the armor and artillery, inflicted massive destruction on cities and towns, and indiscriminately killed thousands of non-combatant civilians. The *chekisti* and *militsiya* were directed by presidential edicts and cabinet decrees through the security council comprised of the leaders of the federal police, security organs, intelligence services, and top government officials. These edicts and resolutions violated not only the laws but the constitution and several international treaties to which Russia is a party. Violations of the constitution included the arbitrary killing of Russian citizens, a gross violation of Article 2 that stipulates that the protection of "the human being, his rights and freedoms" is one of the state's "highest values"; and of Article 20 that guarantees those born to have the right to life. Article 17 "recognizes and guarantees the rights and freedoms of a person and citizen in accordance with the norms of international law," and Article 15 affirms that the government is guided by principles and norms of international law, yet the Geneva Conventions and other international treaties expressly forbid the conduct of state security and MVD forces in Chechnya.[92] Article 40 guarantees citizens a right to housing, yet MVD troops made hundreds of thousands homeless. Article 46 guarantees legal protection of rights and freedoms, yet no such protection was accorded citizens in Chechnya. Article 55, Paragraph 3 states that limitations on rights and freedoms can be imposed "only by federal law and in accordance with the provisions spelled out by the Constitution," yet no laws existed to permit the "limitations" imposed on residents of the Chechnya region. Article 56 permits limitations during a state of emergency, but those limitations do not include extrajudicial killing. Furthermore, President Yeltsin did not order a state of emergency. In order to proclaim a state of emergency, the president must inform both chambers of parliament. Also, Article 102 mandates that the upper chamber must approve this action. However, Yeltsin neither informed the legislature nor received Federation Council approval.[93] Presidential decrees and cabinet decisions authorized measures including body searches, road checkpoints, mass checking of documents, and censorship—measures permitted only in a state of emergency declared in accordance with the law.[94]

Russian leaders have likewise violated every major law concerning the security and law enforcement services. The Law on Defense, Article 5, states that the president may launch military action only with the approval of the Russian parliament, yet Yeltsin neither sought nor received such approval; Article 12 states that internal security forces may be deployed only as permitted by law. The Law on the *Militsiya* stipulates that MVD officers may use firearms only under strict regulations and are forbidden to fire at a suspect if bystanders would be threatened. Yet MVD forces killed thousands and wounded many thousands more in the twenty-month Chechnya conflict.

Protection of human rights is the security organs' first obligation, according to Article 1 of the Law on Security. Provisions in the Law on Operational Work that allow the security organs to conduct covert activities explicitly ban political and military provocations as in Chechnya. The Law on Federal Organs of State Security bans federal security entities not explicitly provided for in law. The security organs' covert recruitment of personnel from other services for Chechnya violated the Law on the Status of Servicemen and the Law on Military Draft and Military Service. Moreover, Article 36 of this law forbids the issuance of illegal orders to service personnel.[95]

The Soviet-era institutional checks still in force are insufficient. All MVD activity is subject to approval of the procuracy. Yet while the federal Procurator General pursued conscripts who had gone AWOL for more than 48 hours, the office failed to attempt to enforce any of the above laws broken by military commanders or the federal leadership.[96] In short, the Chechnya war proved that neither the constitution nor the law restrains the police and secret police today—even though the federal government expressly initiated military action in the name of the constitution and the law.

Lack of Budgetary Controls

Parliament has proven unable to take charge of the purse strings. While the State Duma approves overall budgets for each ministry, it has not sought to approve line-item budgets and lacks the authority to require or forbid certain expenditures. According to members of the Duma budget committee, the law enforcement budget is combined with the military budget. Even then, lawmakers say that the executive branch spends federal funds as it pleases, without checks and balances. Parliament specifically barred federal funds from being used for the Chechnya war, but the government spent the money anyway.[97]

Independent Economic Wealth

Adding to concerns that the security organs, apart from the MVD, are reasserting themselves as states within a state, is their access to wealth and economic power. Control of businesses, front companies, financial transactions, and e-mail open tempting opportunities for large-scale graft and organized crime in a corrupt system free of independent checks and balances. The *chekisti* also keep the secrets of where—and how much—money was illegally stashed abroad by the Communist Party and its leaders in the waning years of the Soviet Union. Some Russian lawmakers argued that it would be in the country's interests to recover the funds as a means of financing a social safety net and national reconstruction. Supreme Soviet investigators tried to find the money for just that purpose. They discovered that the hidden money's paper trails ended at the Ministry of Finance and the External Intelligence Service (SVR).[98] Receiving no cooperation from these or other agencies, the parliamentary commission passed the following resolution:

> Propose to the Russian President that he make the appropriate instruction to task the management of the External Intelligence Service, the Ministry of Defense, and the Apparatus of the President to provide an investigative crew and its experts direct access to the archives of the USSR KGB, the General Secretary of the CPSU CC, the Presidium of the USSR, and other archival material, having tasked the colleagues of these authorities to provide the investigators with all possible help and support in seeking out the documents concerning the financial activity of the CPSU.[99]

Yeltsin did not respond. Effectively blocking the probe, then–SVR Director General Yevgeny Primakov persuaded Supreme Soviet Chairman Ruslan Khasbulatov to terminate the investigative commission.[100] The keys to billions of dollars in illegally gained wealth remain in the hands of the SVR.

While holding the secrets of stolen fortunes, various security and law enforcement organs generate a continued flow of extra-budgetary funding through a range of commercial activities. The Main Guard Directorate under Gen. Aleksandr Korzhakov controlled the government's Rosvooruzheniye arms-export monopoly, as well as the limousine fleets, health centers and stores for government officials.[101] The law permitted the central internal security services to support themselves with "extrabudgetary funds," presumably through front companies, affiliated business operations, and the active reserve.[102] The Federal Agency for Government Communications and Information (FAPSI) owns a large share of one of Russia's largest commercial Internet access providers, controls commercial telecommunications lines, leases out secure lines to private companies, and registers all electronic financial transactions, charging banks and brokerages for the "service." In St. Petersburg, the internal security services reportedly took control over cellular telephone and paging operators. In mid-1996 the State Communications Inspectorate re-registered licenses of Internet access providers, with the proviso that the companies install control devices for the Federal Security Service to monitor all electronic communications.[103]

Conclusion

The evidence on the state of Russian security and law enforcement institutions provided in this chapter shows that instead of a clear cut with the past regime and the development of civil authorities legitimized by a new democratic order, Russia has been saddled with unreformed structures that are deeply undemocratic, have furthered corruption, and undermined the credibility of civil authorities. The major power basis for these old forces over the last years has been their stronghold over valuable economic assets. Much was achieved already during the time of *perestroika*. However, the post-1991 regime has done little to improve transparency and accountability for distribution of valuable economic assets. Privatization served to legitimize *de facto* control rights, but did little to change control structures already in place, and the security forces were able to move quickly once centralized state controls had been weakened. Their control over economic assets has removed the security forces from effective oversight by the legislature. Absent budgetary controls, what remains are directives issued by the executive, which as of now have tended to spare the security forces from reform. The lack of reform and the infiltration of civil service and economic organizations by members of the security forces has far reaching implications for the prospects of economic, political, and legal reform in Russia. Rather than markets, networks of the former *nomenklatura* with connections to the security forces are governing many valuable assets in the country. Many of the original goals for economic reform have been compromised as reformers lacked the political clout to challenge the stranglehold of security forces. Politically, this has undermined the credibility of economic reforms, as the identity of the winners of economic reform is only too obvious. Many well-intentioned legal reform efforts were half-hearted or remained unenforced dead letter laws. For the creation of legitimate law enforcement agencies bound by the rule of law, more was and still is needed than a few general laws or presidential decrees. What is required is strong political will and determination to break with the past. To date, such will and political support to implement it, either within the Russian Federation or among those who wish Russia well, virtually does not exist.

Notes

1. ·The procuracy is an institution that dates back to Peter the Great. It is in charge of overseeing law and order in general. Unlike state prosecutors in the West, its role is not limited to prosecution, but encompasses observance of orders and decrees in all spheres of

life. To this date, the Russian procuracy has the right to launch an appeal in private law suits and to initiate bankruptcy proceedings against companies that have violated the law.

2. For discussions of the KGB as a power structure, see Dziak (1988), Knight (1988, 1990), and Waller (1994a).

3. Shelley (1996), 51–52, and 71, citing the Russian Soviet Federated Socialist Republic Criminal Code.

4. Minutes of the Second All-Russia Conference of Commissars, 2–6 July 1918, cited by Fainsod (1967), p. 27.

5. Bakatin, interview with author, September 19, 1992. Also see Albats (1994).

6. Some observers note that the removal of Dzerzhinsky's imposing statue in front of KGB headquarters in Moscow, and the re-naming of Dzerzhinsky Square to its earlier name Lubyanka, are signs that the central government tried to break with the Cheka leader's legacy. In reality, the statue was removed by city officials when demonstrators tried to topple it.

7. See Popplewell (1991), and Waller (1994a), pp. 221–246.

8. *Izvestiya*, December 31, 1991, union edition, trans. in BBC Summary of World Broadcasts, January 1, 1992, p. SU/1267/B/1.

9. For a greater discussion of the problem, see Handelman (1995).

10. Sheehy (1990), p. 315.

11. Podlesskikh and Tereshonok (1994). The author wishes to thank Victor Yasmann and Glenn Bryant for their assistance with Russian language material. For more on the *vory*, see Vaksberg (1991) and Sterling (1994).

12. Podlesskikh and Tereshonok (1994), pp. 117–123.

13. Knight (1990), p. 98.

14. Timofeyev (1992), p. 117.

15. Timofeyev (1992), pp. 121–128.

16. *Novoye vremya*, No. 43, 1991.

17. A major financial, construction and media group, set up in 1989 by a young Komsomol organizer, ended up housing several top KGB generals in its corporate ranks, including the last two heads of the Fifth Chief Directorate and the KGB's number two official who ran all internal security at the time, First Deputy Chairman Filipp Bobkov. The company claims the *chekisti* were hired only to provide corporate security, but in reality these high-ranking officers played policy roles within the firm. See J. Michael Waller, "Russia's Biggest 'Mafia' Is the KGB," *Wall Street Journal Europe*, June 22, 1994.

18. Borovoi (1994), pp. 83–84.

19. Borovoi (1994), p. 84.

20. Ponomarev and Surkov (1992).

21. Timofeyev (1992), pp. 118–119, citing text of resolution.

22. *Komsomolskaya pravda*, January 22, 1992, trans. in *Soviet Press Digest*.

23. The privatization fund was to have been a Soviet operation, and ought not to be construed as a post-Soviet privatization fund as established by the economic reform team of the Russian Federation under Boris Yeltsin.

24. *Komsomolskaya pravda*. The reports were corroborated by Surkov (1992).

25. Timofeyev (1992), pp. 120–121.

26. Timofeyev (1992), pp. 119–120.

27. S. C. Gwynne and Larry Gurwin, "The Russia Connection," *Time*, July 8, 1996, p. 33.

28. Gwynne and Gurwin (1996), pp. 33–36.

29. Shelley (1996).

30. To trace these changes, see Waller (1994a).

31. Handelman (1995), pp. 1–3, 108–111, 127–129, 269–271.

32. The powers, responsibilities, and structure of the Security Council are defined in Russian Federation Presidential Edict No. 1128, "On Approving the Statute on the Russian Federation Security Council Apparatus," signed by President B. Yeltsin on August 1, 1996, published in *Rossiyskaya gazeta*, August 8, 1996, p. 4, trans. in FBIS-SOV-96-155, August 9, 1996, pp. 16–19.

33. Yan Ulansky, *Kuranty*, March 24, 1994, p. 1, trans. in FBIS-SOV-94-057, March 24, 1994, p. 8; Yasmann (1994b), p. 12.

34. Lev Ponomarev, "On the Parliamentary Supervision of the Security Services," transcript of remarks at IV Roundtable on the "KGB: Yesterday, Today, Tomorrow," Moscow, December 10, 1994, in Isakova, Oyvin and Oznobkina (1996), pp. 118–119.

35. *New York Times*, August 6, 1995.

36. Author's confidential conversations with State Duma and Federation Council members, including senior members of the mentioned committees, April, July, and August 1994, and September 1995.

37. Vladimir Golubev, former Deputy Chief of the Moscow State Procuracy Office Department to Supervise the Investigative Work of the KGB, "The Prosecutor's Oversight of the Counterintelligence Agencies," transcript of remarks at IV Roundtable on the "KGB: Yesterday, Today, Tomorrow," Moscow, December 10, 1994, in Isakova, Oyvin and Oznobkina (1996), p. 124.

38. A well publicized 1992 incident in Yekaterinburg is a case in point. Two former KGB officers-turned-businessmen were prosecuted for allegedly using their contacts improperly to speed export visas and passports for clients. The two maintained that they were singled out in retaliation for their public denunciation of the August 1991 coup attempt, for which they had been pressured to leave the state security service. The tribunal chief ruled that the two could not be prosecuted because it was impossible to determine whether the allegedly improper transactions might have been part of official intelligence operations. See Yasmann (1993a), p. 17.

39. Law No. 2646–1 of the Russian Federation, "On Security," Article 20, Moscow, March 5, 1992, *Rossiyskaya gazeta*, May 6, 1992, first edition, p. 5, trans. in FBIS-SOV-92-088, May 6, 1992, p. 34. The lawmaker who shepherded the bill through the Supreme Soviet was Committee on Defense and Security Chairman Sergei Stepashin, who at the time was also one of Barannikov's deputies in the Ministry of Security, and who ultimately succeeded Barannikov in early 1994 after the ministry was re-named Federal Counterintelligence Service. Stepashin became a member of the so-called "Party of War" that precipitated the military campaign in Chechnya.

40. Law 3246-1/1 "On Federal Organs of State Security," Article 11, in *Rossiyskaya gazeta*, August 12, 1992, pp. 1–4, trans. in FBIS-USR-92-121, September 14, 1992, pp. 21–28.

41. Cases in point: former federal internal security chief Nikolai Golushko and Moscow security chief Anatoly Trofimov, who served in the KGB Fifth Chief Directorate.

42. Gale Colby, "Fabricating Guilt," *The Bulletin of the Atomic Scientists*, October 1993, pp. 12–13; Waller (1994b); and Vil Mirzayanov, fax press statement, Moscow, March 11, 1994. Also see, "Possible Prisoner of Conscience in Fear of Death Penalty," Urgent Action, UA 33/96 (London: Amnesty International, February 9, 1996); and "The Arrest of Alexander Nikitin" (Oslo: Bellona Foundation, April 13, 1996) on Bellona World Wide Web site: http://www.grida.no/ngo/bellona.

43. J. Michael Waller, "Russia's Campaign Against Human Rights," *Washington Times*, March 17, 1995.

44. Tatyana Kuznetsova, in Isakov and Oznobkina (1996), pp. 43–45.

45. Alexei Simonov, "Voina protiv zhurnalistov," in Izakova and Oznobkina (1996), pp. 46–49.

46. Lee Hockstader, *Washington Post*, December 8, 1995.

47. Information provided by John Finerty of the Organization on Security and Cooperation in Europe, U.S. House of Representatives.

48. Former KGB Maj. Gen. Oleg Kalugin, interview with author, April 9, 1994; and Albats (1994), p. 305. Albats reports that Ivanenko "naively" went to Yeltsin with information on alleged corruption by the president's close friend Barannikov, and by Deputy Interior Minister Andrei Dunayev.

49. David Filipov, "Same Old Swan Song," *Moscow Times*, April 15, 1994.

50. Yasmann (1993a), citing *Izvestiya*, February 11, 1993.

51. Filipov.

52. Handelman (1995), Sterling (1995).

53. Gurov (1995).

54. KGB (1989).

55. Albats (1994), p. 57.

56. Rahr (1993), p. 28, citing *Moskovskaya pravda*, September 4, 1992; and *Komsomolskaya pravda*, November 14, 1992; and author's confidential interviews with Russian state security officers. In 1992, Yeltsin decreed that thousands of state security officers would be posted as active reservists in government ministries to "fight corruption." The officers were to act as advisers and consultants under dual subordination to the central government and state security, and would perform the role of overseers, with payment from the security services. Yet four years after the fact, the problem of corruption had worsened. See Yasmann (1993a), p. 18.

57. Albats (1994), p. 57.

58. Albats (1994), p. 59.

59. Law No. 2646-1, "On Security," Article 2.

60. Sergei Stepashin, interview on "Itogi," St. Petersburg Fifth Channel Television, 1800 GMT, January 30, 1994, trans. in FBIS-SOV-94-025, February 7, 1994, pp. 21–22.

61. Basta (1994), Bren (1993), Darski (1991–1992), Engelbrekt (1993), Müller (1992), Sustrova (1992), Toman (1991), Yasmann (1993b).

62. Adams (1992 and 1993), Gauck (1993).

63. Jane Perletz, *New York Times*, January 9, 1996; Anthony Robinson, "Soviet Shadow Is Cast Over Poland," *Financial Times*, January 23, 1996.

64. Lev Ponomarev, *Izvestiya*, February 8, 1992, trans. in FBIS-SOV-92-031, February 14, 1992, p. 55.

65. St. Petersburg Mayor Anatoly Sobchak claimed that as a member of Mikhail Gorbachev's presidential council he witnessed the decision to use Zhirinovsky as a con-

trolled opposition figure. See "Sobchak Alleges Zhirinovsky Has KGB Links," *RFE/RL Daily Report*, No. 7, January 12, 1994, p. 2; Bernard Kaplan, "Zhirinovsky's KGB Ties Eyed," Hearst news service dispatch, *Washington Times*, December 22, 1993, p. 1; Fred Hiatt, "Gorbachev Tied to Zhirinovsky? Ex-Leader Reportedly Ordered KGB to Found 'Alternative' Party," *Washington Post*, January 14, 1994, p. A27.

66. Yevgenia Albats, "Subjects of the KGB," *Moscow News*, No. 14, April 1, 1992.

67. Kazis Uscila, ITAR-TASS, March 26, 1992 and Vladas Burbulis, ITAR-TASS world service in Russian, 1254 GMT, September 14, 1992, trans. in FBIS-SOV-92-179, September 15, 1992, p. 57.

68. Author's interview with Galina Starovoitova, who authored the law.

69. Russian Supreme Soviet Deputy Nikolai Ryabov, deputy chairman of the State Commission to Investigate the Activity of the State Security Organs, *Rossiyskaya gazeta*, September 18, 1991, p. 1, trans. in FBIS-SOV-91-181, September 18, 1991, p. 25.

70. Lev Ponomarev and Alexander Maksimov, interview, trans. Federal News Service, February 4, 1992. Ponomarev was Chairman of the Russian Federation Supreme Soviet Commission to Investigate the Causes and Circumstances of the August Putsch; Maksimov was commission secretary.

71. RSFSR People's Deputy Nikolai Ryabov, *Rossiyskaya gazeta*, September 18, 1991, p. 1, trans. FBIS-SOV-91-181, September 18, 1991, p. 25.

72. Golubev, p. 123.

73. *OMRI Daily Digest*, Vol. 1, No. 225, November 17, 1995, p. 3, citing ITAR-TASS.

74. Natalya Gevorkyan, "Appointments," *Moscow News*, No. 13, April 1994, electronic version. The article did not appear in the printed English-language edition.

75. Author's interview with Moscow KGB chief Yevgeny Savostyanov, December 1991.

76. Yuri Orlov, Honorary Chairman, International Helsinki Association, "Voina v Chechnye: Prestupleniye protiv chelovechnosti," in Isakova and Oznobkina (1996), p. 14.

77. Igor Baranovsky, "Several Versions of an Assassination," *Moscow News*, No. 15, April 1994, p. 15.

78. Candice Hughes, "Yeltsin: Russia a 'Superpower of Crime,'" Associated Press wire story, *Washington Times*, June 7, 1994.

79. First Deputy Interior Minister Mikhail Yegorov, *OMRI Daily Digest*, Vol. 1, No. 115, June 14, 1995.

80. *New York Times*, June 6, 1995.

81. Jonas Bernstein, "How the Russian Mafia Rules," *Wall Street Journal*, October 26, 1994; and author's interviews with Russian Presidential Security Council staff, July 1996.

82. Abstract of *Prestupnost' v Rossii v devianostykh godakh v nekotorye aspekty zakonnosti borby s nei* (Crime in Russia in the 1990s and Several Legislative Aspects of the Fight with It), (Moscow: Russian Criminological Association, 1995), in *Trends In Organized Crime*, Vol. 1, No. 4, Summer 1996, pp. 84–85.

83. Soviet leader Mikhail Gorbachev requested the KGB to supervise drafting the Law on State Security Organs. For the source on the eight laws and 800 secret decrees, see KGB Deputy Chairman Valery Lebdev, TASS in English, 1016 GMT, March 2, 1991, in FBIS-SOV-91-042, March 4, 1991, pp. 26–27. For a review of the drafting, review, and enactment of the Law on State Security Organs, see Waller (1994), pp. 168–178.

84. Vladimir Kryuchkov, address to the USSR Supreme Soviet, transcript in TASS international service in Russian, 1427 GMT, March 5, 1991, trans. in FBIS-SOV-91-044, March 6, 1991, pp. 23–25.

85. Albats (1994), citing Federal Counterintelligence Service Director General Nikolai Golushko, pp. 352–53; and Waller (1994), pp. 168–178; 205–220.

86. Law No. 2646-1 of the Russian Federation, "On Security," Article 12, signed by Russian President Boris Yeltsin at the Russian House of the Soviets, Moscow, March 5, 1992, *Rossiyskaya gazeta*, May 6, 1992, first edition, p. 5, trans. in FBIS-SOV-92-088, May 6, 1992, p. 34. Note: FBIS erroneously cites the date of passage and signature as 5 May 1992.

87. Law 3246–1/1 "On Federal Organs of State Security," Article 11; and Russian Federation Federal Law No. 5, "On Foreign Intelligence," Article 18 (which permits penetration of such institutions, but not for agent-of-influence purposes), in *Rossiyskaya gazeta*, January 17, 1996, pp. 4–5, trans. in FBIS-SOV-96-012, January 18, 1996, pp. 34–41.

88. Rahr (1993), p. 29.

89. Analyzing the decrees, Moscow State University criminologist Ninel F. Kuznetsova argues that Yeltsin's May 1994 proposed program was "developed thoroughly and competently," but "it is two years too late. Had it been adopted earlier in 1992, crime growth could have been slowed." Kuznetsova (1994), pp. 450–451.

90. Sergei Alexeev, "Voina v Chechnye: Retsidiv kommunisticheskogo pravoponimaniya," in Isakova and Oznobkina (1996), pp. 27–28 (trans. pp. 94–99).

91. In the months prior to the December 1994 invasion of Chechnya, the federal Security Service (FSB) covertly contracted members of the armed forces to form irregular paramilitary units to conduct provocative armed actions in the region. These irregular units had no legal status, and violated the Law on Defense which requires the parliament to approve the creation and mobilization of all military units. Former KGB Colonel Aleksandr Kichikhin examines the legal violations in "Rossiiskaya 'Operatsiya Glyaivits' v ispolneii Federalnoi sluzhby kontrrazvedki," in Oznobkina and Izakova (1995), pp. 51–61 (trans. pp. 118–127).

92. M. F. Polyakova, Professor of the Procurator General Office Institute for Personnel Training, "O personalnoi otvetstvennosti Prezidenta i vyschikh dolzhnostnykh lits Rossii," in Oznobkina and Isakova (1995), pp. 32–34 (trans. pp. 102–103).

93. Polyakova; Aleksandr Kichikhin, "Rossiyskaya 'Operatsiya Glyaivits' v ispolneniy Federalnoi sluzhby kontrrazvedki," in Oznobkina and Isakova (1995), pp. 51–61 (trans. pp. 118–127).

94. Polyakova.

95. Kichikhin.

96. Yu. Stetsovskiy, "Ekspertnoye zaklyucheniye dlya Komissiy obshchestvennogo rassledovaniya," in Oznobkina and Isakova (1995), pp. 68–73 (trans. pp. 134–138).

97. Author's conversation with State Duma Budget, Taxation, Banks and Finance Committee Vice Chairman Aleksandr D. Zhukov, and members Viktor V. Gitin and Yuri M. Voronin, July 23, 1996.

98. Yelena Vrantseva, "The Secrets of Personal Accounts," *Megapolis kontinent*, February 25, 1992, p. 4, trans. *Soviet Press Digest*; and Surkov (1992), pp. 295–299.

99. Ponomarev and Surkov (1992), p. 276.

100. L. A. Ponomarev, interview with author, March 1992. The Russian government did go through the motions of trying to hunt down the funds by assigning some officials to follow leads, and by hiring the U.S. investigative firm Kroll and Associates to assist. One of Russia's most effective investigators, Vladimir Kalinichenko, finally quit. "I was no fool," he told journalist Stephen Handelman. "There were plenty of cases in which I could trace the money: I had names, bank account numbers. But not a single criminal proceeding was started as a result of my investigations. I decided fighting corruption in our country is like fighting windmills." Handelman (1995), p. 2.

101. Yasmann (1994b), p. 12.

102. Law No. 2646-1, "On Security," Article 20.

103. *OMRI Daily Digest*, Vol. 1, No. 132, July 10, 1995, p. 2. U.S. intelligence notes that newly installed "electronic fund transfer networks for banks in Russia" are supervised or controlled by FAPSI and other former KGB units. Also see, *Intercon Daily Report on Russia*, July 22, 1996.

CHAPTER 7

Contracting in the Shadow of the State: Private Arbitration Commissions in Russia

Timothy Frye

The importance of creating a law-governed economy in Russia resounds daily in press reports on corrupt officials, shady businessmen, and powerful racketeers. It also invites a re-examination of debates on the relationship between the state, the market, and the rule of law. One prominent view in law and political science suggests that private actors ultimately rely on the state to enforce contracts and protect property rights. Citizens pay taxes to the state to enforce contracts and the state abstains from arbitrary and excessive taxation out of fear of sparking a revolt or capital flight.[1] As Hobbes notes: "before the names of Just and Unjust can have place there must be some coercive power to compel men equally to abide by their covenants by the terror of some punishment greater than the benefit they expect by the breach of their covenant."[2] This view marks a strong state as the foundation of the rule of the law.

A second view argued by a diverse group of scholars suggests that the case for state enforcement of contracts may be overplayed.[3] Theories of self-governance suggest that small groups of homogenous individuals with sufficiently long time horizons can form self-governing organizations (SGOs) to protect property rights as well as the state can. In many instances, members of rotating credit associations, private arbitration courts, and professional organizations transmit information about an actor's reputation, levy sanctions, and thereby deter fraud without turning to the state. As Elinor Ostrom notes: "Communities of individuals have relied on institutions resembling neither the state nor the market to govern some resource systems with reasonable degrees of success over long periods of time."[4] This view places the state in the background and emphasizes the ability of market participants to govern themselves.

The case of commodity exchanges in post-Soviet Russia highlights several interesting facets of this debate. Commodity exchange officials attempted to engage in self-governance by creating private arbitration commissions. Brokers, however, shunned these commissions because providing evidence to the court required revealing information about their trades, which left them subject to high rates of taxation by the state. Brokers were wary of using state courts for a similar reason.[5] This gave individual brokers strong incentives to forsake private arbitration commissions and state courts and use private enforcers.[6]

This brief outline highlights three points for theories of self-governance and state regulation. First, while most works on self-governance study groups beyond the reach of the state and explain the success or failure of self-governance by examining factors internal to the group (the number, heterogeneity, and time horizons of members), this case suggests that when an SGO operates within a territory controlled by a state, state actions often determine the SGO's shape, scope, and survival.

Second, if state actors follow policies that inhibit the flow of information among members of a group seeking to trade, then the prospects for self-governance will be low, regardless of the internal features of the group. This case depicts the state as a "meddlesome Leviathan" that hindered self-governance by pursuing policies that restricted the flow of information in the market.

Third, this case suggests that the rise of private protection organizations in Russia can be usefully viewed as a result of micro-level contracting problems, rather than as emerging from the institutional legacy of the Soviet system, the collapse of the Russian state, or an early stage of capitalism, as has been argued in the literature.

This case suggests that state-centered approaches to the creation of a law-governed economy tell only part of the story. They often fail to appreciate that a state made strong enough to protect property rights is also made strong enough to violate them.[7] Actors who fear high rates of taxation will be reluctant to strengthen the state.

Theorists of self-governance, on the other hand, tend to study groups beyond the reach of the state and rarely incorporate state actors into their models. State policies, however, may alter the incentives of group members to engage in self-governance. For example, high tax rates reduce actors' incentives to share information about their trading practices and reduce the prospect for self-governance. Conversely, policies that reduce the cost of sharing information among group members may promote self-governance. This case suggests that a condition for the creation of a law-governed economy is not simply a strong state. This strength must also be tempered by limits on the power of the state to engage in predatory taxation.

In this chapter, I describe the rise of the commodity exchanges and their private arbitration commissions during the period 1990–1994. I outline the problem facing brokers on the exchange and attribute their reluctance to use private arbitration commissions to the fear of taxation by the state. I then present an interpretation for the rise of private protection organizations and compare the merits of state versus private protection of property rights.

Commodity Exchanges in Russia, 1990–1993

One of the most dynamic economic institutions of the Russian transition were commodity exchanges.[8] The first commodity exchanges opened in 1990, and within 18 months, more than 180 were registered in Russia.[9] Odd alliances of regional branches of the State Supply Agency (Gossnab), private entrepreneurs, managers of industrial enterprises, and former Communist Party officials often provided the human and physical capital to create the exchanges. Unlike their nominal counterparts in the West, commodity exchanges in Russia sought profit by selling seats on the exchange, charging fees to brokers, and selling shares to outsiders. Shareholders often received access to goods before they reached the trading floor, a clear case of insider trading.

Trade on the commodity exchange boomed for two reasons.[10] First, after the collapse of the command economy, the exchanges united buyers and sellers who had little way of finding each other. Second, traders also profited by arbitraging between state and market prices. Commodity exchange goods often sold for two to three times the state price, but the exchanges could provide these goods immediately—an attractive selling point in a shortage economy. The price liberalization of January 1992, however, severely limited these arbitrage opportunities.

Two types of exchanges blossomed. Universal exchanges were often founded with a mix of private and state capital and sold a variety of goods under one roof—from helicopters to computers to clothes. For example, one prominent exchange, the Russian Raw Materials and Commodities Exchange (RCRME), was divided into seven sections: Metals; Construction; Agriculture; Transportation; Energy; Electronics; and a joint Energy and Transportation Sector. By 1991, more than 1000 firms registered as brokers at the RCRME. Moreover, in 1992, the exchange registered over 12,000 deals for a total of over 15.5b rubles.[11] The main rival to the RCRME as a universal exchange was the Moscow Commodity Exchange, which registered more than 20.6b rubles in trade in 1992.[12]

Theories of self-governance suggest that brokers on universal exchanges would find it difficult to govern themselves. Brokers on universal exchanges were typically large in number. On many days, more than 1,000 brokers traded on the floor of the RCRME or the MCE. They came from a heterogeneous group of firms that traded a wide variety of products and had short time horizons because trading on a universal exchange required little training and experience. These internal group features lead us to expect that brokers on universal exchanges would have great difficulty engaging in self-governance.

Specialized exchanges had deeper roots in the former state economy and traded in particular goods, such as oil, metals, or agricultural goods. They often evolved from regional branches of the State Supply Agency or branch ministries that specialized in a particular good. For example, the Moscow Ferrous Metals Exchange was physically attached to the main research institute for the State

Committee on Metallurgy and was dominated by large metal producers. Similarly, the Moscow Oil Exchange had roughly 240 brokers and 80 percent of organizations in the oil industry were shareholders. Not surprisingly, it traded more oil than any other exchange in 1992. Brokers on specialized exchanges should have been more likely to govern themselves than counterparts on universal exchanges. They were typically smaller in number. They were more homogeneous because they usually worked in the same field under the planned economy. Moreover, they often had longer time horizons because the value of their specialized experiences and relationships in the industry was much lower than in other occupations. Thus, we would expect brokers on specialized exchanges to have more success engaging in self-governance than their counterparts on universal exchanges.

Trading on the Exchange

Four actors were involved in each trade on the exchange. Brokers who purchased the right to make trades on the exchange took buy and sell orders from clients who did not enter the exchange. The parties signed contracts obligating the broker to fulfill the client's order. The broker took this order to the exchange and checked the price list to see whether the good was available at the exchange that day. If so, the brokers bid on the item in an auction. If the bid was accepted, then brokers for the buyer and seller signed a contract on the spot and were supposed to register their deal with the commodity exchange and pay a fee of two to three percent of the proposed deal.

Like actors in all sectors of the Russian economy, brokers faced the problem of enforcing contracts. Opportunities for cheating were manifold. Clients or brokers listed their product on several exchanges and then broke contracts with all but the highest bidder. Brokers accepted bids for goods that they did not have in hand. If they failed to find the good, then the contract would eventually be broken. Called "trading in air" (*vozdushnie sdelki*), these deals accounted for many violations.

One survey of brokers conducted by the Institute for Market Research found that 30 percent of contracts went unfulfilled.[13] Another found that 20 percent of deals contracted on the exchange broke down before delivery.[14] When asked to cite the percentage of contracts that go unfulfilled in a third set of surveys, brokers responded as shown in Table 7.1.[15]

Interviews with brokers conducted in the summer of 1992 and 1993 found these figures to be reliable. Moreover, other works on both universal and specialized commodity exchanges in Russia cite contract enforcement as a major problem.[16] This high incidence of contract violations reveals the intensity of the contracting problem facing brokers in Russia.

Contract violations contributed to the rapid decline of trading on all commodity exchanges. In 1993, reported trade on major exchanges fell dramatically. For example, trade in nominal terms at the Moscow Commodity Exchange increased

TABLE 7.1   Survey of Brokers

Unfulfilled Contracts	Percentage of Brokers Responding		
	6/92	9/92	12/92
<10 percent	33 percent	24	34
11–25 percent	18 percent	19	27
26–50 percent	28 percent	33	20
>51 percent	21 percent	14	19

SOURCE: *Rossiyskaya Gazeta,* March 10, 1993, p. 3; "Birzha chestnosti ne garantiruet," *Kommersant',* #21, May 25, 1993, p. 18.

four fold, but these gains were erased by an inflation of more than 800 percent.[17] By 1994, only a handful of commodity exchanges remained active.

Creating an SGO: Private Arbitration Commissions

To mitigate these contracting problems, commodity exchange founders established private arbitration commissions that could hear economic disputes among brokers on the exchange, render compulsory decisions, and levy sanctions. The legal basis for these commissions came from the Law on Arbitration Courts passed in July 1991, the Arbitration Procedural Code of April 1992, and the Temporary Statute on Arbitration Commissions of June 1992.[18]

Exchange founders and their legal advisors studied models of dispute resolution used on foreign commodity exchanges and attempted to adapt them to Russian circumstances. They hired experienced judges—many had worked previously in the state arbitration courts (Gosarbitrazh)—who resolved disputes more quickly and at lower cost than state arbitration court judges. They charged a fee of 3–5 percent of the sum in question to resolve the dispute, while state arbitration courts charged a fee of 10 percent. They also rendered decisions within two months, while brokers often believed that the state courts typically took longer.[19]

For example, the Moscow Commodity Exchange (MCE) Commission was perhaps the most sophisticated in Russia.[20] It was legally and financially independent from the exchange and earned revenue by charging a 3 percent commission on each case.[21] Judges on the MCE Commission had worked in the state arbitration courts, and were well-versed in economic disputes. The MCE Commission had 13 judges and 20 brokers who could serve as arbiters. Three judges heard matters over 300,000 rubles, and one judge heard other cases. The MCE standard contract gave primary jurisdiction to the MCE Commission, thereby accelerating the process and ensuring a rapid decision.[22] Yet, commodity exchange arbitration commissions attracted few customers and had little success in reducing contract violations.[23] The MCE Arbitration Commission handled 123 cases in its first sixteen months.[24] The arbitration commission at the RCRME handled more than 500 matters in 1992 and 1993, but many matters were points of clarification, not binding decisions.[25] Self-governance by arbitration commissions was no more successful at the specialized exchanges. Private arbitration commissions at the Moscow Oil Exchange (MOE) and the Moscow Ferrous Metals Exchange (MFME) handled fewer than ten cases each in 1992–93.[26] These figures are low given the number of reported contract violations.[27]

Why were traders reluctant to use these courts despite the very high rate of contract violations? The enforcement powers of the private arbitration commissions were weaker than state courts.[28] Their decisions were compulsory and subject to immediate compliance, but private arbitration courts had to turn to state courts to issue an order of compliance when their decisions were ignored. State courts could review the process by which the decision was made on their own initiative and could hear appeals brought by one party to a decision, but in practice they usually upheld the decision of the private arbitration commission. Pistor notes that while the vast majority of private arbitration commission decisions were referred to state courts for enforcement, this process was seen as a technicality. She adds that enforcement powers of state courts are more reliable than conventional wisdom suggests.[29] Weak state enforcement does not seem to be the main problem.

Moreover, studies from a variety of fields find that small groups of homogeneous members, as existed on specialized exchanges and on some universal exchanges, can use social sanctions that do not require state action. Low cost punishment strategies included disbarment, charging higher deposits, and listing the names of dishonest traders at the exchange. Like the SGO at the Champaigne Fairs of Medieval Europe and the New York Stock Exchange, post-Soviet commodity exchanges controlled entry to the trading floor to punish brokers.[30] Brokers had to show a pass to enter the trading floor and brokers were, on occasion, barred from the exchange.[31] Thus, brokers had some means to enforce their decisions without turning to the state.

The reluctance of judges to index damages to inflation slowed the number of cases referred to the courts, but brokers responded by writing contracts that indexed damages to inflation, allowing judges to award inflation-adjusted compensation. Moreover, during periods of low inflation brokers were also reluctant to use private arbitration commissions.

The decline in trading on commodity exchanges reduced the number of possible cases that could be referred to the exchange commissions and slowed their development. Of the smaller number of trades concluded on the exchanges in 1993–94, only a handful of cases fell to the commodity exchange arbitration commissions. In addition, traders were reluctant to use the commissions during the boom of 1991–92, as well as the bust of 1993–94.

The roots of the problem lie in the Russian state's punitive taxation towards brokers on all exchanges. Referring a case to a commodity exchange commission required brokers to share information about their trading practices, which left them vulnerable to taxation by the state.[32] The federal government initially set the value added tax at 28 percent and later reduced it to 20 percent. In addition, brokers faced a 45 percent normal profit tax, in contrast to the 32 percent paid by other businesses.[33] Prior to 1992, also brokers paid a superprofit tax on profits larger than 50 percent of the cost of production, based on a sliding scale.[34] As brokers' costs of production were low and their profits were high, they often exceeded the barrier of superprofits. Total estimated taxes on private sector activity fluctuated throughout the period, but often reached as high as 70 percent.[35]

Regional authorities who faced steep cutbacks in federal subsidies often levied high tax rates on the private sector. Moreover, brokers in the private sector were a favorite target for the state tax service.[36] One survey of 265 brokerage houses operating on 16 commodity exchanges concluded that "high taxes on middleman activity encouraged brokerage firms to engage in off-exchange trades and illegal forms of trading."[37] Two surveys of actors who were active on commodity exchanges also bear out the severity of the tax problem. A World Bank survey of small manufacturers in St. Petersburg cited high and arbitrary taxes as their most important problem.[38] A survey of cooperative owners also ranked taxes first among a variety of problems.[39]

Brokers on commodity exchanges were not only highly taxed. They also faced currency restrictions that increased the risk of trading on the exchange. Two monies were widely used in Russia: cash rubles (*nalichnie rubli*), and account rubles (*beznalichnie rubli*). The former included cash held by individuals and are intended for everyday purchases. The central government limited the use of cash rubles and deals for larger than R500,000 (about $5,000) cannot be conducted in cash rubles.[40] The latter were intended to be used by organizations and are processed through the Russian Central Bank. It was more difficult to avoid taxes using account rubles because they leave a paper trail in the banking system. When possible, brokers used cash rubles to discourage inquisitive tax collectors.

Currency restrictions prohibited commodities brokers from using hard currency to settle their accounts. Given the volatility of the exchange rate during the boom period of the commodity exchanges, brokers preferred to trade in dollars to minimize their currency risks. There are no estimates of the volume of trades concluded in hard currency, but the figures are likely large, particularly after inflation jumped in March 1992.

Exiting the Formal Economy

To avoid high tax rates and currency restrictions, traders often took their deals off the exchange by not registering them with the commodity exchange. The number of "off-exchange" deals (*vnebirzhevie sdelki*) is difficult to determine, but one survey from 1991 found that brokers on universal exchanges reported only 25–50 percent of trades while brokers on specialized exchanges reported only 50–75 percent of trades.[41] Later studies suggest that for every deal registered on the exchange twenty deals were concluded off the exchange.[42] Brokers interviewed in the summer of 1992 and 1993 suggested that this figure was accurate. Press reports and scholarly writings on Russian commodity exchanges also cited this as a structural fault of the trading mechanism on all exchanges.[43]

The main advantage of off-exchange deals was their opacity to tax collectors. They benefitted individual brokers who received a commission and individual clients who did not pay a commission to the exchange, but reduced contract compliance by providing no information to the trading community. Brokers were loathe to share information about their trades with private arbitration commissions because this left them subject to punitive taxation by the state. Deals concluded "off the exchange" were not subject to the jurisdiction of arbitration commissions at most exchanges.

Off-exchange deals limited other types of self-governance. Brokers on many exchanges tried to create a black list of unreliable clients and brokers, but the attempt failed because the brokers saw the costs of maintaining such a list as prohibitive.[44] A victim had to investigate and verify a claim to get a broker's name on the list, but because providing evidence is costly, and the victims or brokers who honored the boycott would not receive compensation from a broker that was barred, they had little incentive to provide information about a dishonest trader. Brokers had no assurance that others would honor the boycott of dishonest traders. If trade is expected to be profitable, conducting a boycott will be difficult.

The Private Protection Trap

The problems of trading on both universal and specialized commodity exchanges pushed brokers into the trap of private protection. Despite their best efforts, individual brokers did not give information to private arbitration commissions because this made them vulnerable to high taxation by the state. Moreover, brokers were wary of relying on state enforcement due to a similar fear of taxation. This gave individual brokers strong incentives to rely on private protection agencies that produced gains for individual traders, but prevented movement to a more socially efficient equilibrium. This phenomenon was common discussion among brokers. For example, at its second congress, the Inter-regional Exchange Union issued a statement that "virtually all commercial and middleman activity has shifted to the sector of the shadow economy and the black market" and issued an appeal for greater protection from law enforcement agents against private protection agents.[45]

As brokers and other economic actors withdrew from the formal economy and turned to private agents to enforce contracts, they created a demand for private protection organizations. The extent of organized protection, both legal and illegal, in wholesale trade and other sectors of the economy is widely recognized.[46]

This interpretation of the rise of private protection agencies in this sector differs from other approaches. Some see the roots of this phenomenon in society-specific values or culture. Others trace the roots of private protection agencies in Russia to the institutional legacy of communist systems.[47] Similarity in the methods and practices of the Yakuza in Japan, the Mafia in Sicily, and private protection agencies in Russia suggests that this phenomenon is not unique to countries exposed to the legacy of post-communism. Culture or an institutional legacy seems too broad a variable to account for the origins and presence of private protection across these cases. Moreover, this approach rarely specifies the causal mechanisms that led to the rise of private protection agencies or account for variation in the extent of private protection across sectors within countries.

A second view links the rise of private protection agencies to the collapse of the Russian state and the ensuing power vacuum in the country.[48] On this view, private protection emerges wherever the state is too weak to enforce contracts. This view neglects the potential for market participants to design their own mechanisms to enforce contracts. Self-governance on the currency futures and equities market in Russia seems to have been much more successful than on commodity exchanges. Brokers in these sectors have mitigated the problem of contract enforcement without turning to the state or private protection agencies.[49]

A third view links the rise of private protection to the early stages of capitalism.[50] Again, this view does not account for variations across economic sectors. In addition, as Polanyi suggests the harshness of early capitalism may compel citizens to turn to the state for services, rather than to private protection agencies.[51]

Linking the rise of private protection organizations in commodity exchange trade to microlevel contracting problems has several advantages. First, this method may also be used to explore similar phenomena in other settings, such as the Sicilian Mafia, or the Japanese Yakuza. Second, it provides for micro-level foundations for a macro-level phenomenon.[52] Third, it offers the potential to account for variations in the strength of private protection across economic sectors. Where contracting problems are most severe, the use of private protection agencies should be most widespread.[53]

The Business of Private Protection in Russia

Brokers on commodity exchanges are not the only actors that have used private enforcers. The Ministry of Internal Affairs (MVD) registered the first private protection agency in 1989, and by 1994, more than 8,000 private security agencies employing 800,000 full-time workers were registered in Russia.[54] This figure does not include a large number of unregistered or illegal enforcers. State security agencies complain that private protection agencies are luring their best officers with higher pay. According to the MVD, 17,000 former MVD employees and 12,000 former KGB employees now work for private security agencies.[55]

The per capita number of private security officers—even including unregistered enforcement agencies—is large, but is likely comparable to other developed countries.[56] In 1982, of a population of 250 million, more than 1.1 million

Americans worked in private security—twice as many as in public security.[57] Estimates for 1995 place the number of private security personnel in the US at 1.6 million.[58] In 1978, General Motors employed more than 4,200 security personnel, a figure larger than the police forces of all but the five largest cities in the country at the time.[59] Britain has a population of 56 million, and there are about 100,000 private security personnel.[60] A 1986 study found that the Australian state police totaled about 40,000, while private security personnel numbered roughly 60,000, out of population of 17 million.[61] As Russia's population is 150 million, the number of private security agents is high, but not unreasonable.

Two factors distinguish private protection organizations in Russia from their nominal counterparts in developed economies. First, the Russian state is much less capable of regulating private protection organizations than other governments and the level of self-governance in the industry is almost nil.[62] Members of the industry admit that security personnel are poorly trained and lack experience.[63] According to the Russian Ministry of Internal Affairs, 2,500 private protection agencies lost their licenses over the last two years.[64] Private security officers complain that the police view them as competitors and obstruct their activities.[65]

Second, and perhaps more important, private protection organizations, both legal and illegal, commonly resolve disputes and enforce contracts without sanction from the state. By usurping a central function of the state, these agencies have greatly impinged on state sovereignty.

One of the largest legal private protection organizations in Russia is Aleks.[66] Formed in 1989 by the Isaakov brothers who worked in the Soviet Militia (police), Aleks has clear ties to the old regime. Its headquarters were located in the same building as the local party committee (Sovetskii Raion) in Moscow. Moreover, it received the first license to operate a private security agency in Russia. Aleks gathered a broad clientele by its promise to return any "reasonable damages." Aleks provides body guards and security guards who accompany goods to prevent diversion from their contracted destination. The firm also has an economic security division that acts as a credit and collection agency. Through ties with banks, Aleks claims to be able to provide credit ratings—an important service in an information-poor economy.[67]

As always, enforcement is costly and Aleks's fees are beyond the reach of many firms. Aleks's president declined to specify their rates noting only that they are generally three times less than those charged by a Western security firm.[68] If force is needed to gain compliance, then options other than expensive legal private protection organizations exist. It may be cheaper and as effective to hire someone to throw a rock through an offender's plate glass window or to expropriate the good, than to rely on the state for enforcement.

Private protectors may deter opportunism and raise efficiency even if the social consequences are less benign. If private protectors can allow trades to be made that otherwise would go unmade, so what is the problem? Aren't they just providing a service at lower costs than a court system? How is private enforcement of property different from state enforcement?

While private enforcement does provide some benefits, it is typically more costly than state enforcement. First, private protectors rarely expect to be in "office" longer than state actors and have stronger incentives to exploit their position by charging high rates for their services. Private protectors often have short time horizons due to factional infighting and the threat of arrest. These factors increase the incentive to charge high fees or engage in extortion.[69] This is particularly true for poorly organized crime groups. The high rate of internecine violence among Russian criminal groups suggests that illegal private protectors have a very short time horizon. State actors may also have short time horizons, but are more likely to be constrained by procedures for replacing leaders. State actors with a stake in the future have reason to prevent lame-duck leaders from exploiting private business. The time horizons of private protectors and state actors is an empirical question, but the time horizon of a state actor will likely be longer.

Second, if there is competition, rather than monopoly, among state and private protectors, this competition will produce negative externalities, such as increased violence.[70] If all private protectors have a collective interest in reducing violence, an individual private protector has no incentive to restrict the violence associated with his business. In Russia, the contract killing of private businessmen has sadly become commonplace. The Prosecutor General reported 102 contract killings in 1992 and 562 in 1994.[71] If protection were "sold" by a monopolist like the state, the incentive to internalize these externalities would be greater.

Third, private enforcers are often more difficult to monitor than state enforcers. Since enforcement is costly, once the enforcer receives payment, he has no incentive to actually deliver the punishment in a one-time interaction. Since both the broker and the enforcer can foresee this outcome, the broker does not receive protection, and the enforcer does not receive payment. If the exchange is repeated, however, then an enforcer may have an incentive to gain a reputation for honesty if the gains from future exchanges exceed the costs of defecting with the gains from a single round. One observer noted that legal private protection organizations, like Aleks, operated "like a reverse extortion racket" (*Eto reket, no v obratnuyu storonu*).[72]

Fourth, and perhaps most important, private protectors often inhibit changes in economic institutions that reduce transaction costs and increase efficiency. For example, a thriving private arbitration system would present a threat to private protectors. Diego Gambetta notes that private protection organizations—like the Sicilian Mafia—thrive by injecting distrust into economic relations to create an artificial demand for their services.[73]

State enforcement also presents great problems. The potential for corruption is arguably greater with state protection. Nonetheless, the state is generally seen as a more efficient means of providing the commodity of contract enforcement and protection. Robert Putnam notes that slower growth rates correlate with higher mafia influence across regions of Italy.[74] Charles Tilly argues that the triumph of the state over other organizations set the stage for the great economic development of Western Europe.[75] Finally, North and Thomas attribute the rise of the western world to the efficiency of the state as a protector of property rights.[76]

The state can potentially offer economies of scale and scope in enforcement. Moreover, monitoring state actors as providers of enforcement is typically easier than monitoring private enforcers. If state actors in a competitive system fail to satisfy constituents they can be removed from office. Once private enforcers provide their services it is much more difficult to ask them to leave. Diego Gambetta compares private enforcers to guests who stay too long: they are welcome at first, but become an unbearable burden over time.[77]

Conclusion

Contracting problems on post-Soviet commodity exchanges highlight several salient points about relationships between the state, the market, and the rule of law. First, where economic agents try to create self-governing organizations within a territory controlled by the state, state actions often determine the scope for self-governance. While most studies of self-governance groups are beyond the reach of the state, this case suggests the importance of studying SGOs within the context of a state.

Second, if state actors favor policies that restrict information among members of a group that can realize the gains from trade, then the prospects for self-governance will be low, even where the internal features of the group favor creation of an SGO. In this case the state acted as a "meddlesome Leviathan" that hindered self-governance by choosing policies that restrict the flow of information on the market.

Third, the rise of private protection agencies in Russia is better depicted as a response to micro-level contracting problems facing political and economic actors, than as emerging from the institutional legacy of the Soviet system, the collapse of the Russian state, or an early stage of capitalism.

Finally, the case of commodity exchanges in Russia suggests a reevaluation of the two most prominent views of creating a law-governed economy. Actors contracting in the shadow of a state that levies a predatory tax will not behave as predicted by either of these traditions. They will be reluctant to turn to the state to enforce contracts when they fear state power. Moreover, they will have difficulty engaging in self-governance because they will be reluctant to share information about their trading practices. In this environment they will have strong incentives to rely on private enforcers. Thus, high tax rates may have perverse side effects, such as inhibiting self-governance and promoting the rise of private protection organizations.

Notes

The author gratefully acknowledges support from the National Council on Soviet and East European Affairs, and the Wallis Institute of Political Economy, and would like to thank Joel Hellman, Slava Kokorev, Pavel Mochalov, Katharina Pistor, William Riker, Jeffrey D. Sachs, Jack Snyder, Elena Vinogradova, Dave Weimer, Andrei Yakovlev, and members of the Olin Series Seminar on the Rule of Law and Economic Reform in Russia. All mistakes are my responsibility.

1. North and Thomas (1973); Charles Tilly (1991).

2. Thomas Hobbes (1986).

3. Stewart Macauley (1961), pp. 55–67; Richard Posner (1980); Mark Granovetter (1985), pp. 481–510; Milgrom, North, and Weingast (1990), pp. 1–23; Elinor Ostrom (1990); Robert Ellickson (1991).

4. Ostrom (1990), p. 1.

5. The terms of the Russian court system are doubly confusing. State courts in charge of commercial disputes are typically referred to as arbitration courts (*arbitrazhnie sudi*), while private bodies established to resolve economic disputes are referred to a tertiary courts (*treteiskiie sudi*). To make these terms more accessible I refer to the former as state arbitration courts and the latter as private arbitration commissions.

6. Timothy Frye (1995). This is not the only reason for the failure of self-governance organizations on the commodity exchanges, but it seems to be a theoretically sufficient and often under-appreciated one.

7. Barry Weingast, "Market-Preserving Federalism," ms. Stanford University.

8. Cohen (1991), pp. 11–16; Kokorev (1993); Yakovlev (1991a); see also Institut issledovannia organizovannikh rynkov (1991b); Woodruff (1992); Zhurek (1993), pp. 41–43; Sedaitis (1994).

9. The number of exchanges cited by Russian sources varies. Many diverse organizations called themselves exchanges—*birzhi*. The figure cited above includes only those registered by the State Anti-Monopoly Committee's Commission on Commodity Exchanges.

10. According to official statistics commodity exchanges handled about 3–5 percent of retail trade in 1992. This figure is understated due to the difficulty of gauging trade in the private sector. Many trades at the exchanges went unregistered.

11. Yakovlev (1991a), p. 111.

12. *MTB Godovoi Otchet*, 1993.

13. *Rossiskaya Gazeta*, March 10, 1993, p. 3. Surveys suggest that traders broke contracts strategically. Most violations were for very small or very large amounts.

14. "Birzha chestnosti ne garantiruet," *Kommersant'*, #21, May 25, 1993, p. 18.

15. Survey data from the Institute for Organized Markets provided by Kokorev.

16. Yakovlev (1991a), (1991b), Cohen (1991); Zhurek (1993); Woodruff (1992); Kokorev (1992); Sedaitis (1994).

17. *MTB Godovoi Otchet, 1993*.

18. Elena Vinogradova (1993), for relevant legislation.

19. Pistor (1996a), finds that state courts handled 90 percent of their cases within two months. Brokers interviewed in the summer of 1992 and 1993 seemed to believe the courts to be slower than they were in reality.

20. Vinogradova (1992a).

21. Vinogradova (1992a).

22. Sazhina, *Delevoi Mir*, September 24, 1992.

23. The arbitration tribunals established by the Association of Russian Bankers (ARB) has also handled few cases. In the middle of 1994, the ARB had 800 members and was the dominant lobby for the Russian banking community. Roughly 20 percent of commercial loans by Russian banks end in default, but only 28 cases worth a total of $4.5m had been decided by the ARB Arbitration Court by the summer of 1994, *Bizness i Banki*, #34, 1994.

24. Interview with Leonid Balayan and Elena Vinogradova, the two highest ranking judges on the MCE arbitration commission, July, 1993.

25. *RTSB Godovoi Otchet'*, 1993; interview with RTSB legal department.

26. Interview with legal departments of the MOE and MFME, July, 1993.

27. *Bizness, Banki i Birzha*, #42, 19, 1992, p. 7.

28. Vytransky (1992); Vinogradova (1992b), pp. 85–92; Vinogradova (1992d), pp. 106–114; Vinogradova diss. (1994).

29. Pistor (1996), p. 79.

30. Milgrom, North, and Weingast (1990).

31. Economic actors in post-Soviet Russia have shown great ingenuity and we might expect them to resolve this enforcement problem as well.

32. Litwack (1991a), pp. 77–89. Also Litwack (1991b), pp. 255–279.

33. Kokorev (1992).

34. At the first meeting of the Inter-regional Exchange Union, the Minister of Labor promised that the government would end the superprofit tax, but was contradicted by a representative of the Ministry of Finance. *Kommersant'*, June 10, 1991, p. 2.

35. Anthony Jones and William Moskoff (1991); Kokorev (1992).

36. Jones and Moskoff (1991); Ericson (forthcoming).

37. *Bizness, Banki, i Birzha*, #26, (1992), p. 49.

38. Webster and Charap (1994).

39. Jones and Moskoff (1991).

40. *Kommersant' Daily*, July 10, 1993.

41. Sedaitis (1994), p. 100.

42. *Ekonomicheskaya Gazeta*, #23, June 1992, p. 8.

43. Cohen (1991); Yakovlev (1991a and 1991b); Woodruff (1992).

44. Yakovlev (1991b).

45. Demchenko, *Izvestiya*, May 27, 1992.

46. Economist Intelligence Unit, January, 1995. IMF *Russia*, 1993.

47. Anderson (1995); Handelman (1994).

48. Skaperdas and Syropolous (1994).

49. Tim Frye (1997).

50. This third view may also lack historical validation as well. Private protection agencies were not active in the frontier economy of the US during its early stages of capitalism. Vigilante groups on the frontier were usually composed of the leading members of society and disbanded quickly after their search. Most studies link the rise of organized protection

in the US to two sources: the economic problems of contracting in the large immigrant communities at the turn of the century and the prohibition on the production and sale of alcohol included in the 19th amendment. See Brown (1969), pp. 43–80.

51. Polanyi (1957).

52. On the importance of microfoundations for explanation, see Bates (1987), pp. 31–54.

53. Consistent with the explanation presented above, sectors of the economy that have the most severe contracting problems, banking, insurance, and export, seem to have led the increase in private protection organizations.

54. *Kommersant'*, #10, 1995, p. 43; *Kapital,* July, 18, 1995; the Russian Supreme Soviet passed a Law on Private Security Agencies that allowed private companies to provide security services on March 11, 1992. Zakon RF, "O Chastnoi Okhrannoi i Detektivnoi Deitelnosti," *Izvestiya*, March, 14, 1992, p. 2.

55. *Kommersant'*, #10, 1995, p. 43. Many US states require that certain private security functions be performed only by agents with prior experience in the field. See Nemeth (1989).

56. Schelling and Gambetta have the best discussions of the distinction between extortion and protection. Schelling (1984); Gambetta (1994), pp. 28–33.

57. Cunningham (1985).

58. Telephone interview with William Cunningham, May 8, 1995.

59. O'Toole (1978).

60. Johnston (1989).

61. Johnston (1989).

62. According to Johnston "there is no statutory regulation of private security" in Britain (Johnston, 1993, p. 86). The UK relies primarily on self-governance. In the US state regulations on training, licensing, and monitoring vary widely (Nemeth, 1989).

63. *Kommersant'*, #10, 1995. In Russia, the training course for a security guard costs 500,000 rubles and security firms are obliged to rent their weapons from the state.

64. *Kapital*, July 18, 1995.

65. *Finansoviye Izvestiya*, May, 26, 1994, p. 5. The Moscow City Government has begun to use private security personnel to patrol with regular police. Local police either pay the agencies directly or give them tax breaks. Police forces in the US and Canada commonly contract many services to private security agencies.

66. This information on Aleks was obtained during interviews with the President and Vice President on June 18, 1992. When possible the information was corroborated with secondary sources.

67. The president of Aleks denied threatening violence against those who breach contracts with his clients. He explained that after Aleks operatives present evidence to the alleged violators "they usually make the right choice."

68. Later research found that Aleks charges $4 an hour for an unarmed security guard and $6 an hour for an armed security guard in a typical store. Personal body guards hired for more than a month cost $130 unarmed and $230 armed per day, *Kapital,* July 18, 1995, p. 1, quoting Sergei Fadeev, the General Director of Aleks.

69. Deiermeir, Ericson, Frye, and Lewis (1997).

70. Schelling (1984). A protection agency with a monopoly on the use of force becomes the state.

71. OMRI, Daily Report, April 11, 1995.
72. Interview with Dmitri Abkhimenko, market analyst for Interfax, June, 28, 1992.
73. Gambetta (1994), pp. 15–22.
74. Putnam (1993), p. 146–148.
75. Tilly (1991).
76. North and Thomas (1973).
77. Gambetta (1994).

CHAPTER 8

Developing Commercial Law in Transition Economies: Examples from Hungary and Russia

Cheryl W. Gray and Kathryn Hendley

The transition from plan to market in formerly socialist economies is perhaps most fundamentally a change in the role of the state. The state must withdraw from everyday control over most aspects of economic life, and the central economic controls associated with the state's central planning apparatus must be replaced by decentralized, objective rules of the game, i.e., the "rule of law." The patron-client networks and the resulting particularism that characterized economic relations under state socialism have to give way to relationships based on universalistic rules. The state's role must become facilitative. Its functions in this area are twofold: (1) to build a body of substantive law that is clear, transparent, feasible, efficient and stable, and (2) to create legal institutions with sufficient authority and independence to enforce these laws (even against the politically powerful).

What does it take to develop such "rule of law" in transition settings? Most observers and providers of technical assistance focus on the *supply* side, i.e., on what key laws and institutions have to be in place before decentralized markets can function. They recognize the importance of well-crafted legislation and institutions that facilitate efficient and largely self-enforcing economic outcomes. However, while a supply of key legislation is undoubtedly critical, such supply is not enough on its own to ensure rule of law. There must also be a deep-seated *demand* for rule of law by existing or potential market players. What generates such demand? It springs from a desire for *stability*—a desire for objective "rules of the game" that apply across the board rather than on a case-by-case basis (as was typical under socialism). This desire in turn will arise only if these players must truly depend on the market for survival; that is, if they no longer view the state as an assured safety net in times of trouble. State intervention can perhaps be conducted in an ad hoc fashion; widespread market interactions among strangers, in contrast, depend on reliable, objective rules to lower transaction costs. In sum, the withdrawal of the state may to a great extent be a *sine qua non* for the development of rule by law.

The goal of this chapter is to illustrate the process and requirements for developing rule of law in transition economies. It focuses on a specific example of commercial law reform in each of two transition countries, Hungary and Russia. While each country's experience is in a narrow sense unique, in broader respects Hungary is quite representative of Central Europe, while Russia shares many characteristics with other former Soviet republics. While the key problems associated with transition in the two regions are similar in *kind*, the detailed comparison of Hungary and Russia underlies our belief that the problems of legal development in the two regions are different in *magnitude*, due to two factors: (1) different legacies and experiences under socialism, and (2) different degrees of state withdrawal from post-socialist economic activity. The shorter period of socialism in Central Europe, its presocialist legal and institutional legacy, and its closer links (even during socialism) with Western Europe ease the task of developing rule of law. The legacy is particularly important; Hungary had a well-functioning legal system and rule of law before World War II, while Russia was never a society or economy ruled fundamentally by law. The highly instrumental use of law by the Communist Party elite during the Soviet period further eroded trust in law and legal institutions. Furthermore, Hungary's longer experience and greater progress to date in implementing economic reforms that separate private actors from the state help provide the incentives needed for rule of law to become reality.

The specific examples of legal reform addressed in this paper are somewhat different in the two countries. This reflects in part the different areas of concern that have highlighted the reform agenda in the two countries since 1992. In Russia the focus is on company law, which has been a primary means through which the Russian government has tried to change the behavior of ostensibly privatized firms. In Hungary the focus is on bankruptcy law, which has taken center stage as a means to change enterprise behavior in that country since the adoption of the transition world's most modern and aggressive bankruptcy law in late 1991. Thus, each specific area of law reflects a major initiative of that country in trying to change enterprise behavior in the past half-decade.[1] To what extent have these laws been followed in practice, and how effective have these initiatives been in changing behavior?

What Is Required for Fundamental Legal Change?

The specific cases to be analyzed illustrate three interlocking requirements that are essential for decentralized legal frameworks to be implemented effectively in any setting—reasonable laws, adequate institutions, and market-oriented incentives. All three must exist together, and in socialist economies must often be built from scratch. Developing any of the three is a major challenge, and progress along all three necessarily takes time. The question to ask at any point in time is not whether there is or is not "rule of law," but whether the country is moving in the right direction along these three dimensions.

A Reasonable Legal Framework

The first necessary (but not sufficient) condition for the development of "rule of law" is a formal legal framework that:

- provides all players with clearly delineated rights and responsibilities, including clear norms of fiduciary duty;
- embodies market-friendly economic policies that are to a large extent "self-enforcing";
- has been internalized into local legal culture and understanding through an airing and acceptance by a basically democratic political process; and
- is reasonably well-known by the population, stable, and predictable in enforcement.

This is by no means an easy first requirement, especially given the wide range and scope of the policy debate, the intense political pressures, the shortage of experience with market mechanisms, the limited analytical skills and the fragility if not the absence of democratic institutions typical of transition settings. While getting the economic signals "right" is itself an enormous challenge, perhaps even more difficult is defining principles of individual responsibility, particularly for those acting in a fiduciary capacity for others. The socialist system undermined the mutual trust among the people that is so essential for decentralized markets to function, and the state, acting through new laws and institutions, must now undertake the formidable task of reinstating that trust and of convincing individuals that it will also be governed by law. Unfortunately, the failure of this first step may have systemic costs beyond mistakes in individual laws themselves. When laws are passed with major inconsistencies, uncertainties, economic flaws, or clear avenues for abuse by some at the expense of others, these new laws can act to deepen public mistrust in law even further.

What are the possible sources for transition countries to turn to in formulating substantive legal frameworks? Essentially there are two options: (1) "home-grown" law (either from "first principles" or from old pre-war legislation), as has typically been true of most of the legislation adopted since the late 1980s in Central and Eastern Europe[2]; or (2) legislation transplanted in part or in whole from advanced market economies. Although imported laws have the benefit of supplying "pre-tested" models, they are inherently risky, because they do not grow out of local legal culture and so may not take root when transplanted without having undergone an internal process of formulation and drafting. An intermediate model—borrowing general ideas from "best practice" models abroad, but then internalizing them through a thorough process of indigenous legal drafting and political debate—is probably optimal in most cases.

Supportive Institutions

A second necessary (but still insufficient) condition for the development of "rule of law" is the existence of institutions capable of supporting the legal framework and enforcing it at the margin. Even if the formal body of laws is economically sound and potentially self-enforcing to a large extent, it may well lie dormant without basic institutional support.

The first obvious supporting institution is the court system. For an individual or the state, taking action to enforce a law is often time-consuming and costly, particularly when information is scarce. The potential end result must make it worth the effort. In particular, there must be some assurance that the court (or other legal institution involved) has the power and capacity to decide the substantive question objectively and enforce the judgment. These assurances were absent under state socialism. The administrative-command system led to a general marginalization of law within the economy, and formal judicial institutions atrophied in the economic sphere. Managers tended to turn to ministerial or party officials if a trading partner reneged, rather than pursuing legal remedies. This was a pragmatic approach. Appealing to the bureaucracy solved their problem in that the ministry or the party had the power to order, for example, that key inputs be delivered. As a rule, the courts could only award money damages and fines. In a non-monetized economy, such remedies were cold comfort to enterprise managers seeking to fulfill the plan. With the transition to the market, the remedial role of the state bureaucracy must be supplanted by arm's-length dispute resolution and enforcement institutions.

While formal legal institutions such as judges, prosecutors, arbitrators, and court functionaries (including, for example, bailiffs and bankruptcy trustees) are of course the primary law interpreters and enforcers, the list of institutions needed to undergird the rule of law in any country goes well beyond them. For arm's-length legal norms to be useable by market participants in everyday commerce, perhaps the *most* important institutions are those that produce and distribute information and monitor those participants, i.e., the "watchdog" institutions such as accountants, credit rating services, securities regulators, the private bar and investigators (including the press). These institutions provide the information that is absolutely critical for laws to be enforced (whether "self-enforced" by the participants themselves or enforced by formal institutions) and thus for economic policies to have their intended effects.

Early yet careful attention to institutional needs is warranted, because institutional development is reinforcing, as each successful case of law enforcement and information provision creates a demonstration effect that builds overall trust in the legal process. Institutions do not arise in a vacuum but are themselves shaped by the substance of the new transition-era laws and by the institutional legacies of state socialism.[3] The state creates formal legal institutions through enabling legislation. In doing so, the goal should be to develop institutions that are generally autonomous from the day-to-day political process of government and able to operate unobtrusively. The state continues to be involved, in that it provides financial support and lends its legitimacy to these institutions (which can be important when enforcing judgments against the political or economic elite). As to the "watchdog" institutions that facilitate both official and self-enforcement, the state's role is more limited, both in terms of their creation and operation. Indeed, if such institutions are to be successful, they must arise from societal demand rather than being imposed from above by bureaucrats.

Market-Based Incentives

Finally, a third necessary condition for rule of law to develop in any country is a set of incentives for individual market participants themselves that motivates them to take full advantage both of the rights granted by the formal legal framework and of the information and enforcement capacity provided by supportive institutions. Once again, the role of the state is critical. As noted earlier, parties will have strong incentives to take advantage of legal rights and abide by legal responsibilities primarily to the extent they depend on the market—and their reputation in it—for survival. For example, banks and other creditors may not avail themselves of the rights provided under bankruptcy laws unless they are convinced that state bail-outs are not likely to be available and thus that aggressive debt collection is necessary for survival. Similarly, managers in private firms may be tempted to ignore shareholder protections and other checks and balances laid out under corporate law unless their access to inputs and their ability to sell products and raise capital depends on a law-abiding reputation. If they can raise capital by turning to the government or state banking system for subsidies, or if they have a monopoly position in the market (either as output seller or as input purchaser), why worry about reputation in private markets?

In sum, market-oriented incentives complement market-oriented laws and institutions. All three are—for better or worse—inextricably interlinked. One cannot proceed far without the others, and all three are essential for the development of rule by law.

Hungary's Experience with Bankruptcy Reform

To translate the rather abstract discussion above into real-world relevance, let us take as a first example the case of bankruptcy reform in Hungary. We look in turn at the pros and cons of the formal law, the state of institutional support for such law, and the incentives of the parties supposedly affected by the law's provisions.

The Legal Framework: Hungary's Bankruptcy Legislation

Hungary's experience with bankruptcy reform since 1992 is unique among the transitional economies. Hungary adopted a tough new bankruptcy law in late

1991 that took effect January 1, 1992. The law required managers of all firms with arrears over 90 days to any creditor to file for either reorganization or liquidation within 8 days (the so-called "automatic trigger") and provided a rather sympathetic framework for them to do so.[4] The law immediately resulted in a wave of filings, with some 3500 filings in April, 1992, alone (90 days after the law took effect). From 1992 through 1994 over 25,000 cases were filed under the law, a level far beyond the expectations of policy makers when the law was adopted.

The Hungarian law provides a modern and quite reasonable economic and legal framework for judicially directed reorganization and liquidation. It is similar in structure to the U.S. bankruptcy regime, as policy makers imported contemporary thinking from advanced market economies while attempting to tailor it to Hungarian conditions. Under the law debtor firms may file for either reorganization or liquidation, while creditors may file only for liquidation of the debtor firm. If a debtor files for reorganization, incumbent managers may stay in place and have three months to present a reorganization plan to creditors, who then negotiate and vote to accept or reject it. If either party files for liquidation, a liquidator is appointed once the court reviews and decides to proceed with the case. The liquidator is supposed to notify creditors, draw up a list of assets, sell the assets, and divide the proceeds among creditors in order of priority (with liquidation costs first, followed by creditors secured by mortgage, other creditors, and equity holders, in that order). The entire liquidation process is supposed to be completed within two years.

Under the first version of the law, a debtor firm filing for reorganization received automatic relief from debt service and asset foreclosures for the first three-month period (further extendible by one month), during which the reorganization plan was to be prepared. Unanimous approval by all creditors was required for the plan to be adopted; otherwise the case reverted automatically to liquidation. A firm with a successful plan could not file again for reorganization for at least three years. Trustees and creditors' committees were not required in reorganization cases but could be organized at the discretion of creditors.

Numerous important changes were made to the law in September, 1993, drawing from the first one and a half years' experience with the 1991 law. The unanimous creditor approval requirement was considered too tough, so it was replaced by a requirement of creditor approval by one-half in number and two-thirds in value of outstanding claims. The automatic three-month stay on debt service was considered too generous and easy to abuse, and it was replaced by a discretionary stay that required the same level of creditor approval. Liquidators' compensation was considered too low and was increased. To stem the unanticipated flood of cases, both the "automatic trigger" and the automatic reversion of failed reorganizations to liquidation were eliminated. Finally, trustees were made mandatory in all reorganization cases.

In sum, while there were some design flaws in both the original and the amended bankruptcy laws,[5] the adoption of the 1991 law was a step forward in Hungary and provided a reasonably efficient economic framework for the reorganization or exit of problem firms. Was it implemented? Yes it was, due in large part to the powerful nudge provided by the automatic trigger. Was it implemented as it would have been in advanced market economies, or even as anticipated by its designers? No it was not, and to understand why one must turn to institutions and incentives.

The Institutional Base: Hungary's Legal and Commercial Institutions

When the bankruptcy law was adopted in Hungary, the institutions needed to implement it were extremely weak. First, there were very few bankruptcy judges—only 8 in the entire Budapest court[6] in mid-1992 (handling about 4000 cases)—and even fewer with a clear understanding of the issues involved. Second, the professions that we tend to take for granted in advanced market economies and that are so critical in bankruptcy proceedings—accountants, lawyers, appraisers, trustees—were in their infancy. Third, banks and other creditors (including trade and government creditors) lacked employees trained in market-based financial analysis and workout negotiation techniques. Fourth, the economy lacked the institutions—whether trained and motivated bank supervisors, wary depositors, or interested owners—that markets depend on to oversee bank management and counteract fraud and inefficiency. Finally, financial and cost accounting systems were poorly developed within debtor enterprises themselves.

All of this institutional weakness added up to a huge asymmetry in access to information concerning debtor enterprises. Creditors suffered from a vacuum of information (with little place to turn to reliably generate it), while only senior managers within the debtor firms had full access to this important information. This contrasts markedly with the situation in advanced market economies, where both judicial and "watchdog" institutions insure much broader access to relevant information in bankruptcy cases among both debtors and their various creditors. What happens when information is asymmetrically distributed? Those with access have greater opportunity to use the information for their own ends, as discussed further below.

Demand for Law? The Incentives Surrounding the Bankruptcy Process

Even with a well-designed law and sufficient information, would the Hungarian bankruptcy law have been implemented as intended by policy makers and as a similar law would be in advanced market economies? This depends in large part on the incentives of the various parties, which depend in turn on the extent of their independence from the state and thus their dependence on the market for survival. The major parties whose incentives matter in bankruptcy reorganizations are the debtors and their creditors. Added to this in liquidation cases are the liquidators themselves.

Debtors.   Beginning with debtors, one can differentiate between owners and managers of debtor firms, whether public or private. To the extent that an owner owns 100 percent of the firm and is also the manager, the incentives of owners and managers are one and the same. If the owner-manager's ownership interest is less than 100 percent, or if the owner is not also the manager, the incentives of these two parties are likely to differ. Hungarian managers, like managers everywhere, are likely to obtain satisfaction from two sources—the performance of their firms and their own personal economic remuneration. The mix between these objectives varies from manager to manager and firm to firm, but in most cases each plays some role. As is well-known in Western literature, agency costs (including managers' pursuit of personal agendas, even at the expense of shareholder value) are likely to be higher when shareholder monitoring is weak. For example, a manager of a state-owned firm may have a strong incentive to "spontaneously privatize" the firm's assets,[7] particularly if those assets are readily transferable and if such transfer is unlikely to harm his or her reputation because the owner (i.e., the state) is either disinterested or uninformed. The manager of a private firm may face the same incentives to the extent there are many widely dispersed owners without adequate incentive to monitor management. Similarly, a partial owner who manages a private firm may have an incentive to transfer assets of the enterprise to another firm more fully owned by that person. In any case, one common incentive of managers in many transition settings is to increase their ownership of valuable assets while decreasing their ownership of costly liabilities—or to "privatize" assets and "socialize" liabilities.

In the Hungarian case, privatization has moved quite slowly, due in large part to the country's dedication to the sales approach and its eschewing of any form of mass privatization. Yet, unlike in Poland or the former Yugoslavia, Hungary's state-owned enterprises do not have a long tradition of worker activism and control. This, combined with the practical difficulties faced by Hungary's state asset management agencies in their attempts to monitor the activities within hundreds of individual firms, has essentially left managers in almost total control of state-owned firms, with little oversight by owners or workers.

Creditors.   At the same time that some managers face strong incentives to divert assets of firms, many creditors in transition economies lack strong incentives to stop them. In Hungary the principal creditors are government agencies, trade creditors, and banks, each holding roughly equal proportions of the debt of the large problem enterprises.[8] The government creditors include the tax office, the social security service, and the customs office. These authorities were not known for active law enforcement and collection of arrears; in contrast, their legacy carried over from socialism was one of pervasive bargaining and redistribution from profitable and loss-making firms.[9] Habits and attitudes do not die easily. Although there is some evidence that budget pressures have made government creditors more vigilant, tax and social security arrears clearly continue to be a major source of financing for firms in financial distress.[10]

The incentives of trade creditors depend in large part on their links with the state, and these are changing quite rapidly with the growth of the private sector in Hungary. As with government debt, a significant portion of the debt to trade creditors consists of overdue receivables, many which arose in 1991 and 1992 when the enterprise sector in both countries was subject to serious demand and liquidity shocks. These shocks led to a network of inter-enterprise credits that itself undercut discipline due to the fear of "domino" bankruptcies if any one party attempted to collect debts. There is evidence, however, that trade creditors are slowly becoming more active in preventing the emergence of new overdue receivables by requiring payment in advance before goods are shipped to problem firms.

The third major category of creditor is banks. Credit from banks represents less than half the total liabilities of troubled firms in Hungary. Nonetheless, banks play an important if not pivotal role among creditors in maintaining borrower discipline and forcing workouts or liquidations in problem firms. Banks are the only source of financing available now to most Hungarian firms, apart from self-financing and temporary involuntary financing from government, trading partners, and employees through arrears. In advanced market economies banks are clearly key players in bankruptcy processes.

Yet the incentives of large state-owned Hungarian banks in the early 1990s have been complex and confused. As in most transition economies, many of the state-owned commercial banks in Hungary were insolvent by 1992 when evaluated using internationally accepted accounting principles. These insolvencies resulted from several causes, including bad loans inherited from the socialist "monobank," transition-induced defaults on existing loans, and defaults on new credits extended after the onset of relative price reform.[11] As in many other countries, Hungary moved to reinvigorate existing banks via recapitalization. A one-time recapitalization may be needed early in the transition to establish viable institutions, given the undercapitalized state of most commercial banks when initially separated from the monobank. However, growing experience from around the world is showing that recapitalization is itself a risky undertaking, particularly if undertaken repeatedly. If it leads bank managers to believe that future losses will also be offset by the government, it can encourage fraud and moral hazard and further undercut the incentives of banks to expend time and energy pursuing delinquent borrowers.[12] Hungarian banks were effectively recapitalized four times between 1991 and 1994, with a total value of some $3.4 billion—equivalent to about 9 percent of 1993 GDP. Yet little else was done to create strong market-based incentives within banks. The government did not carry out independent, in-depth portfolio or operations reviews before the recapitalizations or implement performance-oriented management contracts. Managers did not have strong and clear incentives to undertake actions that would increase the value of the banks they managed. The government failed to formulate a clear plan for state-bank privatization, although two banks (the foreign trade bank and Budapest Bank) have recently attempted to privatize (the first successfully, the second not yet so) largely on their own initiative. Most observers agree that banking supervision has been weak. In sum, banks have continued to rely on government support, and this has arguably undercut their aggressive pursuit of debt collection.

The Outcome: Rule of Law?

To what extent is Hungary's bankruptcy experience evidence of the development of "rule of law"? In other words, to what extent did the introduction of a new bankruptcy law in Hungary change the behavior of those ostensibly subject to it, and in ways envisioned in the law? The evidence is mixed. On the one hand, the automatic trigger unequivocally resulted in an enormous wave of filings, as managers evidently took seriously the civil penalties they could personally incur if they failed to file. Furthermore, evidence gathered from a recent survey of 117 bankruptcy cases filed in 1992 and 1993[13] indicates that the rough outlines of the mandated legal procedures were more or less followed. Debtors filing for reorganization did benefit (until September 1993) from automatic stays on debt service and collateral foreclosure, and they did generally put forward reorganization plans within the 3–4 month period provided in the law. The cases of firms whose plans were not approved reverted automatically to liquidation. In liquidation cases there is clear evidence that appointed liquidators maintained strong control over the liquidation process and made at least partial attempts to fulfill their legal duties and requirements. More important than adherence to process, however, is the fact that bankruptcy outcomes appear broadly to follow some degree of economic logic. Of the 117 firms surveyed, those that successfully emerged from reorganization were on average less heavily indebted and had better profit performance (i.e., smaller losses) than either those that filed in reorganization (and thus reverted to liquidation) or those that avoided reorganization altogether and filed directly for liquidation. This economically sound outcome can arguably be considered a real success, given the newness of the process and the underdeveloped state of the institutions involved.

On the other hand, the actual outcomes of the bankruptcy process still appear to differ substantially from what was envisioned in the law. The differences arise in large part from the underdevelopment of norms of fiduciary responsibility, the tremendous asymmetry of information access, and the weak incentives of some creditors to oversee the process and assure the maximum possible return on their outstanding credits. First, there is ample anecdotal evidence (not easily verifiable through surveys) that many managers take advantage of the bankruptcy process as a means to privatize assets and socialize liabilities. In some cases they transfer valuable assets to separate private firms prior to filing, leaving the less valuable assets and the liabilities to enter the bankruptcy process. Creditors may also be involved in asset diversion, by colluding with the debtor firm to transfer assets and thus repay that particular creditor prior to bankruptcy at the expense of other creditors.[14] In advanced market economies, such transfers in anticipation of bankruptcy are void or voidable by the trustee. They are by law also voidable in Hungary, but liquidators report tremendous difficulty obtaining necessary evidence, due in large part to the underdevelopment of the "watchdog" institutions.[15] Furthermore, in advanced market economies well-developed laws and traditions of fiduciary responsibility inhibit such behavior, but these laws and traditions are not yet well-developed in transition environments such as Hungary's.

Second, liquidators and the managers of debtor firms may in many cases be following the letter but not necessarily the spirit of the law. It appears that liquidation is to a large extent perceived by all parties more as reorganization than as pure liquidation. This has become even more true since late 1993, when the number of reorganization cases began a steep decline[16]—i.e., when liquidation appears in effect to have replaced reorganization as the primary restructuring process. Interviews with liquidators and firms suggest that many if not most liquidators see themselves as active restructurers, representing first of all the interests of employees or the public rather than the interests of creditors. Virtually all "real" firms (as opposed to "shells" or firms with minimal assets, of which there are plenty) stay alive during the liquidation process as the liquidator looks for ways to privatize their viable parts.[17] This approach is encouraged by a design feature added to the law itself in 1993: the provision that liquidators earn 2 percent of gross proceeds of firms in liquidation as long as the firms are still in operation.[18] While this outcome may be good for restructuring and privatization, it is not necessarily good for creditors, who may lack either sufficient information and institutional enforcement power or sufficient motivation to challenge liquidators' actions. In the end, of course, this lack of a viable creditor-led "exit" and debt collection mechanism can be costly to firms, because it increases the cost and reduces the flow of credit in the economy.

In sum, Hungary's experience with bankruptcy reform indicates the difficulty of pushing economic and legal change "from above," given the lack of well-established norms of fiduciary responsibility, institutional weakness (leading to serious information bottlenecks), and continued soft budget constraints on the part of certain creditors. However, it also illustrates some progress can be made in a relatively short time period if a country undertakes strong forward-looking policy initiatives. Not only has the concept of bankruptcy gained some legitimacy it lacks in so many other transitional economies, but Hungary's initiative has contributed toward building the institutions needed for rule of law to take hold. The process has stimulated the development of a cadre of professional trustees and liquidators with in-depth knowledge of techniques of financial and organizational restructuring. Hungary has been willing to license both foreign and domestic firms as liquidators, and the foreign participation has brought outside knowledge and expertise into the picture. It has also led to an increase in the number and commercial expertise of judges and in the sophistication of the banks' understanding and approach to debt collection. Finally, for better or worse, it has probably been one of the main stimulants of privatization (both of assets and of parts of going concerns) in the Hungarian economy since 1992, and thus has furthered the separation of the economy from state control that is so essential to the healthy development of rule of law. In its reforms of bankruptcy law, Hungary appears to be moving generally in the right direction, albeit certainly not without some difficulty along the way.

Russia's Experience with Company Law

Russia presents a somewhat different case from Hungary. Its experience with state socialism was twice as long and infinitely more intense. Consequently, the behavioral patterns that grew out of socialist incentives and institutional structures were more deeply entrenched and arguably more resistent to change.

One of the key elements of Russian economic reform (as in Hungary and other transition economies) was the legalization of private property and the subsequent privatization of the state industrial sector. Although the state retained an interest in most enterprises, the privatization process brought about a profound change in the ownership structure, as state enterprises were transformed into private entities. But privatization was only a means to an end. The goal was to increase the efficiency of Russian firms and, ultimately, to make them capable of competing in the global marketplace. Privatizing a firm is necessary, but not sufficient, to achieve that goal. More important is effecting a change in *how* the business is run. Such change comes about slowly. The state cannot unilaterally compel change in enterprise behavior. At best, the state can reshape the environment within which the enterprise operates, and thereby have some influence at the margins.

The Legal Framework: Russian Company Law

The technical problems of Russian law (including company law) are legion. Merely finding the law can be a struggle—to say nothing of the difficulty of interpretation. Laws are often internally contradictory or make cross-references to laws that either do not yet exist or do not say what the first law claims. The desire to make the market reforms irreversible has led to impatience with the long debates within the legislature, and to a preference for executive decrees. Ruling by decree is easier in the short run, but does little to move society towards the rule of law. Decrees are inherently non-democratic; they are conceptualized and introduced in a top-down fashion that often ignores local legal culture. None of these shortcomings are unique to Russia, but they are particularly troubling in the Russian context because they tend to deepen the general distrust of the legal system that lingers on from the Soviet period.

The changes in company law over the past decade have generally tracked macro-level economic reforms, though they have often lagged a step or two behind. They began with the 1988 Law on State Enterprises,[19] which represented the first tentative move away from administrative controls towards greater enterprise autonomy. The years that followed brought new laws on property and business organizations that reflected an increased (and sometimes grudging) willingness to accept private property and passive investment interests. By 1990, both Soviet[20] and Russian[21] legislation recognized privately owned business organizations of various types.

While not yet contemplating full privatization, these early laws opened the door to experimentation with new forms of corporate organization. Some adventuresome managers, for example, took advantage of these opportunities to engage in "spontaneous privatization" on the enterprise and sub-enterprise level.[22] Yet these laws were superficial and provided little if any guidance on organizational structure, fiduciary duty or shareholders' rights. For example, the Soviet laws purported to create "collective enterprises," but the legislative language was unclear and incomplete.[23] Basic questions, such as whether equity interests were alienable, whether equity owners could be called on for capital contributions, or the extent to which they could participate in management, were left unanswered.

During the last few years of the Soviet Union, the Russian legislature (led by Yeltsin) was consistently more committed to market reforms than its Soviet counterpart. Consequently, Russian company law represented a significant improvement over Soviet law.[24] In particular, the Statute on Joint-Stock Companies (1990) set forth guidelines on the rights and duties of shareholders and directors. But even this law fell short of creating a complete framework. In particular, it was silent on remedies and fiduciary duty. Shareholders had no legal mechanism for enforcing their rights, and had only minimal rights to information about the operation of the company.

Incremental changes were made in company law during the next few years,[25] but attention was largely focused on privatization. The periodic omnibus privatization decrees addressed certain aspects of company law, but not in a comprehensive manner. For example, one decree included a "standard" charter that implicitly addressed certain aspects of fiduciary duty, and several other decrees designed to protect shareholders' rights were issued on the specific topic of registries.[26] The privatization decrees were typically lengthy, making it difficult to find the relevant provisions. Moreover, they applied only to enterprises that privatized through traditional routes, not to the many enterprises who fashioned their own route. In principle, how an enterprise is privatized should not affect the law that governs it subsequently as a privatized entity. A more comprehensive approach came only with the new Civil Code and the new Law on Joint-Stock Companies.[27] Indeed, simultaneously with their passage came the nullification of many laws that had previously governed corporate affairs.

In sum, in contrast to Hungary's one-shot introduction of a new, coherent, and universally applicable framework for bankruptcy, the potential impact of company law reform in Russia during the first few years of the transition period was dissipated by its piecemeal nature, its incomplete coverage, and its failure to adequately address many fundamental issues.

The Institutional Base: Russian Legal and Commercial Institutions

While they were weak in Hungary, the institutions needed to support a market economy were extremely feeble if not entirely nonexistent in Russia in the 1990–1994 period. Consider first the courts. In Russia, economic disputes are generally resolved by the state arbitration courts (*arbitrazhnie sudi*). During the Soviet period, these tribunals, then known as "State *Arbitrazh*," dealt with disputes between state enterprises.[28] This was not high-profile work and did not attract the most talented or competent jurists. They emerged from the Soviet period with a besmirched reputation and a consequent lack of legitimacy. Recent years have witnessed major institutional reforms, including an expansion of the jurisdiction of the tribunals and their reconstitution as "courts," thereby raising the status of the decision-makers. While these reforms represent a step in the right direction, they are only the beginning. Questions persist about the remedies available (legal vs. equitable) and about the power of the *arbitrazh* judges to enforce their decisions.[29] A deep distrust of formal legal institutions persists, arguably much deeper than in Central Europe.

Other potentially supportive "watchdog" institutions in Russia are in their infancy. Since the late 1980s, the private business bar has experienced a remarkable regeneration, but its target clients are entrepreneurs, not disgruntled shareholders. Procedural rules stymie any possibility that lawyers would take on shareholder-generated claims against management. Such claims are costly and tedious as a result of the inability to aggregate them into class action lawsuits, and the unavailability of contingent fees gives private lawyers little incentive to pursue such claims.[30]

Institutional support is also needed to give meaning to financial disclosure requirements. Although Russian law requires that open joint-stock companies publish an annual report, a balance sheet and an income statement,[31] this requirement is difficult to enforce in practice. Many companies have responded by deeming such information "commercial secrets," and their flouting of the law has had few repercussions. State regulation of securities is in its infancy in Russia and thus is still largely ineffective. Even if the information is published, the lack of uniform accounting standards can render it virtually meaningless. An independent accounting profession that is capable of valuing assets and auditing ongoing operations is only beginning to form in Russia. As a result, financial statements are often prepared in-house, and put the best possible face on the situation.

Finally, an additional "watchdog" institution in the area of company law might be shareholder advocacy groups which, in recent years, have begun to form around the country. Yet their efforts tend to focus on legislative lobbying, rather than on the protection of shareholders' interests at individual enterprises. Moreover, the absence of any class action mechanism within the civil procedure code renders the collective action hurdle almost insurmountable and makes it unlikely that advocacy groups will take up violations of fiduciary duty.[32]

Demand for Law? Incentives Within the Firm

How do the laws and institutions, inadequate as they may be, translate into behavior in the firm? And to what extent is there a demand for better laws and institutions? The answer to these questions depends in large part on the incentives of the parties—in particular the managers and shareholders, whether insiders or outsiders to the firm.

Russian managers, like managers in Hungary and elsewhere, obtain satisfaction from both the performance of their firms and their own personal economic remuneration. During the Soviet period, law was largely irrelevant for state enterprise managers in the pursuit of either objective. Personal relationships, rather than rules of general application, were the glue that held economic transactions together. Law was to be avoided; many managers regarded it as an oppressive instrument of the state. The idea that law could be used affirmatively as a means to create an optimal form of business organization still strikes most Russian managers as absurd.

In theory, the combination of market-based economic reform and political fragmentation could generate a "demand" for law on the part of managers. No longer is any single group (e.g., the Communist Party) capable of dictating the rules of the game. Instead, a plethora of groups have emerged that need to find some way to co-exist. At the same time, private property has been legalized, giving rise to a nascent middle class eager to preserve its gains.[33] Under such conditions, law has the potential to emerge as a compromise solution for all concerned.

However, the peculiar nature of the Russian privatization, which left many firms in the hands of insiders, may have reduced managers' "demand" for law. Private connections remain critical in obtaining supplies and making sales, thereby to some extent obviating the need for universalistic rules. Similarly, as long as a firm can be internally financed, or can be financed through continued state subsidies (whether directly or through the banking system), neither the firm nor its managers need necessarily develop a reputation for following consistent standards and norms. That is not to say, however, that managers can run roughshod over shareholders. Managers of employee-owned firms still need to develop a community of trust between labor and management to boost productivity and performance in the firm, and this may require some degree of (at least perceived) fairness and openness in the running of the company.

With regard to more "private" goals of managers, at a minimum they almost certainly want to maintain their jobs and as much control over the firm as possible (considering the need for at least a perception of fairness as noted above). In addition, Russian managers, like those in Hungary, may face a substantial incentive to skim profits or transfer assets of companies to their personal use.

Who are the potential overseers that might temper the power of management and minimize profit-skimming and insider dealing in privatized firms? For firms that must raise money from equity markets or banks, these outside owners or creditors may be able to exert some controls if (as discussed earlier for Hungary) they are themselves motivated by profit-maximizing concerns. For privatized firms with primarily insider ownership and the capacity for self-financing (even through decapitalization if necessary), the task falls to the shareholders and their representatives on the board of directors. But many Russian shareholders are also workers and so have conflicting loyalties. With no alternative management team waiting in the wings, shareholders are reluctant to throw out the existing managers. On a more personal level, an individual shareholder-worker has little incentive to rock the boat, fearing that the trouble-makers will be the first to be laid off. Board members themselves are likely to be employees also—often other officers of the company. The incestuous nature of an employee-owned company makes it particularly difficult for insiders to hold board members accountable.

The Role of Law in the Russian Enterprise: The Rule of Law?

While the picture in Hungary may be mixed, the picture in Russia appears more one-sided. To date there is little evidence of an underlying respect for law, of a perceived duty to abide by law, or of a clearly articulated demand for the development of rule by law. Illustrating and supporting such a conclusion is difficult in the abstract. Therefore, we have chosen to describe in some detail the experience of one privatized firm during the 1991–1994 period. Although no two firms are exactly alike, we believe the attitudes and actions of this firm are a typical response to the laws, institutions, and incentives now prevailing in the Russian environment.

The company is the Saratov Aviation Plant (*Saratovskii Aviatsionnyi Zavod* or "SAZ"), a large industrial enterprise that produces 125-seat passenger airliners (see Box 8.1 for a more in-depth description). SAZ was privatized in January 1991, pursuant to a decree of the USSR Council of Ministers. In essence, SAZ purchased the assets of the enterprise on behalf of its workforce (then numbering in excess of 15,000), and thereby transformed itself from a state enterprise into a collective enterprise. In early 1993, the stakeholders in the collective enterprise reconstituted the entity as a closed joint stock company (*aktsionnernoe obshchestvo zakrytogo typa*).

SAZ is something of an anomaly, in that it privatized early. As a result, it did not go through the "corporatization" process later mandated and administered by the State Property Committee.[34] But our primary interest is not in privatization per se, but in how privatized enterprises actually function. SAZ is also somewhat peculiar in that it emerged from privatization as a one-hundred percent employee-owned company. At no point in SAZ's privatization process did the state possess any kind of equity interest. This was not an option available to enterprises that privatized later.[35] As one of very few Russian enterprises that was, from 1991, totally private, SAZ provides an ideal setting in which to study the role of law.

There are two discrete stages in SAZ's post-privatization development. The first is the transition from collective enterprise to closed joint-stock company, which took place during 1992 and culminated in a shareholders' meeting in February 1993, at which the reorganization was formally approved. The second is the operation of SAZ as a joint-stock company during 1993 and 1994. In each stage, law played a peripheral role in shaping enterprise behavior.

Transition to Joint-Stock Company.   The catalyst for the transition to joint-stock company did come from the law. The collective enterprise (*kollektivnoe predpriatie* or "KP") was a form of business organization recognized under Soviet law but not under Russian law. With the collapse of the Soviet Union, SAZ's legal status became rather precarious.

But this technical legal problem was not the real reason for abandoning the KP form. The dissatisfaction went deeper. It stemmed from a failure to define the rights and obligations of the various participants at the outset. With the purchase of SAZ assets from the state in early 1991, all SAZ employees automatically became "co-owners" (*so-vladel'tsy*) and received "membership units" reflecting an equity interest in SAZ.[36] Neither the charter (*ustav*) nor the bylaws (*polozheniia*) of the KP clarified the role of co-owners, and the law provided no guidance (as noted earlier). No certificates representing ownership of "units" were issued. This created considerable uncertainty among co-owners as to whether their ownership interests were real. Because the co-owners worked at SAZ, and the primary goal of privatization had been to spur productivity, top management felt compelled to take action.

SAZ management had consulted with Soviet experts when drafting the organizational documents for the KP. Their inexperience with market-based business organizations, combined with the shortcomings of the law, contributed to the creation of an entity that served no one's interests. The intermediary institutions, such as securities regulators, shareholder advocacy groups and private lawyers,

---

BOX 8.1 ECONOMIC CHALLENGES FACING SAZ

SAZ shares many characteristics of other Russian enterprises, particularly its locus within the transitional Russian economy and its consequent struggle for survival. Its key output is the Yak-42 civilian airliner. It also produces many unrelated items (e.g., bicycles, teapots, cutlery, baby carriages). During the Soviet period, SAZ was part of the military-industrial complex, but the conversion to civilian production has been less painful than for many other defense plants, since SAZ had the option of expanding already-existing lines of production, rather than having to completely reconfigure. Now SAZ receives almost no government subsidies.

SAZ's primary challenge lies not in defense conversion, but in selling its planes. The market for planes in the former Soviet Union collapsed as Aeroflot split apart and the spin-offs and new airlines struggled for survival. SAZ's response has been to seek new markets, but its ability to compete effectively is limited by inexperience and by the fact that the Yak-42 is not certified in the West. Like many other large Russian enterprises, SAZ has had to face its own mortality. In order to avoid a stockpile of unsold planes, it now initiates production only upon receipt of a confirmed order. As a result, the plant went onto a three-day work week in the spring of 1994, with corresponding cuts in pay. When these measures failed to achieve the desired cost reductions, the plant ceased production for several months during the summer. This allowed SAZ to repay its debts, both to banks and to workers. During the summer, top management successfully negotiated the sale of several planes to China, which led to a partial resumption of production in the fall of 1994. An analysis of whether SAZ can overcome these short-term challenges is beyond the scope of this paper. A basic awareness of their existence is important for understanding the pressures brought to bear on SAZ management for internal organizational change.

---

that in principle could have provided assistance were almost non-existent in Russia in 1991–1992. When seeking to remedy the situation, the general director sought assistance from foreign specialists.

The decision to reorganize as a joint-stock company brought SAZ within the ambit of the new set of Russian laws, which, as noted earlier, were somewhat better than the old Soviet legislation but still failed to define fiduciary duties or provide for adequate disclosure or remedies. The SAZ managers had a choice: whether to structure SAZ according to the statutory requirements or to go beyond those minimal requirements and create additional internal standards. They chose the latter. In the short run, the choice is puzzling. After all, the gaps in the law would seem to work to their benefit, in that they enhanced management's capacity to maintain control of the company. Over the long run, however, any such manipulative behavior would undermine the goal of creating a community of trust between labor and management, which the SAZ managers believed essential for employee ownership to work.[37] In this way privatization did create some demand for objective limits on managerial discretion. For example, the charter limits the amount of stock that any single person (or entity) can own.[38] Along similar lines, the bylaws governing the board of directors make an effort to forbid conflicts of interest.[39] These bylaws also hold directors accountable for losses to SAZ resulting from the "dishonest" or "unconscientious" (*nedo-brosovestnoe*) fulfillment of their duties, and imply that such a cause of action can be pursued in the courts.[40]

The organizational documents evidence a strong commitment to the one share–one vote principle. SAZ created its own system of proxy voting; it abandoned the old system of selecting delegates to the conference, which smacked of the Party system and facilitated managerial manipulation of the results.[41] Moreover, management took steps (not required by law) to ensure that worker-shareholders understood the reorganization process. Virtually every 1992 issue of the weekly factory newspaper contained articles about some aspect of the joint-stock company. Drafts of the organizational documents were published in this newspaper, giving workers an opportunity to comment. Top management held open meetings and answered questions. The stated purpose was to open up the process to all shareholders.

Neither law nor supporting institutions was critical in changing SAZ's behavior in this first stage of its development as a privatized company. The institutions were non-existent, and the written law was patently inadequate. Moreover, management was highly skeptical about the relevance of law to its situation. But the willingness to impose additional duties on directors reflected a desire—albeit inchoate—for rules of the game that would work over the long run. Thus, SAZ management's decision to reorganize as a joint-stock company and to impose minimal fiduciary duties on directors was to some extent the result of privatization and the beginnings of market-based incentives. The goal was a profitable company that was capable of competing with Western aviation firms. The SAZ managers believed that productivity would increase only if workers participated in the changes—that this would generate a sense of trust and community. The beginnings of a demand for fair and objective norms—if not yet overarching law— are noticeable.

Operation as a Joint-Stock Company.   Thus far, we have only a static vision of SAZ based on its organizational documents. More important in terms of assessing the prospects for the rule of law is what happened after the registration of the joint-stock company. Did management abide by its self-imposed rules? Did it pay any attention to subsequent changes in the statutory law?

At the beginning the reorganization created a sense of enthusiasm within the plant. The first election of the board of directors was taken quite seriously, and the candidates outnumbered the available seats.[42] They represented a wide variety of interests within the plant, and were not exclusively the hand-picked disciples of the general director. Similarly, the board that was finally elected, while made up of top managers, included individuals who had been known to disagree with the general director.

However, any hope that the board of directors would be a genuine decision-making body died a quick death. From the start, board meetings were elaborately choreographed; no real debate was permitted. The general director exercised dictatorial power. This is, of course, not unique to Russian companies, but it is particularly troubling in the Russian context because it creates an impression of "business as usual"—of a continuation of hierarchical Soviet-style "one-man management."[43] The unwillingness of the board members to challenge the general director in a quasi-public forum made board approval of any decision virtually automatic. Not surprisingly, this deflated the post-reorganization enthusiasm and caused many to believe that the transition from state enterprise to KP to joint-stock company had been only a change in form, not in substance. By 1993, elections for the board had become routinized, with the number of candidates equalling the number of open spots. When questioned, those who ran unsuccessfully in 1992 said they had no interest in being on a board that merely rubber-stamped the decisions of the general director. Three outside directors were elected to the board in 1994, but they had been hand-picked by the general director for strategic business reasons. Since their election, not one of them has attended a board of directors meeting.

While this provides some sense of the atmosphere that prevailed at SAZ, the more important question is whether the legal obligations imposed by the charter and bylaws have been enforced. The record is mixed. The restrictions on the amount of stock that can be owned by any shareholder have been enforced. Obviously, this is critical in an employee-owned firm, since a concentration of ownership (particularly within management) would undercut the rights of worker-shareholders. SAZ has continued to operate as a relatively open company. In fact, it consistently exceeds the disclosure mandated by law. A detailed financial report is published in the factory newspaper before each annual shareholders' meeting, and additional information can be found in the newspaper throughout the year. In 1994, a list detailing the stock ownership of all board members was published. A booklet containing the charter, bylaws, and form documents for buying and selling SAZ stock and for voting by proxy has been printed and distributed to interested shareholders. Though shares may be voted by proxy, annual meetings continue to be open to all. There has been no reversion to the Soviet system of electing delegates, who then vote the shares of their work collectives.

On the other hand, the self-imposed rules on fiduciary duty lie dormant. Allegations of profit-skimming and insider dealing on the part of board members are rampant within the plant, but have resulted in no formal charges. Along similar lines, the general director is subject to no meaningful oversight. He often makes significant contractual commitments on behalf of SAZ without prior board approval (or even knowledge). He has also brought SAZ into major joint ventures with Russian and foreign entities without seeking shareholder approval. This is not to say that these transactions are not in the interest of SAZ. Perhaps they are, but they still legally require vetting by the board and/or the shareholders. Certainly the general director speaks with great passion about his commitment to SAZ and to the workers. The point is that he feels no obligation to comply with legal niceties.

A related question is whether SAZ has complied with company laws and decrees passed since its 1992 reorganization as a joint-stock company. Although a technical argument can be made that SAZ (as a closed joint-stock company) was not bound by these laws, it is important to recognize that SAZ management believed these laws were relevant. Part of the reason for looking to the general law was the absence of laws addressing the company's specific circumstances. As has been argued above, in certain spheres SAZ met and even exceeded the minimum required by law (e.g., disclosure). Looking beyond the law itself to the policy underlying it, SAZ has flagrantly defied the state policy against large closed joint stock companies. It has consistently refused to allow outsiders to purchase stock without the prior consent of a majority of shareholders. The new law on joint stock companies has restricted its options, but it does not require SAZ to become open.[44]

Why can SAZ and its managers and directors disobey both the law and the company's own charter and bylaws? The reason lies in the absence of individuals or institutions that have the power and/or the will to force compliance. For example, although insider dealing is clearly prohibited by the organizational documents, no one has pursued the persistent allegations of insider dealing in SAZ. One reason is institutional weakness—namely the dearth of qualified lawyers, the high cost of proving wrong due to weak "watchdog" institutions, and the deep-seated mistrust of formal enforcement institutions such as the courts. Yet even if weak institutions undermine outside enforcement, why are potential violations of the duties owed by board members to SAZ not raised in internal forums, such as the periodic meetings between workers and managers or the annual shareholders' meeting? Even at the 1994 annual meeting, which followed on the heels of the introduction of the three-day work week and the announcement of impending layoffs, the questions posed to the board were not confrontational. Perhaps the language of the bylaws, which does not clarify who has standing to bring such charges, has discouraged potential lawsuits. The more likely proximate cause is the absence of individuals or institutions with the means and incentive to instigate an investigation or sue. Arguably, SAZ itself (acting through the board) could bring a claim. The board of directors of SAZ has established committees to handle various issues, including an ethics committee. In principle, this committee should be monitoring potential conflicts of interest. In practice, however, the committee has done little. The membership of the committee also undermined its ability and/or willingness to act. The chairman of the ethics committee is the vice president for production; he is also a member of the board. Thus, it is difficult to see how the committee could assume a "watchdog" function. Shareholders are also unlikely to pursue an action against either managers or directors, for many of the reasons laid out above. Not only is there a conflict of interest arising from insiders' dual role as shareholders and employees, but precisely what remedies might be available to shareholders who attempt to hold directors accountable for breaches of fiduciary duty are not clear. Even if a shareholder prevails, it might well be an empty victory, in that enforcement is unlikely. In a world of interlocking self-dealing and shareholders beholden to managers for their jobs, who would initiate strong oversight actions?

In sum, the motivation for managerial behavior in SAZ is rarely influenced by the letter of the formal law, or even the requirements implied by SAZ's self-imposed standards. Indeed, there is little evidence of an underlying respect for law or standards of any kind. We do not believe that SAZ is unique among Russian enterprises. It is responding rationally to the existing legal framework (still incomplete and in flux), the institutions that support and enforce it (still in their infancy), and the underlying incentives currently existing within insider-dominated privatized firms.

Summary and Conclusions

This paper has attempted to lay out three fundamental requirements for the rule of law to grow and flourish in transitional economies. These three requirements include a reasonably well-designed "supply" of written laws, a functioning set of institutions to generate the information and take the actions necessary to enforce such laws, and market-based incentives for the actors involved to generate the "demand" for rule by law and the use of laws and institutions once they exist. The absence of any one of the three requirements introduces major distortions and dooms the system to inadequacy if not utter failure. Laws or institutions without each other or without a supportive framework of incentives are likely to lie dormant, while incentives by themselves will be frustrated without a reasonable legal framework and institutions to support and enforce them. The problem in transition settings is that all three must to a large extent be created from scratch. Not only must new laws be drafted (a daunting task in and of itself, but still perhaps the easiest of the three), but they must be accompanied by the growth of supportive institutions (including not only formal judicial institutions but also the "watchdog" institutions that we almost take for granted in advanced market economies) and of economic reforms—whether privatization (particularly with outside owners) or banking reforms—that separate actors from the state and reinforce market-based incentives.

Two case studies—Hungarian bankruptcy law and Russian company law—have been used in the paper to illustrate the interaction of these three requirements in practice. These particular cases illustrate our general view that Central Europe is somewhat further along on all of these dimensions than Russia. Quite well-designed laws are in place in many commercial areas, as evidenced by the Hungarian bankruptcy example discussed in this paper, and the presence of these laws is stimulating the development of the legal and commercial institutions needed to implement them (among which, in this example, are courts, trustees, and banks). Russia is not as advanced in the development of either laws or institutions, among other reasons because it lacked Hungary's pre-war legacy and it started its economic reforms much later. With regard to incentives, in both cases relevant actors exert weaker demand for proper implementation of the laws on the books than one would expect in more mature market economies. In the Hungarian case, creditors' (particularly banks') potential demand for a well-functioning bankruptcy system has been arguably weakened by their ability to turn to the state for recapitalization support rather than having to depend for survival on debt collection mechanisms. In the Russian case the demand for a corporate law with strong corporate governance potential and shareholder protections has been compromised by the preponderance of employee ownership and the resulting conflicts of interest that make employee shareholders reticent to assert ownership rights.

Our framework and our cases belie any simplistic notion that the rule of law can be mechanically dictated from above. Indeed, there is constant tension between the desire of policy makers to push social and legal change from above and the need to generate legal norms from actual practice and acceptance below. But there is more the government can do than simply pass legislation; its policies can profoundly affect incentives and institutions as well. In the case of bankruptcy law in Hungary, top-down legislative reform appears to have been at least marginally successful in changing expectations and behavior, in part because it stimulated the growth of new supporting institutions. It might have been even more successful if other areas of government policy had created more complementary incentives, particularly in banks. In the case of company law in Russia, attempts at top-down legislative reform appear to have been less effective to date, in large part because of the almost complete absence of either supporting institutions or incentives for shareholder monitoring. The hope is that the law on paper will eventually come closer to the law in practice as continued economic reforms move enterprises away from dependence on the state toward dependence on the market.

Notes

1. Russia has hardly begun to implement bankruptcy law, and thus it does not provide a meaningful comparison of experience in this area to Hungary. Hungary adopted a new company law in 1988, but it was not accompanied by the same type of rapid privatization as in Russia, and thus it did not serve to the same extent as a tool of change.

2. For specific examples, see Gray and Associates (1993).

3. For further discussion of the Leninist legacy and the path-dependent nature of the transition to the market, see respectively Jowitt (1992) and Stark (1992).

4. For purposes of this paper, we use the term "bankruptcy" for the entire framework and "reorganization" and "liquidation" for the two specific procedures provided in the law. This differs from the specific Hungarian terminology, which used the term "bankruptcy" to refer to the specific reorganization procedure rather than the broader overall framework.

5. For details, see Gray, Schlorke, and Szanyi (1996). For a somewhat different view, see Bonin and Schaffer (1994).

6. Mizsei (1993).

7. "Assets" here should be read broadly to include valuable intangibles such as customer lists, service contracts, or the working time of productive employees.

8. Baer and Gray (1996).

9. Kornai and Matits (1984), Vodopivec (1994), Schaffer (1989).

10. Bonin and Schaffer (1994).

11. Indeed, while some of the problem was inherited from the breakup of socialism, much of it arose from lending made during the 1990–1991 period. Abel (1994) provides supportive data for Budapest Bank.

12. For further discussion, see Baer and Gray (1996).

13. See Gray, Schlorke, and Szanyi (1996).

14. The incentive for such creditor collusion is partly attributable to the weak legal protection given to collateral and the resulting difficulties that secured creditors face in collecting debts through formal and transparent legal means.

15. To avoid detection, managers or creditors could either wait one year to file in order to avoid the period during which liquidators could retroactively void transfers, or they could destroy the records so that the transfers were not later traceable by creditors, trustees, or liquidators.

16. Several factors have contributed to this decline, including (a) a natural decline after the initial glut of cases; (b) the elimination in September 1993 of the automatic trigger; (c) the elimination at the same time of the automatic 3-month moratorium on debt service (which motivated many filings); (d) the substitution of a separate process—"debtor consolidation"—for bankruptcy in many cases; and (e) the requirement, added in September 1993, that a trustee must be appointed in all bankruptcy cases.

17. Gray, Schlorke, and Szanyi (1996).

18. If the assets are sold, the liquidator earns 5 percent of sales proceeds, which in many cases is substantially less than 2 percent of ongoing revenues.

19. *Vedomosti SSSR*, No. 26, Item 385, 1987. The law was passed in July 1987 and went into effect in January 1988.

20. E.g., "On cooperatives in the USSR," *Vedomosti SSSR*, No. 22, Item 355, 1988; Fundamentals of Legislation of the USSR on the Lease, *Vedomosti SND SSSR*, No. 25, Item 481, 1989; "On property in the USSR," *Vedomosti SND SSSR*, No. 11, Item 164, 1990; Law on enterprises in the USSR, *Vedomosti SND SSSR*, No. 25, Item 460, 1990; Statute on joint-stock companies and limited liability companies, *Sobranie Postanovlenii Pravitel'stva SSSR*, No. 15, Item 82, 1990.

21. E.g., "On enterprises and entrepreneurial activity in the RSFSR," *Vedomosti RSFSR*, No. 30, Item 418, 1990 (amended on June 24, 1992); "On property in the RSFSR," *Vedomosti RSFSR*, No. 30, Item 417, 1990; Statute on joint-stock companies, Order No. 601, 25 December 1990 (amended on April 15, 1992, Order No. 255, and on November

24, 1993, Order No. 2004). With the collapse of the Soviet Union, Soviet laws became null and void to the extent that they contradicted existing Russian law.

22. Johnson and Kroll (1991), Burawoy and Hendley (1992).

23. This example is relevant to our case study. Article 2 of the USSR Enterprise Law recognized collective enterprises as a legitimate form of business organization. The subsequent articles failed to articulate the rights and obligations of holders of property interests in collective enterprises. Law on enterprises in the USSR, *Vedomosti SND SSSR*, No. 25, Item 460, 1990. See also Article 12, "On property in the USSR," *Vedomosti SND SSSR*, No. 11, Item 164, 1990.

24. This first wave of market-oriented business legislation was largely home-grown. This is not to say that Russian reformers were not influenced by foreign models. Certainly they were. But the influx of foreign advisors did not begin in earnest until 1992, when the collapse of the Soviet Union and the liberalization of retail prices signaled the beginning of serious market reforms. See generally, Rutland (1994) and Boyko, Shleifer and Vishny (1993).

25. For example, the Russian statute on joint stock companies was amended on April 15, 1992 (Order No. 255), and on November 24, 1993 (Order No. 2004). The Russian enterprise law was amended on June 24, 1992.

26. E.g., "On the Protection of Investors' Interest," No. 1233, 11 June 1994 (as amended on 4 November 1994), *Sobranie zakonodatel'stva Rossiiskoi Federatsii*, no. 8; Statute on Joint-Stock Company Shareholders' Register, No. 840-r, 18 April 1994, "Rynok tsennykh bumag," *Financy*, part 4, 1994; "On Measures to Ensure the Rights of Shareholders," No. 1769, 27 October 1993, *Rossiiskie vesti*, 2 November 1993; "On the Privatization of State and Municipal Enterprises in the Russian Federation," No. 701-r, 4 November 1992, *Ekonomika i zhizn'*, no. 47, 1992.

27. The first part of the Civil Code (*Sobranie zaknodatel'stva RF*, no. 32, art. 3301, 1994) came into effect in January 1995. The second part of the Civil Code (*Sobranie zaknodatel'stva RF*, no. 5, art. 410, 1996) came into effect in March 1996. The Law on Joint-Stock Companies (*Sobranie zaknodatel'stva RF*, no. 1, art. 10, 1996) was passed after this chapter was written, and so is beyond the scope of our analysis. For a brief analysis see Pistor in this volume.

28. See Pomorski (1977).

29. "On the state arbitration courts in the Russian Federation," *Vestnik Vysshego Arbitrazhnogo Suda* RF, no. 6 (1995), 6–21; "The State Arbitration Procedural Code of the Russian Federation," *Vestnik Vysshego Arbitrazhnogo Suda* RF, no. 6 (1995), 25–79. See also Hendley (1995), Pistor (1996), and *Kommentarii k arbitrazh nomu protsessual'nomu kodeksu RF* (Moscow: Kodeks, 1995).

30. See Easterbrook and Fischel (1991), 100–102.

31. Article 97-1, Civil Code.

32. In some of the more notorious pyramid schemes (e.g., MMM), defrauded shareholders have attempted to persuade the legislature to reimburse them for their losses and to criminalize the activities of the fund's organizers. Whether such collective actions represent movement towards the rule of law or merely a reversion to old habits of relying on the state for a bail-out is questionable.

33. See Weber (1978), vol. 1, ch. X; Unger (1976).

34. Taken together, the various laws and decrees on privatization required that a state enterprise transform itself into a joint-stock company *prior* to privatizing. See Frydman, Rapaczynski, Earle, et al. (1993).

35. See generally, Rutland (1994).

36. All SAZ employees received units worth 600 rubles. Additional units were distributed according to a formula based on seniority, salary and qualifications that was set forth in the bylaws. Notwithstanding the fact that property interests in SAZ resembled stock, we use the word "unit" to describe them because the SAZ organizational documents purposely avoid describing them as stock (*aktsia*), referring to them as lots (*dolya*).

37. For an analysis of why SAZ managers acted in their long-term interests, see Hendley (1992).

38. The chairman of the board of directors can not own more than 0.2 percent of the total outstanding shares. Other members of the board are limited to 0.15 percent, and ordinary shareholders are limited to 0.1 percent. Note that the analysis of the charter and bylaws of SAZ relates to their pre-1996 form. In the spring of 1996, in response to the new Law on Joint-Stock Companies, these organizational documents were rewritten.

39. The bylaws provide that: "Members of the board of directors do not have the right indirectly or directly to receive [outside] compensation for exerting influence on the decision-making process of the board of directors."

40. The mechanism by which such a cause of action might be pursued was not specified in the bylaws, nor was it to be found in statutory law. In all likelihood, it was a symbolic right. No SAZ director was ever prosecuted under this provision. A recommendation to include a more straightforward right of shareholders to sue directors was rejected out of hand. Management contended that the courts' lack of familiarity with such cases would cause them to be dismissed. Proposals to get around this problem by making such shareholder claims subject to private arbitration were likewise rejected, suggesting that management was not eager to encourage shareholders to mobilize their rights.

41. Cf., Pistor in this volume.

42. A two-part election was necessary to winnow down the field.

43. See generally, Berliner (1957) and Granick (1960).

44. See Art. 94, pt. 4, Law on Joint-Stock Companies (1996).

CHAPTER 9

Company Law and Corporate Governance in Russia

Katharina Pistor

With the completion of mass privatization programs in a number of former socialist countries, policy makers and scholars have shifted their attention from the
best procedure for transferring state owned enterprises into private hands to corporate governance. Corporate governance has become a catch phrase not only in
academic debate, but also in the relevant countries for solving the so far unresolved problems of enterprise reform. As mass privatization alone apparently
does not lead to immediate and extensive restructuring, improvements in the
governance structure of firms shall now bring about the desired increase in efficiency of enterprises in transition economies. The key question addressed by
scholars and policy makers alike is who should be the best agent for corporate
control: should banks own shares; should control be exercised though capital
markets; what would the right level of ownership by top management be in order to mitigate agency problems?[1] Little attention has been paid to the role of
the legal framework, particularly of corporate law, in enabling or facilitating
changes in ownership and providing a mechanism for new owners to effectuate
their rights.[2]

This chapter attempts to identify the function of corporate law in the governance of firms by drawing mostly from the experience of two Western legal systems, Germany and the United States. It discusses the particular challenge posed
by the transition context, and finally analyses in detail the role of corporate law in
the Russian privatization process. The argument presented in this chapter is that
the function of corporate law in the governance of firms—in developed market
economies as well as in the transition context—is to grant shareholders procedural rights. In the transition context, the importance of enforceable procedural
rights is especially pronounced, because privatization, as well as the post privatization battle for control is comparable to a take-over scenario, in which new
owners try to establish control rights that previously had been captured by company insiders.

The Role of Company Law in
Corporate Governance

At the heart of the corporate governance problem lies the question of how to mitigate the monitoring and control problems that arise with the separation of ownership and control in publicly held corporations. This debate, which was initiated in the United States by Berle and Means in the early 1930s,[3] has in recent years led to a fascinating comparison of various institutional arrangements across different countries that provide or were believed to provide a definable set of different institutions that have been associated with different country models of corporate governance.[4] The prevalent models are the Anglo-American model, the German model, and the Japanese model. The Anglo-American model is usually characterized as governance through external capital markets with take-over mechanisms; the German model as monitoring by large banks in the role of equity, and even more importantly, proxy voting-rights holders with representation on companies' supervisory boards; and the Japanese model as a network of companies with dense cross-shareholdings, including a house bank, which is called a *keiretsu*. The comparative advantage of any these three models has been subject of a so far unresolved debate.[5] Meanwhile, new studies have increasingly questioned the accuracy with which these models capture the actual governance structures in the three countries. A recent analysis of the role of German banks does not find sufficient evidence to support the view of banks as important monitors, but concludes that the prevailing feature of the German corporate landscape is large blockholdings by other large firms, including, but not dominated, by banks.[6]

Structural Differences in Corporate Laws

With the explanatory power of different governance models increasingly in question, what role does corporate law play in shaping corporate governance systems?[7] The answer for the three countries mentioned would probably be—little, if at all.[8] A look at the Japanese corporate law, which closely resembles US American corporate laws, explains why. The enactment of this legal transplant has proved to be quite compatible with a very different governance model. Moreover, when focusing on the core of norms pertaining to the internal governance structure of a corporation, we discover that the paper form of laws across countries—including common law and civil law countries—differs less than might be suspected, and certainly less than the ownership structure of firms, or the regulatory framework for financial intermediaries in these countries.[9] This does not exclude the existence of structural differences in various countries' corporate laws. Indeed, on paper, the German two-tier management structure differs considerably from the Anglo-American one-tier management structure. Under German law, the shareholder meeting elects a supervisory board,[10] which in turn appoints the members of the executive board. However, both structures work more similarly in practice than their paper forms predict. Although German law reinforces the independence of the supervisory board from the management board by prohibiting concurrent membership on both boards, the interests of those serving on the two boards are in fact not far apart. German chief executives frequently move on to the supervisory board after they retire. Moreover, the CEO (*Vorstandsvorsitzende*) has a decisive influence on who will be elected to the supervisory board, which—not surprisingly—often results in the chief executives of other companies occupying most seats on the supervisory boards. In the US, not the board of directors, but the executive officers manage the company. In both countries, directors and members of the supervisory board have to rely on information made available to them by management.[11] Their most effective tool is to dismiss the chief executive officer (or the management board), a measure that is taken only as last resort.

This suggests that differences in the formal governance structure do not necessarily materialize into significant practical differences. A simple and straightforward explanation for this is that "private parties are quite resourceful in adapting their affairs to minimize the adverse effects of regulation."[12]

Procedural Function of Corporate Law

Any set of rules can be effective only to the extent these rules cannot be easily circumvented, enforcement mechanisms exist, and rights are allocated to guarantee that those whose rights are infringed upon may seek remedies. Thus, the major function of corporate law is to provide a procedure for enforcing rights allocated to different interest groups in the corporation. Procedural rights include internal or "self-enforcing" mechanisms that enable shareholders to strengthen their position, i.e., through voting rules,[13] as well as external mechanisms that rely on court enforcement.

In the United States, the procedural function of corporate law is usually assumed, because the judiciary takes an important part in the interpretation of corporate contracts and the creation of new corporate law.[14] In a more explicit recognition of the role of courts in corporate law in this country, mandatory judicial oversight has been referred to as the essence of legal constraints remaining at the end of a long trend of liberalizing corporate law that left few other mandatory provisions.[15]

By contrast, continental European legal systems show a much lower degree of court involvement. In comparison to the United States, a low number of corporate litigation appears to be not simply the result of a lower level of litigation in general, but is part of the legal design. German law, for example, provides only few procedural rights for shareholders.[16] Moreover, no explicit provisions for shareholder or derivative suits exist in German corporate law and courts have long refused to grant remedies, because judges and law makers perceive conflicts between the corporation and its shareholders as internal matters which are not subject to judicial oversight. As recently as 1982 the Supreme Court acknowledged a shareholder suit by ruling that the statutory provisions of German corporate law do not grant sufficient protection to shareholders.[17] Nevertheless, shareholder suits have remained a rarity and many scholars and judges still view judicial interference as detrimental to a company's affairs.[18] This view reflects a belief that the interests of the company have priority over those of special interest groups, whose historical roots go back to the late 19th century.[19] Ironically, the underdevelopedness of effective procedural rights has resulted in corporate law playing a far less active role in shaping corporate governance in the carefully structured German system, than in the more liberal system of the United States.

Corporate Law in the Transition Context

The transition from planned economies to market-based economies creates new challenges for corporate law. In most developed market economies, corporate law was invented or implemented at the outset of industrial development and its basic structure only slightly altered over time. Few companies that were established under one corporate law ever had to adjust and reorganize their internal framework to major changes in corporate legislation. In other words, little evidence can be found on the effects of changes in formal laws on the actual governance structure of companies.[20]

In the former socialist countries, however, corporate law was assigned the function to facilitate, if not execute changes in the management of companies. The transformation of state enterprises into joint stock companies was supposed to serve three major functions. First, corporatization was seen as an essential step in streamlining the governance structure of state owned enterprises, particularly in countries such as Poland, where workers' councils had gained increasing influence over company management.[21] Second, corporatization was the first step in privatizing state owned companies, because the sale of shares is the simplest form of asset transfer. And third, corporate law had to provide the framework for new owners to establish control rights in privatized companies. The following discussion will concentrate on the role of corporate law in privatized companies and will examine whether the Russian corporate law fulfilled its assigned function.

Corporate Law Post Privatization

Privatization was not simply a transfer of assets from the state to private parties. It amounted to a large scale reallocation of economic and political assets.[22] At the company level this required wrestling control rights from management who had effectively become *de facto* owners by the new *de jure* owners, making privatization akin to a take-over situation. However, a privatization take-over differs substantially from its counter part in a developed market economy. In the latter case, a raider usually acquires a substantial block of shares which allows him to impose new policies on the company. This case is most closely mirrored in privatization policies that use case-by-case sale methods. In comparison, mass privatization often results in the dispersion of assets among a relatively large number of shareowners who are less able to capitalize on the acquired equity position. Not only do shareholders oftentimes lack the necessary expertise to turn a company around, but decisive shareholder actions are also undermined by collective action problems. Russia, for example, is said to now have 40 million shareholders in roughly 14,000 companies.[23] According to survey data, the largest single block holder in a company owns on average hardly more than 10 to 15 percent of total shares.[24] While these numbers appear to be quite high by American standards—given the extent of insider domination in Russian firms and the absence of other external control devices, such as developed capital, managerial labor, or even product markets—the benchmark for effective control in a Russian company is much higher. In many cases, it is likely to require nothing short of majority ownership.[25] It is possible that shareholdings will be consolidated on the secondary market and that the actual take-over scenario will occur only after the completion of privatization programs through a market driven secondary privatization. However, the success of secondary privatization depends on the effectiveness of corporate law, because it requires easy entry and exit, the availability of reliable information, and the possibility to exercise "voice." Company insiders, particularly management, are unlikely to give up control rights voluntarily; therefore, new owners will need an option to enforce their rights in case they encounter resistance.

The Case of Russia

Russia embarked on a mass privatization program in late 1992, and privatized around 14,000 companies over the course of 18 months.[26] The privatization procedure described in detail elsewhere[27] followed the following basic steps: the Russian privatization agency or one of its regional branches corporatized companies by re-registering state owned enterprises as joint stock companies. Upon corporatization and approval of the companies' privatization plan, GKI transferred the company's shares to the Property Fund for execution of the privatization plan. Depending on the privatization option chosen, between 40 and 51 percent of shares were first offered to insiders in a closed subscription. As a result, company employees became majority shareholders in most companies. Subsequently, shares were offered to the public at voucher auctions (on average a block of 18 percent). Company insiders could also participate in voucher auctions and managed to increase their holdings to on average 65 percent of voting stock. The remaining shares were partly transferred to an employee-shareholder trust (5–10 percent of total voting stock), and either sold in additional voucher or cash auctions, or investment tenders, or remained under the control of the property fund.

Company Law and Enterprise Organization
Prior to Privatization

Not having a pre-revolutionary corporate law to fall back on, Russia adopted her own rudimentary version of a corporate law in 1990, the statute on joint stock companies confirmed by a Council of Ministers Decree (Decree 601). This decree, which was passed prior to the 1991 Russian privatization law, came to provide the legal basis for the corporatization of companies slated for privatization.[28] It was one in a series of normative acts adopted during the period of *perestroika*.[29]

As a result of the *perestroika* reforms, a large number of companies had already experimented with changes in their organizational form when privatization arrived. In fact, many companies had changed their legal form more than once, either to improve management control rights,[30] or to comply with Russian legislation after the demise of the USSR.[31] In most instances, top management turned out to be the main beneficiaries of change. The onset of privatization posed an imminent threat to the position they had established for themselves without offering tangible benefits. In recognition of this fact, Russian reformers concluded that privatization was impossible without the support of management. The reformers decided to co-opt management into privatization by yielding to their demands and gave insiders the option for initial control over the majority of shares. They hoped that actual change in the ownership structure and governance of privatized firms would be accomplished by transactions on the secondary market post-privatization. They thereby assigned a crucial role to corporate law.

Company Law and Privatization Take-Overs

The legal basis for corporatizing state owned enterprises slated for privatization was a model statute adopted by Presidential Decree on 1 July 1992.[32] It supplemented but did not supersede Decree 601 on joint stock companies. Additional norms scattered across various presidential decrees and privatization programs were enacted during the process of privatization as particular weaknesses of the legal regime became apparent.[33] However, a comprehensive corporate law was enacted only on 1 January 1996, that is eighteen months after the completion of mass privatization.[34] The subsequent analysis will focus primarily on the legal regime for corporate law as it was in effect during the privatization process followed by an overview of the major changes introduced by the new corporate law. The analysis focuses on the allocation of rights between management and shareholders, procedural rights vested with shareholders, and possible remedies available for shareholders in case of violations of their rights.

Internal Governance Structure.   As in western corporate laws, the corporation under Russian law has three main corporate organs: the shareholder meeting, the board of directors, and the executive board, which may consist of the general director only. But the functions of these bodies and the allocation of powers to the different bodies differs from western type corporate laws. The shareholder meeting, for example, was defined as the highest management organ of the corporation. Only in the intervals between shareholder meetings should the board of directors—and only in the intervals between the board meetings should the executive board—manage the company.[35] As the highest organ in the corporation, the shareholder meeting also had the exclusive power to hire and fire the general director. Allocating the key control right of replacing top management to shareholders rather than the company board in effect reduces the threat of replacement. In order to dismiss a chief executive officer, a shareholder meeting must be convoked.[36] Moreover, the dismissal will only be effective if support by a majority of shareholders can be ensured with the decision making process likely to be hampered by serious collective action problems.

The 1990 regulation did not specify the role of the board of directors, which continued to be only a nominal body. The model statute enhanced the role of the board by allocating a number of powers to the board. However, most of these powers required either cooperation with the general director, which included issues such as the appointment and dismissal of additional members of the executive board, or they amounted only to recommendations to the shareholder meeting, which had the final say over decisions concerning dividend payments or the establishment of subsidiaries.[37] The only powers exclusively vested with the board of directors were the development of accounting standards and of principles concerning loans, credits, and guarantees, and decisions on investment projects involving less than 10 percent of the companies' capital, because larger projects required approval by the shareholder meeting.[38]

Not only did the design of corporate law lack effective control rights allocated with the board of directors, but the very first board encountered by companies was put firmly under insider control. The model statute mandated four members: the general director, whose influence was further increased by granting him two votes, a member of the company's working collective, a representative from the local state administration, and a representative of the privatization agency in charge (either GKI or the property fund). Thus, insiders could easily outvote the state representatives. However, anecdotal evidence from interviews with property fund employees in various regions, and data from a recent survey of voucher funds, suggest that state representatives and management often do not represent opposing interests, and in fact often have formed alliances.[39] These alliances have made the position of new outsider shareowners even more precarious: they are facing company boards under the firm control of company insiders who hold the majority of voting shares in roughly 70 percent of privatized companies.[40]

In an attempt to enhance control rights by outsiders, the 1994 Privatization Program provided that shareholders who are concurrently employees[41] of a company may not occupy more than 1/3 of the seats on the board. Following the enactment of the program, a few more outsiders were placed on the boards. Data collected in a joint research project by Blasi and Shleifer[42] suggest that the number of companies with some outside board representation increased from 40 percent to 76 percent. However, this was apparently not the result of competitive elections, but of a deal reached by outsider investors with the top management in charge.[43] Even this type of friendly board representation has so far remained an exception to the rule, rather than the rule. Only 2 of the 40 enterprises sampled by Blasi and Shleifer actually complied with regulations mandating 2/3 outsider representation on the board, and 3 companies implemented (mandatory) cumulative voting rights.[44] Thus, the typical board structure in Russian companies at the end of privatization had the following composition: one outsider, one state representative, and four insiders from among the company's management.[45]

Voting Rules.   Russian corporate law at the time of privatization spelled out few and straight-forward voting rules. The basic rule was "one-share–one-vote." Shareholder meetings required a 50 percent quorum for the first meeting. For most decisions taken by the shareholder meeting, a simple majority sufficed. However, for a number of decisions, a qualified majority of 3/4 was required. They included changes in the corporate statute, the charter capital, or the reorganization or liquidation of the company, and the sale or lease of substantial amounts of assets.[46] The 1994 Privatization Program tightened these requirements by increasing the quorum requirement for said decisions from 50 percent to 75 percent. In other words, 75 percent of all shareholders had to be represented at a meeting where, i.e., decisions on charter amendments should be taken and a decision needed to be supported by 75 percent of those that were present. The effects of this new rule are somewhat ambiguous. The purpose of majority and super majority requirements is to protect minority shareholders against changes imposed by the directors or controlling shareholders. However, the stringent super-majority requirement, enacted by the 1994 Privatization Program, made any charter amendments—including those that could potentially benefit outside investors (i.e., by transferring the right to appoint and dismiss the general director from the shareholder meeting to the board of directors)—almost impossible.[47] In its mission to strengthen the internal governance structure of firms, the 1994 privatization program also made cumulative voting mandatory.[48] However, empirical evidence suggests that this rule has largely been ignored.[49]

   In practice, even the simple one-shareholder-one-vote rule proved to be quite difficult to implement. Workers conferences and enterprise boards had previously operated with a much simpler rule, namely one worker one vote, exercised publicly by raising hands. In fact, decisions to be taken at a shareholder meeting were often pre-decided by insiders in their production brigades in that same old fashion.[50] In many cases, management ensured that not all workers attended a shareholder meeting and organized the election of representatives also on a "one-worker-one-vote" basis. Even where the per-share rather than the per-capita voting rule was acknowledged in principle, its implementation at shareholder meetings depended largely on the number of shareholders present and the length of the agenda. Shareholders usually voted by raising cards that indicated the number of shares they held. As a result, counting votes was a time consuming procedure, which required that for each vote, the number of shares every single shareholder represented must be counted. Therefore, this rule was often changed in favor of voting by simply raising hands in order to speed up the process. The one-share-one-vote rule was thereby changed into a one-shareholder-one-vote rule which dilutes the influence of large shareholders.[51]

Exit and Entry.   Because privatization resulted in majority control by insiders in most companies, major changes in ownership structure and management of privatized firms were expected through the secondary market, but have largely failed to materialize. Russian corporate legislation provided that, in an open corporation, every shareholder had the right to freely sell his or her shares. But freely selling and buying shares proved to be quite difficult, mostly because companies' shareholder registers were, and still are, under the control of company management. Preventing workers from selling, refusing or delaying registration of shares acquired by new owners, or erasing shareholders from the company register,[52] have been often reported defense strategies.[53] A presidential decree of October 1993[54] addressed the problem by stipulating in detail the requirements for registering shares and for providing that the refusal to register, despite the fact that all necessary documents were submitted, could be challenged by referring to the company's revision commission or filing a law suit. In addition, companies with more than 1,000 shareholders were required to transfer their register to a bank, investment company, or similar organization. Apparently, this decree was ignored by many companies. A survey of 3,400 of Russia's largest companies revealed that 44 percent of the companies with more than 1,000 shareholders had not surrendered control over their shareholder register.[55] Moreover, many of the broker or financing houses conducting shareholder registers on behalf of companies are controlled by these companies, and their "independence" is therefore a pure formality.[56]

Control over shareholder registers has given companies ample opportunity to raise transaction costs for share trading. Shareholders are often required to pay for registration.[57] In addition, administrative entry barriers are a common occurrence. Companies frequently require not only documentation of the transaction, which in turn needs to be certified by a specially authorized firm with a notarial certified copy of the licenses of this firm attached, but also a variety of other documents, including, but not limited to, a formal application by the new shareholder to open an account, powers of attorney by the seller or buyer—certified by a notary in case they send an agent to perform registration, as well as proof that taxes were paid on the transaction.[58]

In response to these practices, rating firms have started to evaluate companies according to the ease with which shares can be re-registered.[59]

Information and Disclosure Requirements.   Information on companies' past and present performance is a necessary precondition for monitoring firms and exercising governance. In the Russian context, monitoring through evaluating company information is extremely difficult because of the lack of information available in general and the cost involved in receiving whatever information there is. This is the result of the culture of commercial secrecy, but also of the lack of accounting principles that would establish standards for meaningful comparison. The obligation to share data with outside shareholders and even the public at large runs counter to established Soviet business practices. A number of laws and regulations explicitly require companies to disclose information. Under the Civil Code enacted in 1995, every open joint stock company is required to publish financial data once a year, irrespective of whether shares are publicly traded.[60] Companies whose shares are publicly traded are obliged to publish quarterly reports.[61] The compliance rate with these regulations appears to be low. The majority of voucher investment funds, for example, had little access to financial information even about companies they held in their portfolio.[62] Where information is made available, it is not necessarily very meaningful, because bookkeeping for the most part still follows outdated Soviet accounting standards. Finally, the obscure tax structure, as well as the high level of tax rates, creates powerful disincentives for disclosure.

Remedies Available to Shareholders.   Voting rights, entry and exit, as well as information rights are essentially procedural rights whose purpose is to enable shareholders to effectuate their ownership rights in an informed manner. Spelling out these rights on paper is only the first step. Another question is whether these rights are truly enforceable. One may, of course, argue that influential investors will be able to impose their will on companies irrespective of the written rules, and that in the absence of influential investors, procedural rights will remain mostly unenforced. But this view is too simplistic in the context of transition economies. The emergence of influential investors is to a large extent contingent on an environment that facilitates their operation. This includes a legal environment that ensures the enforceability of contractual as well as property rights.

Russian corporate law prior to the enactment of the new law on joint stock companies, and Russian procedure law for commercial litigation[63] have made it extremely difficult for investors to defend and ultimately enforce their rights. In order to file a suit in the state arbitration courts (*arbitrazhnie sudi*), the court system in charge of economic disputes, a claimant needs to be either a juridical person, or must be registered as an entrepreneur,[64] a requirement that entails not only red tape, but also tax consequences. Individual shareholders not registered as entrepreneurs have only the option to address the ordinary civil courts, which have little experience with corporate law. Moreover, the combination of a relatively high fee level[65] and the uncertainty about the outcome of a court procedure have provided further disincentives for seeking enforcement through the court system.

Once procedural barriers are overcome, a claimant needs to state his case on the basis of substantive law. But laws, presidential decrees, or government regulations, are often inconsistent, contradict each other, or are ambiguous. They only rarely spell out the specific remedies private parties may seek. Under the corporate law regime described above, it was impossible to establish who, if at all, could sue the management of a corporation for misconduct. According to the model statute, directors and executive officers are responsible vis-à-vis the corporation for damages caused by their misconduct. This can be construed as a right of the company to take action against management. However, as a juridical person, the corporation needs to be represented by somebody, and this, according to the law, is the chief executive officer. This apparent circularity is usually solved in Western jurisdictions by having the board of directors represent the company in cases against the General Director, but such a provision is absent in the Russian law. Alternatively, shareholders could be granted the right to sue either directly or on behalf of the corporation, but Russian law does not provide for this possibility.[66] Similarly, if a shareholder could benefit from the implementation of—according to the 1994 Privatization Program—mandatory cumulative voting rights that were ignored, it is unclear whether he could successfully state his case in court, if only to demand new elections. Finally, shareholders or directors who were not notified about either shareholder or board meetings were not able to challenge the validity of decisions taken without them on a firm legal basis.

Other laws often deferred a right-holder to general remedies "in accordance with Russian civil or criminal legislation," which often simply did not exist yet or provided remedies which were clearly ineffective. In the aforementioned decree on the protection of shareholder rights, for example, a shareholder who was denied registration in a company's shareholder register could turn to the courts. The stipulated remedy was that, within two weeks after the final court ruling, the company was required to register the shareholder. Not only was it not clear what happened if the company still did not comply, but there was also no mention of compensation for damages incurred. The regulation thus ignored the fact that the failure to register shares entailed economic damages, including failure to receive dividends (share registration was not invoked retroactively), and the inability to benefit from reselling these shares.

Russian Corporate Law in Historical Perspective

The discussion of the previous section raises a more general question beyond the details of corporate law and shareholder suits, namely the role of law in Russia's transition context. From a formal point of view it is worth noting that most normative acts pertaining to privatization or corporate law, issued since introduction of economic reforms in 1992, were presidential decrees. Their primary goal was to regulate specific aspects of the reform process, without being necessarily consistent with each other, or with underlying legislation. The latter is part of the basic dilemma of the reform process. Even if the legislature had been willing to support reform, it would have been unable to keep up with its pace. As a result, contradictions between new normative acts and old laws would have been unavoidable under more favorable conditions.[67] More important than this formal aspect is the nature of the normative acts that were passed. Regulations related to corporate law are mostly flat orders or prohibitions: the president states what is or what is not to be done. What is missing is an attempt to vest private parties with rights that would enable them to fend for themselves.[68] During the first three years of economic reforms, law was used by reformers as an instrument to implement reforms and was akin to the Soviet ideology that generally perceived law as an instrument of the ruling party to achieve short term political goals. The deferral of more comprehensive legal reforms to a later date may have been justified, given the political struggle between reformers and representatives of the old regime. Nevertheless, for the corporatization of thousands of companies, a comprehensive corporate law would have been desirable.

The lack of change in legal culture is also apparent in the style of normative acts passed. The majority of norms reveals a systematic lack of appreciation of the importance of norm clarity and consistency. This tendency is difficult to explain, unless it is seen as the continuation of a legal culture that paid little attention to a rational and predictable legal system.

The lack of regard for rule of law principles is further evidenced by the fact that Russia has followed soviet, and pre-revolutionary Russian legal tradition,[69] by continuing a practice of "special laws for special cases" and wide-spread case by case exemptions from general laws.

Many of the case by case exemptions from existing legislation take the form of bribing bureaucrats, police men, procurators, and judges. But while we may interpret this as a sign of an underdeveloped or degenerated legal culture, exceptions granted through the issuance of special normative acts are more likely to undermine the respect for the rule of law, as such practice formally legalizes the habit of granting special privileges. Examples for special laws can be drawn not only from the anti-reform camp in the Russian government, but include presidential decrees. For example, a number of decrees amended existing privatization legislation specifically for the companies they address. Thus, Yeltsin issued special decrees on the privatization of two large factories, *AvtoVAS* and *GAZ*,[70] which amended their privatization plans already confirmed by GKI. Special privatization procedures and corporate rules were also established for various industry sectors (as opposed to single companies) that were not included in the list of companies mandated for privatization. According to Russian privatization legislation, companies in certain industry sectors could be privatized only with approval by GKI, and others only with approval by the Russian government. For all of these sectors, special privatization rules were established, which granted privileges for acquiring shares in privatization to insiders, suppliers, or subsidiaries, and in effect created a whole subset of privatization legislation.[71] Most of these regulations are the result of intense behind-closed-doors bargains, with the most unequitable in the highly valuable natural resource sectors. The privatization of *Gazprom*, for example, excluded participation by non-insiders through a sophisticated scheme consisting of cross-shareholdings between the holding company and its subsidiaries, generous insiders participation, the designation of large blocks of shares to privatization in selected regions, mostly where gas companies included in *Gazprom* holding are located, and buy-back schemes for the company's own shares, which facilitated the channeling of shares to designated insiders. As a result, it is simply impossible to add up *Gazprom's* shares to 100 percent on the basis of relevant privatization regulations issued for that company.[72]

In addition to special rules for privatization, the Russian government and *GKI* approved special corporate statutes for sectors and individual companies. The extent to which these regulations allowed deviations not only from the Model statute, but also from *Decree 601* can be sensed from a closer examination of the company bylaw of one of the 4 large oil holding companies, *Surgutneftegaz*, which had been confirmed by the Russian government.[73] The most prominent features of this statute are the creation of upper ceilings for share acquisitions in general—and specifically by foreign investors—as well as preemptive rights for the company to acquire shares before they are offered to third parties. Any shareholder who intends to acquire shares in excess of 1 percent of total stock must obtain approval by the board of directors, and foreign investors are prohibited from cumulatively holding shares amounting to 5 percent or more of total stock. In an attempt to control the transfer of shares, the corporate statute also provides that shares must be offered to the company before they can be sold to an independent third party. Shares exceeding these established limits or acquired in violation of the preemptive rule do not confer either voting rights or rights to receive dividends.

Russia's New Corporate Law.   On 24 November 1995, the Russian Duma adopted the Law on Stock Companies which entered into force on 1 January 1996, making it the first comprehensive company law in Russia's history. The enactment of the law is a major hallmark in Russia's legal history in general and the post-socialist structural reforms in particular.[74] The law applies to existing and new stock companies. It replaces most of the patchwork legal regulations on corporate law that had been put in place during the privatization process. Existing companies are required to bring their statutes and corporate by-laws in conformity with the new law by 1 July 1996. All provisions that contradict the law will be held null and void thereafter. The law does not, however, overrule the provisions on corporate law that were included in the first part of the Russian Civil Code, which entered into force on 1 January 1995.[75] One may even argue that the major impediment to a more far reaching reform of the internal structure of the corporation was the inclusion of such provisions in the Civil Code.

The Civil Code retained the notion of "direct democracy" for joint-stock companies, which had been established in earlier company legislation.[76] As before, the shareholder meeting is the highest "management" organ of the corporation and elects not only the Council of Directors, but also the chief management organ of the corporation.[77] The new corporate law had to retain this basic structure, because a special provision in the Civil Code mandates that all subsequent legislation must comply with the provisions of the Civil Code.[78] In particular, the new corporate law could not change the general principle that the chief executive is directly elected by the shareholder meeting, which leaves the board of directors with little real leverage over the executives. The law merely provides that individual corporate statutes may delegate this function to the board of directors.[79] Members of the board of directors are elected for a one-year term, but their term in office may be renewed indefinitely. The company statutes may provide cumulative voting for the election of members of the board of directors. For companies with more than 1,000 shareholders, cumulative voting is mandatory. This is a deviation from the 1994 Privatization Program, which had established mandatory cumulative voting for all companies. The new corporate law also does away with another provision of the 1994 Privatization Program, which states that not more than one third of the members of the board of directors could be employees of the company. Instead, it establishes that members of the executive board may not make up the majority of members of the board of directors.[80] Thus, membership in both boards is not incompatible, but a complete capture of the board of directors by executives has been avoided. What is incompatible, however, is the chairmanship of the board of directors with the position of the chief executive.

The new corporate law is a substantial improvement in shareholder rights. It not only defines shareholder rights and provides clear standards for the right of equity holders in corporate entities, but also arms them with procedural rights, including self-enforcing and justiciable rights.[81]

Several provisions in the law establish principles for shareholder rights that may not be subject to change. They include the principle of equal rights for all shareholders of common stock and the rule of "one-share-one-vote" for holders of common stock, with the exception of cumulative voting procedures. They designate most rights allocated to the shareholder meeting as exclusive rights, which may not be delegated to another organ of the corporation.[82] Moreover, they establish quorums (of 50 percent) for shareholder meetings including decisions taken by ballots, and stipulate majority and, in selected cases, super-majority voting rules. The law does not stop at this rather standard allocation of shareholder rights, but in a rather educative fashion spells out details on how these rights shall be implemented. The law includes, for example, detailed provisions for the preparation of the shareholder meeting. In addition to prior notification by registered mail or publication in mass media, the company must establish a list of eligible shareholders sixty days prior to the shareholder meeting. Shareholders have the right to request information about their eligibility. Moreover, the company is obliged in a number of instances to inform its shareholders about their rights. This is the case, for instance, when the company is placing voting or convertible stock, and the company statutes allow existing holders of common stock to exercise a preemptive right. No less than thirty days prior to the placing of such securities shall eligible shareholders be informed about their rights. Similarly, the company must inform shareholders about their rights to redeem their shares in the cases provided by the law.[83]

The law creates various procedural rights for shareholders, including self-enforceable rules, such as voting rules, information rights, and redemption rights, which can be exercised without recourse to the court. The obligation for companies with more than 1,000 shareholders to implement cumulative voting rights is designed to improve the position of minority shareholders who without this device, would not have a chance to influence the composition of the board of directors. Whether or not this rule will be implemented remains to be seen. In any case, the position of shareholders to enforce this rule has been improved, for they may now challenge decisions that were adopted in violation of voting rules.[84] In order to ensure proper voting procedures, the company law provides that a special counting commission shall be established in companies with more than 100 shareholders. Its task is to establish that quorum requirements have been met and voting rights are being observed. The members of the commission shall be proposed by the board of directors and confirmed by the shareholder meeting.

Other self-enforceable rights include exit options. The corporate law guarantees the right of shareholders in an open stock company to freely sell their shares. A valid transfer of shares requires their registration in the company register. As in the case of previous regulations, the law attempts to reduce control by company insiders over the register by establishing that companies with more than 500 shareholders must transfer management of the register to a special registry. In view of the difficulties many newly incoming shareholders have had with registering their shares, the law provides that registration must be conducted within three days after the necessary documents were submitted. Moreover, the company law clarifies that the documentation requirements for registration shall be regulated by Russian legislation, and not by individual company's fiat. In the event that the registration requirements have not been met, the company must issue a written explanation for the rejection within five days after the request for registration had been submitted. A shareholder may challenge the decision to refuse to register his shares in court.[85]

A more forceful exit option exists for shareholders—those who have been outvoted or did not participate in a decision to reorganize the company—to sell a substantial amount of the company's assets or to change the company's statutes in ways that limit their rights.[86] In these cases, they may redeem their shares. The effectiveness of these rights depends on the price for the redeemable shares. The law refers to the market value of the shares and defines market value as "the price at which a seller—who has full information about the value of the asset [share] without being forced to sell—would be willing to sell, and a buyer—with full information about the value of the asset without being forced to buy—would be willing to purchase it."[87] Where the price of shares or other securities that are regularly quoted in the press shall be determined, their quoted price shall be taken into account. The board of directors is in charge of determining the market value; however, the advice of an independent accountant may also be sought. Since the shares of most companies are not traded regularly, and in view of the fact that most company shares were highly undervalued in privatization, these provisions still leave much discretion to the board. Still, there is hardly a better way to arrive at a market price in the absence of a market.

Shareholders may also mobilize the law in order to gain influence on basic company strategies and decisions. Not only may shareholders who cumulatively hold at least 10 percent of the voting stock call an extraordinary meeting,[88] but shareholders are given comparatively extensive rights to influence the agenda of the yearly annual meeting. Shareholders representing as little as 2 percent voting stock may submit up to two items for the annual shareholder meeting and may nominate candidates for the board of directors and the inspection commission by filing a written request at least thirty days after the end of the financial year.[89] The law states that these requests shall be included in the agenda, unless shareholders do not meet the formal requirements—deadline, number of shares they represent, etc.—or the proposal violates existing legislation. Furthermore, a shareholder who holds at least 10 percent of total stock may request a full list of shareholders eligible to participate at shareholder meetings.[90] This enables relatively large shareholders to build coalitions and prepare proxy fights.

The law explicitly refers shareholders to the courts in a number of instances. First, shareholders may sue the company, in case the registration of shares is refused.[91] Second, a shareholder has the right to appeal against decisions taken by the shareholder meeting, in case they violate the corporate law or any other federal legislation, provided that the litigating shareholder voted against that decision and the decision violates his rights under the law.[92] Third, the law states that decisions in violation of conflict of interest rules may be declared null and void and that those violating these rules are liable for damages that may accrue to the company.[93]

Conclusion

The corporatization and privatization of Russian companies took place without a comprehensive corporate law in place. The rights of new private shareholders were only vaguely defined, and therefore often unenforceable. This proved particularly damaging in an environment that had ceded majority control rights to company insiders. New outsider owners who were already weakened by the fact that they by design could become only minority shareholders, faced considerable problems in asserting their property rights. To a large extent this can be attributed to the lack of more effective legislative backing. Consequently, where shareholders tried to legally enforce their rights, shareholder suits were often rejected by the courts. The absence of a more comprehensive corporate law not only weakened the primary owners who acquired shares in the privatization process, but also created serious obstacles for subsequent reallocation of shares in the so-called secondary privatization, because shareholders faced considerable problems in exiting and entering companies. Even where entry by new owners was successfully accomplished, the rights of outsider owners could be diluted in companies' by-laws, which were frequently amended to enhance the role of the insider dominated executive board.[94]

Russia has meanwhile adopted a comprehensive corporate law that has considerably enhanced shareholder rights and the prospects for their enforcement. On the basis of the foregoing analysis, this raises the question about the possible impact of a new corporate law, which was enacted long after completion of mass privatization and well after the initial boom of secondary privatization had passed. Managers have already developed a routine in adjusting changes in the formal organizational structure of the company to their needs, and have proved to be quite resistant to legislation that was supposed to enhance shareholder rights. They have also been resourceful in bargaining with the relevant state authorities for defensive provisions in their charters. Thus, many have weathered not only formal changes, but even the more substantive changes brought about by changes in the ownership structure of their firms. The new company law attempts to strengthen the formal position of shareholders in that it defines shareholder rights in more detail and spells out the remedies shareholders have whose rights are violated. This alone, of course, does not ensure that shareholders will mobilize these new rights or will succeed in enforcing them. It should, however, give them more leverage and prevent courts from simply refusing shareholder cases.

Whether these legal changes will improve corporate governance will remain to be seen. Not too much hope should be put into short term effects. First, it will take companies some time to adjust their statutes and by-laws, to register such changes, and most importantly, to implement them by shareholder meetings, electing members of the board of directors, appointing management, etc., according to the new rules. Second, the economic and institutional environment is still largely underdeveloped. In view of the weakness of the existing courts and the state of markets, the law has taken pains to design internal or self-enforcing mechanisms. However, they will be effective only if the ultimate threat to sue directors and officers who violate these rules or refuse to implement them is viable. This will depend largely on the ability of the courts to enforce this law, as well as on their credibility in the eyes of shareholders and creditors. It should also be considered that many new private shareholders whose attempts to become more active were once frustrated, may have been crowded out by now. The opportunity to vest them with enforceable rights at the outset was certainly forgone by adopting a comprehensive corporate law after, not before, privatization. Whether a different law adopted at the outset of privatization would have resulted in a substantially different outcome will remain an unresolved question. But it is hard to imagine a legal system that would have made changes in the ownership structure and management of companies more difficult than the Russian corporate laws that governed the privatization and immediate post-privatization process.

Notes

1. See the issues treated in Frydman, Gray, and Rapaczynski (1996).

2. See, however, Black, Kraakman, and Hay (1996), although the authors' discussion does not focus on the role of corporate law in privatization.

3. Berle and Means (1932).

4. For an overview, see Roe (1993).

5. Roe (1993); critical Romano (1993).

6. Edwards and Fischer (1994).

7. The term corporate law is used here to include only the set of norms regulating publicly held companies with limited liability and excludes securities legislation, as well as norms regulating stock exchanges or financial intermediaries.

8. See also Meier-Schatz (1988), p. 477, who attributes to a legal governance scheme a "manifest incapacity to disarm the de facto internal power structure."

9. In fact, most comparisons of different corporate governance systems focus on these aspects, rather than corporate law in the narrower sense.

10. Note that depending on the size of the company, co-determination legislation requires 1/3 to 1/2 of the members of the supervisory boards to be elected by employees rather than shareholders.

11. For evidence on how even powerful banks represented on the supervisory board can be misguided, see the Metallgesellschaft-case. Within weeks after the supervisory board had renewed the appointment of the CEO, the company almost collapsed. On the law suits now pending, see *The Economist*, 4 February 1995, 71.

12. Romano (1993), p. 2022.

13. See Black, Kraakman and Hay (1996).

14. Coffee (1989); see, however, Black (1990), who challenges the view that judge-made law is still an important source of corporate law.

15. See Coffee (1989): ". . . what is most mandatory about corporate law is not the specific substantive content of any rule, but rather the institution of judicial oversight" at p. 1621.

16. According to the law on joint stock companies (AktG), shareholders (as well as members of the corporate board) may, however, sue to declare a decision taken at a shareholder meeting null and void, see para. 241, 243, 245 AktG. The claim must be filed against the corporation (para. 246 AktG).

17. BGH 25.2. 1982–II ZR 174/80 published in JZ 1982, 602. The case dealt with a decision of the executive board to transfer valuable assets to a newly founded subsidiary without prior approval by the shareholder meeting. For a comment on the decision see Grossfeld and Brondics (1982).

18. Hopt (1992).

19. See Schmidt (1992) with reference to v.Gierke, Genossenschaftstheorie (1887) who developed the theory of the "personhood of the enterprise."

20. One of the few counter examples is Japan, where the 1950 corporate law, and subsequently the 1981 amendments, changed the basic allocation of power between shareholders and managers, with the 1981 amendment attempting to promote shareholder democracy. For a cautious evaluation of the effects of these amendments, see Taniguchi (1988).

21. Lipton and Sachs (1990).

22. Frydman, Rapaczynski (1994), chapter 6.

23. See Yeltsin's statement of 1 July 1994, in *Kommersant' weekly* No. 25, 12 July 1994, p. 56.

24. See Blasi and Shleifer (1996), Table 2; voucher funds who are among the most important outsider shareholders hold on average only 6.89 percent of total shares, see Frydman, Pistor and Rapaczynski (1996), Table 5.

25. Voucher funds, which are legally prevented from acquiring more than 25 percent of a companies' shares, often view majority ownership as the only way to establish new control rights in a company. Ignoring the legal prohibition, 47 funds (32.6 percent of the funds surveyed) expressed that they need a majority stake to protect their investment, and 45 funds (31.25 percent) said that this was necessary in order to implement their own restructuring plans in a company. For a full account of the results of this survey, see Frydman, Pistor, and Rapaczynski (1996).

26. A total of 15,797 voucher auctions were held. However, for numerous companies more than one voucher auction took place. The total number of companies privatized through this procedure is therefore closer to 14,000. See Boycko, Shleifer and Vishny (1995), Table 5.1.

27. Frydman, Rapaczynski, and Earle (1993), p. 38.

28. The new Civil Code (Part I), which became effective on 1 January 1995, also includes a number of provisions on corporate law (for joint stock companies see Arts. 96–104). Unless otherwise indicated, the source for Russian laws is Garant data base *ekonomicheskoe zakonodatel'stvo Rossii*.

29. For an account of *perestroika* legislation pertaining to corporate law, see Gray and Hendley in this volume.

30. See Hendley (1992) on the Saratov plant reorganization from a leased company into a closed corporation.

31. The RSFSR Supreme Soviet upon ratifying the treaty that created the CIS, which had provided that none of the USSR laws should be applicable in any of the signatory states, ruled that all laws except those that either contradicted the RSFSR constitution or RSFSR substantive law would be applicable until the relevant RSFSR legislation had been passed see Resolution of the Supreme Soviet of the RSFSR No. 2014–1 of 12 December 1991. Since the RSFSR had adopted its own statute on joint-stock companies, the USSR regulation on joint stock companies was overruled and companies required to re-register under Russian legislation.

32. Presidential Decree No. 721 of 1 July 1992.

33. See Presidential Decree No. 1769 of 27 October 1993 on Protecting Shareholders' rights; section 9.10 of the 1994 Privatization Program, 4 January 1994; Presidential Decree No. 1233 of 11 June 1994 on Protecting Investors' rights.

34. Law on Joint Stock Companies of the Russian Federation, *Rossiiskaya Gazeta*, 29 December 1995, 1 (hereinafter company law).

35. Note that prior to 1950, Japan followed a similar concept, see Taniguchi (1988).

36. In case an extraordinary meeting needs to be convened, a minimum of 10 percent of voting stock is required to demand its convocation.

37. Section 6.3 of the model statute confirmed by Presidential Decree 721 of 1 July 1992 (hereinafter model statute).

38. Section 9 of the model statute.

39. According to survey data on voucher funds, 51 percent of funds in the sample and 75.3 percent of those funds that reported that the state is forming alliances with other shareholders stated that the state was forming coalitions with top management, see Frydman, Pistor, Rapaczynski (1996), Table 12.

40. This number is based on reports by voucher funds, see Frydman, Pistor, Rapaczynski (1996), Table 11. Blasi and Shleifer (1996) report that in the companies surveyed, insiders owned on average 65 percent of all shares, see Table 1.

41. The Privatization Program (section 9.10.4) refers only to "*rabotniki*," which could be interpreted to include only blue collar workers. However, it appears to have been interpreted to include all insiders.

42. See Blasi and Shleifer (1996), p. 14 and Table 8.

43. Surveyed voucher investment funds assert that cooperation with management is important for obtaining a board seat, with 82.7 percent of the funds reporting that this was a crucial factor in obtaining a board seat, see Frydman, Pistor, Rapaczynski (1996), Table 16. See also *Financial Times* of 12 April 1995, p. 2, "American joins board in Siberia," reporting that Irkutskenergo, a large utilities company in Siberia, was actively seeking board representation by a foreign investor. Presumably the underlying rationale is to enhance the reputation of the company. To the extent this becomes a primary motivation for including outsiders on the board, this could in fact strengthen the position of outsiders over time.

44. Blasi and Shleifer (1996), Tables 3 and 4.

45. Blasi and Shleifer (1996), Table 8.

46. Art. 6.4 model statute in conjunction with Art 6.3 (1), (2), (9), (10), (11), (12) model statute.

47. The purpose of this rule was apparently to prevent companies from changing their bylaws subsequent to privatization in a way that would undermine control rights by outsiders. For evidence on this trend, see Pistor (1995).

48. Section 9.10.4 of the 1994 Privatization Program.

49. See footnote 61.

50. Pistor (1995). Additional interviews were conducted with 20 companies in four regions in January 1994; unpublished pilot study, CEU privatization project.

51. At a shareholder meeting attended by the author on 28 January 1994, shareholders decided to vote on a per capita basis until they were challenged by a large outside shareholder who controlled 6,000 rather than the usual 9 shares held by a simple worker. However, even this shareholder did not oppose subsequent switching back to the per capita rule when less crucial issues were on the agenda. Interviews with outsider investors that attended the meeting as well as with voucher funds confirmed that this was not a singular practice. Notes on shareholder meeting at *A/O Serveyi Kommunar* on file with the author.

52. In the widely publicized case of *KraZ*, the Krasnoiarsk Aluminum Factory, management erased most of the 10 percent holdings of Zalogbank and of MFIK Russian Capital (see *Kommersant-Daily* No. 224, 25 November 1994, p. 6). The General Procurator of the

Russian Federation declared this decision to be illegal, see *Delovoi Ekspress* No. 4, 31 January 1995, p. 1.

53. Thirty-six percent of voucher funds surveyed in the summer of 1994 report that a major obstacle to share acquisitions on the secondary market is that shares are not registered, see Frydman, Pistor, and Rapaczynski (1996). Moreover, the very establishment of shareholder registries has often been delayed. For example, *Gazprom* completed voucher auction at the end of June 1994. By December 1994 the company had still not established its shareholder register. This was at least partly the result of the company's strategy to disperse shares widely, which left the company with hundreds of thousands of individual shareholders, see *Kommersant-Daily* No. 238, 15 December 1994, p. 6.

54. Decree No. 1768, 27 October 1993.

55. The survey was conducted by the "Gruppa monitoringy fondovogo rynka" (GMFR) attached to the Russian Securities Commission (KZB), see *Kommersant'* No. 7, 28 February 1995, p. 42.

56. Ibid.

57. The fee level differs from company to company. Some companies require a fixed fee, others a percentage payment for each registered share, or the total price paid for a block of shares; see *Kommersant'*, ibid.

58. See Table at p. 43 in *Kommersant'* No. 7, 28 February 1995, listing documents required by selected 29 companies, including large oil, gas, aviation, and other companies.

59. *Delovoi Mir* of 12 January 1995, p. 3, reports that the rating firm AK&M has rated 163 privatized firms according to these criteria and publishes the rating of the top 25 firms.

60. Art. 97.1 civil code.

61. Presidential Decree 1233 of 11 June 1994 on Protecting Investors' rights explicitly rules that open joint stock companies are required to publish financial statements quarterly in mass media.

62. See Frydman, Pistor, and Rapaczynski (1996), III.1; Tables 8 and 9.

63. A procedural code for the state arbitration court system was enacted on 5 March 1992 as amended in June 1995.

64. Art. 2 state arbitration procedure code, as amended.

65. Initially, a fee of 10 percent of the value of the dispute was leveled for most claims, see Art. 69 state arbitration procedure code. The fee structure has meanwhile been overhauled with an effective reduction of the fee level to a maximum of 2–5 percent of the value of the claim, see Presidential Decree No. 1930 of 17 September 1994, "On State Fees."

66. Some judges have acknowledged the right of a shareholder to sue, if provisions of the company's bylaws were blatantly violated. Interview with Aprachin, deputy chairman of the St. Petersburg state arbitration court, 21 March 1995.

67. The contradictions between privatization legislation and previously enacted laws has, however, resulted in numerous law suits where enterprises often successfully challenged GKI decisions or regulations on the grounds that they violated "old" law, see the summary decision by the supreme state arbitration court of 17 September 1992 on disputes concerning the 1990 RSFSR Law on Ownership, in *Zakon* #2 February 1993, pp. 74, and the commentary by V.V. Vitriianski (deputy head of the supreme state arbitration court) on this decision, ibid., pp. 76.

68. A new approach to lawmaking that is based on self-enforcing rights has been developed by Black, Kraakman, and Hay (1996).

69. See Owen (1991) and Owen in this volume.

70. Presidential Decree on "Special aspects of the privatization of Volzhckii car factory" No. 1190 of 12 October 1992, and Presidential Decree on "Special aspects of the privatization of GAZ" No. 1484 of 30 November 1992.

71. The relevant industry sectors for which special rules were established and published include air, water, and ground transport; agro-industrial complex; bread production; electro-energy; television and radio broadcasting; consumer goods and basic foods; forestry; coal industry; oil and gas industry.

72. According to Presidential Decree No. 1333 on "Transforming the state gas concern 'Gazprom' into the Russian joint stock company 'Gazprom'" of 5 November 1992, 40 percent of Gazprom's shares were to be retained by the state; 15 percent were designated for employees of enumerated subsidiaries, 20 percent were originally earmarked for voucher privatization. See also Presidential Decree No. 1559 of 8 December 1992, "Transforming into joint stock companies and privatizing state enterprises, amalgamations, and organizations of the gas sector in the Russian federation." However, later regulations provided that 5.2 percent of shares should be sold exclusively in Iamalo-Nenetskii autonomous okrug and a total of 28.7 percent in regions where Gazprom companies are located. See Presidential Regulation No. 58-rp of 26 January 1993 on "The board of directors of the Russian joint stock company 'Gazprom' and the distribution of its shares among citizens of the Russian Federation." Moreover, the company was explicitly granted the right to buy up to 10 percent of its own shares on condition that it resold these shares over the period of one year to "the market." Section 4, Presidential Regulation No. 58-rp of 26 January 1993.

73. See resolution of the Russian government No. 271 of 19 March 1993.

74. For an account on the failed attempts to enact a corporate law prior to the October Revolution, see Owen (1991).

75. Note that by including extensive sections on corporate law, the Russian Civil Code has been more inclusionary than its continental European models. In these countries, the Civil Code may include rules on partnerships, but leaves more complex organizations typically to either the Commercial Code or separate legislation on company law.

76. Art. 103 Civil Code.

77. Art. 103 Civil Code.

78. The drafters of the Civil Code have ensured that the Civil Code in fact becomes something like the constitution for civil law relations by providing that all other legislation on civil law rights "must" confirm with the provisions of the Code (Art. 3.2. Civil Code). This principle differs from the general principles found in other civil law systems, namely that the *lex specialis* and the *lex posterior* supersede earlier and more basic legislation. The application of the latter rule would have given the drafters of the corporate law more flexibility.

79. Arts. 48–8, 65–10, company law.

80. Art. 66.2 company law.

81. For the concept of self-enforcing rights in the context of Russia's current institutional and economic environment, see Black, Kraakman, and Hay (1996).

82. These rights include decisions concerning the following: changes in the company charter, reorganization of the company; its liquidation; election of the board of directors; determining the number of authorized shares; decreases in the charter capital; election of members of the inspection commission and approval of company auditors; approving an-

nual reports and financial statements; deciding share splits and share consolidations; approving huge transactions as defined by the law, among others (see Art. 48 company law).

83. Shareholders have the right to redeem their shares, if a company is reorganized or instigates huge transactions, and these shareholders have voted against such a decision (Art. 75 company law).

84. Art. 49.8 company law.

85. Art. 45.2 company law.

86 Art. 75 company law.

87. Art. 77.1 company law.

88. Art. 55.1 company law.

89. Art. 53.1 company law.

90. Art. 51.4 company law.

91. Art. 45.2 company law.

92. Art. 49.8 company law.

93. Art. 84 company law.

94. See Pistor (1995).

Bibliography

Abel, Istvan. 1994. "A gradual approach to banking reform: the Hungarian bad loans problem." Paper presented at International Conference on Bad Enterprise Debts in Central and Eastern Europe, Budapest, Hungary, 6–8 June.

Adam, Jan. 1993. "Transformation to a Market Economy in the Former Czechoslovakia." *Europe-Asia Studies*, 45:4.

Adams, Jefferson. 1993. "Destasification: A Midcourse Appraisal." *Demokratizatsiya: The Journal of Post-Soviet Democratization*, Vol. I, No. 3, Summer, 98–103.

Aer, Anneli. 1995. *Patents in Imperial Russia: A History of the Russian Institution of Invention Privileges under the Old Regime.* Helsinki: Suomalainen Tiedeakatemia.

Ajani, Gianmaria. 1992. "The Rise and Fall of the Law-Based State in the Experience of Russian Legal Scholarship: Foreign Patterns and Domestic Style." From *Toward the "Rule of Law" in Russia? Political and Legal Reform in the Transition Period*, edited by Donald D. Barry. Armonk, NY: M. E. Sharpe.

Albats, Yevgenia. 1994. *The State Within a State: The KGB and Its Hold on Russia's Past, Present and Future.* New York, NY: Farrar, Straus & Giroux.

Alesina, Alberto, and Allan Drazen. 1991. "Why are Stabilizations Delayed?" *The American Economic Review*, 81:5.

American Law Institute. 1994. *Principles of Corporate Governance: Analysis of Recommendations*, Vol. 1 and 2, ALI Publishers.

Anderson, Annelise. 1995. "The Red Mafia: A Legacy of Communism," *Reform in Eastern Europe: Lessons and Prescriptions.* Stanford, CA: Hoover Institution Press.

Åslund, Anders. 1991. *Gorbachev's Struggle for Economic Reform*, 2nd ed. New York, NY: St. Martin's Press.

_____. 1995. *How Russia Became a Market Economy.* Washington, D.C.: The Brookings Institution.

Baer, Herbert L., and Cheryl W. Gray. 1996. "Debt as a Control Device in Transitional Economies: The Experiences of Hungary and Poland," in Frydman, Gray, and Rapaczynski, eds., *Corporate Governance in Central Europe and Russia.* Budapest: Central European University Press, Vol. 1.

Basta, Jaroslav. 1994. "How Czechoslovakia Confronted the Security Police: Successes and Pitfalls in Dismantling the StB." Paper delivered at the International Studies Association National Conference, Washington, D.C., March 31.

Bates, Robert. 1987. *Essays on the Political Economy of Rural Africa.* Berkeley, CA: University of California Press.

Bates, Robert H., and Anne O. Krueger. 1993. "Generalizations Arising From the Country Studies." In *Political and Economic Interactions in Economic Policy Reform*, ed. Robert H. Bates and Anne O. Krueger. Cambridge, MA: Blackwell.

Belykh, Vadim. 1994. "Gruzinsky sled rossiiskoi mafii." *Izvestiya*, November 9, 1994.

Berle, Adolf A., and Gardiner C. Means. 1932. *The Corporation and Private Property*. New York: Macmillan.

Berliner, Joseph C. 1957. *Factory and Manager in the USSR*. Cambridge, MA: Harvard University Press.

Berman, Harold J. 1963. *Justice in the U.S.S.R.* Cambridge, MA: Harvard University Press.

———. 1983. *Law and Revolution: The Formation of the Western Legal Tradition*. Cambridge, MA: Harvard University Press.

———. 1991. "Counterrevolution or Transition: A Response to 'Human Rights and the Emergence of the State of the Rule of Law in the USSR.'" *Emory Law Journal*, 40:903–9.

Black, Bernard. 1990. "Is Corporate Law Trivial?: A Political and Economic Analysis," *84 Northwestern University Law Review*, 542.

Black, Kraakman, and Hay. 1996. "Corporate Law from Scratch." In Frydman, Gray, and Rapaczynski, eds., *Corporate Governance in Central Europe and Russia*. Budapest, London, New York: Central European University Press, Vol. 2.

Blasi, Joseph, and Andrei Shleifer. 1996. "Corporate Governance in Russia: An Initial Look." In Frydman, Gray, and Rapaczynski, eds., *Corporate Governance in Central Europe and Russia*. Budapest, London, New York: Central European University Press.

Blum, J. 1961. *Lord and Peasant in Russia: From the Ninth to the Nineteenth Century*. Princeton, NJ: Princeton University Press, Vol. 2.

Bonin, John, and Mark Schaffer. 1994. "Banks, Firms, Bad Debts, and Bankruptcy in Hungary 1991–1994." Paper presented at Workshop on Enterprise Adjustment in Eastern Europe, September, The World Bank, Washington, D.C., 22–23.

Borovoi, Konstantin. 1994. "KGB i rynochnaya ekonomika." Transcript in *KGB: Vchera, Segodnya, Zavtra, III Mezhdunarodnaya Konferentsiya, Doklady i diskusiy*. Moscow: Glasnost Public Foundation.

Boycko, Maxim, Andrei Shleifer, and Robert W. Vishny. 1993. "Privatizing Russia." *Brookings Papers on Economic Activity*, 2, 139–92.

———. 1995. *Privatizing Russia*. Cambridge, MA: MIT Press.

Bren, Paulina. 1993. "Lustration in the Czech and Slovak Republics." *RFE/RL Research Report*, Vol. 2, No. 29, July 16, 16–22.

Burawoy, Michael, and Kathryn Hendley. 1992. "Between Perestroika and Privatization: Divided Strategies and Political Crisis in a Soviet Enterprise." *Soviet Studies*, 44:3, 371–402.

Butler, W.E. 1988. *Soviet Law*. 2nd edition. London, UK: Butterworths.

Chandler, Alfred D., Jr. 1962. *Strategy and Structure: Chapters in the History of the American Industrial Enterprise*. Cambridge, MA: MIT Press.

Christian, David. 1994. "A Neglected Great Reform: The Abolition of Tax Farming in Russia." In *Russia's Great Reforms*, edited by Ben Eklof, John Bushnell, and Larissa Zakharova. Bloomington, IN: Indiana University Press.

Clark, Robert C. 1986. *Corporate Law*. Boston and Toronto: Little, Brown and Company.

Coffee, John C., Jr. 1989. "The Mandatory/Enabling Balance in Corporate Law: An Essay on the Judicial Role." *89 Columbia Law Review*, 1618–1691.

Cohen, Ariel. 1991. "The Developing Soviet Market: Commodity Exchanges." *Report on the USSR*, May 17.

Darski, Jozef. 1991–1992. "Police Agents in the Transition Period." *Uncaptive Minds*, Vol. 4, No. 4, Winter, 15–18.

Davies, R. W. 1991. Editor of *From Tsarism to the New Economic Policy: Continuity and Change in the Economy of the USSR*. Ithaca, NY: Cornell University Press.

Deiermeir, D., J. Ericson, T. Frye, and S. Lewis. 1997. "Credible Commitment and Property Rights: The Strategic Interaction of Economic and Political Actors," in *The Political Economy of Property Rights: Institutional Change and Credibility on the Road From Serfdom*, ed. Dave Weimer. New York, NY: Cambridge University Press.

Dziak, John J. 1988. *Chekisty: A History of the KGB*. New York, NY: Lexington Books.

Easterbrook, Frank H. and Daniel R. Fischel. 1991. *The Economic Structure of Corporate Law*. Cambridge, London: Harvard University Press.

EBRD. 1994. *Transition Report*. London: European Bank for Reconstruction and Development.

_____. 1995. *Transition Report*. London: European Bank for Reconstruction and Development.

Edwards, Jeremy and Klaus Fischer. 1994. *Banks, Finance and Investment in Germany*. Cambridge, UK: Cambridge University Press.

EECR. 1993. "Special Reports: Crisis in Russia." *East European Constitutional Review*.

_____. 1994. "Focus: Crisis in Russia." *East European Constitutional Review*. Fall/Winter.

Ellickson, Robert. 1991. *Order Without Law*. Cambridge, MA: Harvard University Press.

Elster, Jon. 1993. "Constitution-Making in Eastern Europe: Rebuilding the Boat in the Open Sea." *Public Administration*.

_____. 1994a. "The Constitution-Making Process." Mimeo.

_____. 1994b. "The Impact of Constitutions on Economic Performance." Mimeo.

Engelbrekt, Kjell. 1993. "The *Stasi* Revisited." *RFE/RL Research Report*, Vol. 2, No. 46, November 19, 19–24.

Ericson, Joel. 1997. "Private Firms, City Government, and Arbitration: The Case of St. Petersburg." *The Political Economy of Property Rights: Institutional Change and Credibility on the Road From Serfdom*. Dave Weimer, ed. New York, NY: Cambridge University Press.

Erlanger, Steven. 1995. "Images of Lawlessness Twist Russian Reality." *New York Times*, June 7.

Esser, Josef. 1988. "Bank Power in West Germany Revised." *West European Politics*, Vol. 13 No. 4, 17.

Flathman, Richard. 1994. "Liberalism and the Suspect Enterprise of Political Institutionalization: The Case of the Rule of Law." In *The Rule of Law*, ed. by Ian Shapiro. New York, NY: New York University Press.

Freedom House. 1994. *Freedom in the World: 1993–1994*. New York, NY: Freedom House.

Frydman, Roman. 1993. With Andrzej Rapaczynski, John Earle, et. al., eds. *The Privatization Process in Russia, Ukraine, and the Baltic States*. Budapest, London, New York: Central European University Press.

Frydman, Roman, and Andrzej Rapaczynski. 1994. *Privatization in Eastern Europe: Is the State Withering Away?* Budapest, London, New York: Central European University Press.

Frydman, Roman, Cheryl W. Gray, and Andrzej Rapaczynski. 1996. *Corporate Governance in Central Europe and Russia,* Vols. 1 and 2. Budapest: Central European University Press.

Frydman, Roman, Katharina Pistor, and Andrzej Rapaczynski. 1996. *Investing in Insider-Dominated Firms, A Study of Russian Voucher-Privatization Funds,* in Frydman, Gray, and Rapaczynski, eds., *Corporate Governance in Central Europe and Russia.* Budapest, London, New York: Central European University Press.

Frye, Timothy. 1995. "Caveat Emptor: Institutions, Contracts, and Commodity Exchanges in Russia." *Institutional Design.* Dave Weimer, ed. Boston, MA: Kluwer Academic Press.

_____. 1997. "The State and the Market: Governing the New Russian Economy." Ph.D. dissertation, Columbia University.

Gambetta, Diego. 1994. *The Sicilian Mafia: The Business of Private Protection.* Cambridge, MA: Harvard University Press.

Gatrell, Peter. 1994. *Government, Industry and Rearmament in Russia, 1900–1914.* New York, NY: Cambridge University Press.

Gauck, Joachim. 1993. "Disposing of the Stasi Legacy: Germany's Experience with the Preservation and Disposal of GDR Secret Police Files." *Demokratizatsiya: The Journal of Post-Soviet Democratization,* Vol. I, No. 3, Summer, 104–107.

Gaus, Gerald F. 1994. "Public Reason and the Rule of Law." In *The Rule of Law, Nomos* 36, edited by Ian Shapiro. New York, NY: New York University Press.

Geddes, Barbara. 1994a. "Challenging the Conventional Wisdom." *Journal of Democracy* 5:4.

_____. 1994b. *Politician's Dilemma: Building State Capacity in Latin America.* Berkeley, CA: University of California Press.

Girard, L. 1965. "Transport." In *The Cambridge Economic History of Europe,* Vol. 6: *The Industrial Revolution and After,* Part 1, edited by H. J. Habakkuk and M. Postan. New York, NY: Cambridge University Press.

Goldman, Marshall I. 1995. "Comrade Godfather." *The Washington Post,* February 12.

Goskomstat Rossii. 1994. *Sotsial'no-ekonomicheskoe polozhenie Rossii.* Moscow, 1995, 73–74.

Gorbachev, Ivan A. 1910. *Zakony o tovarishchestvakh ... .* Moscow: Pravovedenie.

Granick, David. 1960. *The Red Executive.* Garden City, NY: Doubleday & Company, Inc.

Granovetter, Mark. 1985. "Economic Action and Social Structure: The Problem of Embeddedness." *American Journal of Sociology,* November, 91:3, 481–510.

Gray, Cheryl W., and Associates. 1993. "Evolving Legal Frameworks for Private Sector Development in Central and Eastern Europe." World Bank Discussion Paper 209, July.

Gray, Cheryl W., Sabine Schlorke, and Miklos Szanyi. 1996. "The Bankruptcy Experiment in Hungary, 1992–1993: Findings from an In-Depth Survey." *World Bank Economic Review,* September.

Gregory, Paul R. 1994. *Before Command: An Economic History of Russia from Emancipation to the First Five-Year Plan.* Princeton, NJ: Princeton University Press.

Greif, Avner. 1992. "Cultural Beliefs and the Organization of Society: A Theoretical Reflection on Collectivist and Individualist Societies." Stanford, CA, November.

Haggard, Stephan, and Robert Kaufman. 1995. *The Political Economy of Democratic Transitions*. Princeton, NJ: Princeton University Press.

Handelman, Stephen. 1994. "The Russian Mafiya." *Foreign Affairs*, Vol. 73, No. 2, March/April.

_____. 1994. *Comrade Criminal: The Theft of the Second Russian Revolution*. London: M. Joseph.

_____. 1995. *Comrade Criminal: The New Russian Mafia*. New Haven, CT: Yale University Press.

Hardin, Russell. 1989. "Why a Constitution?" In *The Federalist Papers and the New Institutionalism*. Bernard Grofman and Donald Wittman, eds. New York, NY: Agathon Press.

_____. 1994. "Constitutional Economic Transition." Mimeo.

Häsemeyer, Ludwig. 1980. *Der interne Rechtsschutz zwischen Organen, Organmitgliedern und Mitgliedern der Kapitalgesellschaft als Problem der Prozeßführungsbefugnis*, ZR, 265.

Hendley, Kathryn. 1992. "Legal Development and Privatization in Russia: A Case Study." *Soviet Economy* 8.

_____. 1995. "The Spillover Effects of Privatization on Russian Legal Culture." *Transnational Law and Contemporary Problems*. Forthcoming.

Hersch, Seymour M. 1994. "The Wild East." Boston, MA: *The Atlantic Monthly*, June.

Hintze, Otto. 1975. "The Preconditions of Representative Government in the Context of World History." In *The Historical Essays of Otto Hintze*, edited by Felix Gilbert. New York, NY: Oxford University Press.

Hogan, Heather. 1993. *Forging Revolution: Metalworkers, Managers, and the State in St. Petersburg, 1890–1914*. Bloomington, IN: Indiana University Press.

Holmes, Stephen. 1993a. "Back to the Drawing Board." *East European Constitutional Review*. Winter.

_____. 1993b. "The Postcommunist Presidency." *East European Constitutional Review*. 2/3:4/1.

_____. 1994. "Superpresidentialism and Its Problems." *East European Constitutional Review*. 2/3; 4/1.

_____. 1995. "Conceptions of Democracy in the Draft Constitutions of Post-Communist Countries." In *Markets, States, and Democracy: The Political Economy of Post-Communist Transformation*, ed. Beverly Crawford. Boulder, CO: Westview Press.

Hopt, Klaus J. 1992. "Directors' Duties to Shareholders, Employees, and Other Creditors: A View from the Continent," in Ewan Mc Kendrick's (ed.), *Commercial Aspects of Trusts and Fiduciary Obligations*, 115.

Horn, Norbert, and Jürgen Kocka, eds. 1979. *Recht und Entwicklung der Grossunternehmen im 19. und frühen 20. Jahrhundert (Law and the Formation of the Big Enterprises in the 19th and Early 20th Centuries)*. Göttingen: Vandenhoeck & Ruprecht.

Huskey, Eugene. 1992. "From Legal Nihilism to *Pravovoe gosudarstvo*: Soviet Legal Development, 1917–1990," 23–42. In *Toward the "Rule of Law" in Russia? Political and Legal Reform in the Transition Period*, edited by Donald D. Barry. Armonk, N.Y.: M. E. Sharpe.

International Monetary Fund, 1993. *Economic Review: Russian Federation*. Washington, D.C.

Isakova, Liliya, and Elena Oznobkina, eds. 1996. *Voina v Chechnye: Mezhdunarodnyi Tribunal, II Rabochaya vstrecha, Stokgolm, 15–16 Dekabrya 1995*. Moscow: Obshchestvennyi Fond Glasnost, bilingual edition in Russian and English.

Isakova, Liliya, Vladimir Oyvin, and Elena Oznobkina, eds. 1995. *KGB: Vchera, segodnya, zavtra, III-IV Kruglyye stoly, Zakonodatelstvo Rossiiskoi Federatsiy o spetsluzhbakh*. Moscow: Obshchestvennyi Fond Glasnost.

Johnson, Juliet. 1994. "The Russian Banking System: Institutional Responses to the Market Transition." *Europe-Asia Studies*, 46:6, 971–89.

Johnson, Simon, and Heidi Kroll. 1991. "Managerial Strategies for Spontaneous Privatization," *Soviet Economy* Vol. 7, No. 4, 281–316.

Johnston, Les. 1989. *The Rebirth of Private Policing*. London: Routledge Press.

Jones, Anthony, and William Moskoff. 1991. *Ko-ops: The Rebirth of Entrepreneurship in the Soviet Union*. Bloomburg, IN: Indiana University Press.

Jowitt, Kenneth. 1992. *New World Disorder: The Leninist Extinction*. Berkeley, CA: University of California Press.

Kahan, Arcadius. 1989. *Russian Economic History: The Nineteenth Century*, edited by Roger Weiss. Chicago, IL: University of Chicago Press.

Kaiser, Daniel H. 1980. *The Growth of the Law in Medieval Russia*. Princeton, NJ: Princeton University Press.

Karlova, Enna. 1990. "Russia: Financial-Industrial Groups (FIGs), Industrial Policy and Competition." Paper presented to the Tenth Plenary Session of the OECD Advisory Group on Privatization, Paris, September, 26–27.

Kartashkin, Vladimir A. 1991. "Human Rights and the Emergence of the State of the Rule of Law in the USSR." *Emory Law Journal*, 40:889–902.

Keenan, Edward L. 1986. "Muscovite Political Folkways." *The Russian Review*, 46:115–81.

Kelman, Mark. 1987. *A Guide to Critical Legal Studies*. Cambridge, MA: Harvard University Press.

KGB (*Komitet Gosudarstvennoi Bezopasnosti*). 1989. *Politicheskaya Razvedka s Territorii SSSR*. Moscow: Krasnoznamennyi Institut KGB CCCP imeni Yu. V. Andropov.

Kipp, Jacob W. 1994. "The Russian Navy and the Problem of Technological Transfer: Technological Backwardness and Military-Industrial Development," 115–38. In *Russia's Great Reforms*, edited by Ben Eklof, John Bushnell, and Larissa Zakharova. Bloomington, IN: Indiana University Press.

Knight, Amy. 1988, 1990. *The KGB: Police and Politics in the Soviet Union*. Boston: Unwin, Hyman.

Kokorev, Rostislav. 1993. *Brokerstvo kak institut organizatsii rynka v perekhodnoi ekonomike*. Dissertation. Moscow State.

Komitet s'ezdov predstavitelei aktsionernykh kommercheskikh bankov. 1917. *O zhelatel'nykh izmeneniiakh v postanovke aktsionernogo bankovogo dela v Rossii*. Petrograd: Al'fa.

Kornai, Janos and Agnes Matits. 1984. "Softness of the Budget Constraint–An Analysis Relying on Data of Firms." *Acta Oeconomica* 32/3–4.

Kovalevskii, Vladimir I. 1991. "Vospominaniia V. I. Kovalevskogo," edited by Leonid E. Shepelev. *Russkoe proshloe*, 2:5–96.

Kreps, David. 1990. "Corporate Culture and Economic Theory." Eds. James Alt and Kenneth Shepsle. *Perspectives on Positive Political Economy.* New York, NY: Cambridge University Press, 90–143.

Kuznetsova, Ninel F. 1994. "Crime in Russia: Causes and Prevention." *Demokratizatsiya: The Journal of Post-Soviet Democratization,* Vol. II, 3:442–452.

Levi, Margaret. 1988. *Of Rule and Revenue.* Berkeley, CA: University of California Press.

Lincoln, W.B. 1990. *The Great Reforms: Autocracy, Bureaucracy, and the Politics of Change in Imperial Russia.* Dekalb, IL: Northern Illinois University Press.

Lipton, David and Jeffrey D. Sachs. 1990. "Privatization in Eastern Europe, The Case of Poland." *Brookings Papers on Economic Activity,* No. 2, 293.

Litwack, John. 1991a. "Legality and Market Reform in Soviet-Type Economies." *Journal of Economic Perspectives,* 5:4, 77–89.

———. 1991b. "Discretionary Behavior and Soviet Economic Reform." *Soviet Studies,* 43:2, 255–279.

Lurie, Jonathon. 1991. *The Chicago Board of Trade, 1859–1905.* Urbana, IL: University of Illinois Press.

Macauley, Stewart. 1961. "Non-Contractual Relations in Business: A Preliminary Study." *American Sociological Review,* 55–67.

Maine, Henry. 1861. *Ancient Law.* London: J. Murray.

Marks, Steven G. 1991. *Road to Power: The Trans-Siberian Railroad and the Colonization of Asiatic Russia, 1850–1917.* Ithaca, NY: Cornell University Press.

Marnie, Sheila, and Albert Motivan. 1993. "Rising Crime Rates: Perceptions and Reality." *RFE/RL Research Report,* Vol. 2, No. 20, May 14.

Mauro, P. 1995. "Corruption and Growth." *The Quarterly Journal of Economics,* Volume CX, Issue 3, August, 681–712.

McCaffray, Susan P. 1996. *The Politics of Industrialization in Tsarist Russia: The Association of Southern Coal and Steel Producers, 1874–1914.* De Kalb, IL: Northern Illinois University Press.

McDonald, Lynn. 1982. "Theory and Evidence of Rising Crime in the Nineteenth Century." *The British Journal of Sociology,* Vol. 33, No. 3, September 1982.

McGregor, James. 1994. "The Presidency in East Central Europe." *RFE/RL Research Report,* 3:2.

Meier-Schatz, Christian J. 1988. "Corporate Governance and Legal Rules: A Transnational Look at Concepts and Problems of Internal Management Control." *The Journal of Corporation Law,* Vol. 13, No. 2, 431.

Merryman, John Henry. 1969. *The Civil Law Tradition.* Stanford, CA: Stanford University Press.

Mertens, Hans-Joachim. 1990. *Organstreit in der Aktiengesellschaft? Eine rechtspolitische Kritik.* ZHR, 24.

Meyendorff, John. 1976. "The Church," in R. Auty and D. Obolensky, eds., *An Introduction to Russian History.* New York, NY: Cambridge University Press.

Mikhailovskaya, Inga B. 1994. "Crime and Statistics. Do the Figures Reflect the Real Situation?" *Demokratizatsiya,* Vol. 2, No. 3, Summer.

Milgrom, Paul R., Douglass C. North, and Barry Weingast. 1990. "The Law Merchant, Private Judges, and Champaigne Fairs," *Economics and Politics,* 2:1, 1–23.

Mironov, Boris. 1990. "The Russian Peasant Commune After the Reforms of the 1860s," in B. Eklof and S. Frank, eds., *The World of the Russian Peasant: Post-Emancipation Culture and Society*. Boston, MA: Unwin Hyman.

Mizsei, Kalman. 1993. "Bankruptcy and the Post-Communist Economies of East Central Europe." Institute for East West Studies.

Moore, Barrington, Jr. 1966. *Social Origins of Dictatorship and Democracy: Lord and Peasant in the Making of the Modern World*. Boston, MA: Beacon Press.

Müller, Pawel. 1992. "The Gauck Commission." *Uncaptive Minds*, Vol. 5, No. 1, Spring, 95–98.

Nelson, Joan M. 1993. "The Politics of Economic Transformation: Is Third World Experience Relevant to Eastern Europe?" *World Politics*.

Nemeth, Charles. 1989. *Private Security and the Law*. Cincinnati, OH: Anderson Publishing.

North, Douglass, C. 1990. *Institutions, Institutional Change, and Economic Performance*. New York, NY: Cambridge University Press.

_____. 1993. "Institutions and Credible Commitment." *Journal of Institutional and Theoretical Economics*, 149:1.

North, Douglass C. and Robert Paul Thomas. 1973. *The Rise of the Western World: A New Economic History*. New York, NY: Cambridge University Press.

North, Douglass C., and Barry Weingast. 1989. "Constitutions and Commitment: The Evolution of Institutions Governing Public Choice in Seventeenth Century England." *Political Economy Working Paper*, 129.

O'Donnell, Guillermo, and Phillippe C. Schmitter. 1986. *Transitions from Authoritarian Rule: Tentative Conclusions about Uncertain Democracies*. Baltimore, MD: The Johns Hopkins University Press.

Olson, David M. 1993. "Dissolution of the State: Political Parties and the 1992 Election in Czechoslovakia." *Communist and Post-Communist Studies*, 26:3.

_____. 1994. "The Sundered State: Federalism and Parliament in Czechoslovakia." In *Parliaments in Transition*, ed. Thomas F. Remington. Boulder, CO: Westview Press.

Ostrom, Elinor. 1990. *Governing the Commons: The Evolution of Institutions for Collective Action*. New York, NY: Cambridge University Press.

O'Toole, G. 1978. *The Private Sector: Private Spies, Rent-a-Cops, and the Police-Industrial Complex*. New York, NY: Norton and Company.

Owen, Thomas C. 1981. *Capitalism and Politics in Russia: A Social History of the Moscow Merchants, 1855–1905*. New York: Cambridge University Press.

_____. 1985. "The Russian Industrial Society and Tsarist Economic Policy, 1867–1905." *Journal of Economic History*, 45:587–606.

_____. 1991. *The Corporation under Russian Law, 1800–1917: A Study in Tsarist Economic Policy*. New York, NY: Cambridge University Press.

_____. 1992. "RUSCORP: A Database of Corporations in the Russian Empire, 1700–1914." Machine-readable database, Louisiana State University, rev. ed. Distributed by the Inter-University Consortium for Political and Social Research, Ann Arbor, Michigan.

_____. 1995. *Russian Corporate Capitalism from Peter the Great to Perestroika*. New York: Oxford University Press.

Oznobkina, Elena, and Liliya Isakova. 1995. *Voina v Chechnye: Neobkhodimost provedeniya Mezhdunarodnogo Tribunala, VI Kruglyi stol, Mockva, 15 Iuliya 1995.* Moscow: Obshchestvennyi Fond Glasnost, bilingual edition in Russian and English.

Pehe, Jiri. 1994. "Czech Republic's Crime Rate Slows Down." *RFE/RL Research Report,* Vol. 3, No. 8, February 25.

Persson, Torsten, and Guido Tabellini, eds. 1994. *Monetary and Fiscal Policy.* Cambridge, MA: The MIT Press.

Pistor, Katharina. 1995. "Privatization and Corporate Governance in Russia—An Empirical Study," in Michael McFaul and Tova Perlmutter (eds.), *Privatization, Conversion, and Enterprise Reform in Russia.* Boulder, CO: Westview Press.

_____. 1996a. "Supply and Demand for Contract Enforcement in Russia: Courts, Arbitration, and Private Enforcement" *Review of Central and East European Law,* 22: 1,55.

Pistor, Katharina, and Andrew Spicer. 1996b. "Investment Funds in Mass Privatization and Beyond." HIID Development Discussion Papers No. 565, December.

Podlesskikh, Georgy, and Andrei Tereshonok. 1994. *Vory v Zakone: Brosok k Vlasti.* Moscow: Khudozhestvennaya literatura.

Polanyi, Karl. 1957. *The Great Transformation.* New York: Basic Books.

Pomorski, Stanislaw. 1977. "State Arbitrazh in the U.S.S.R.: Development, Functions, Organization." Rutgers, NJ: *Camden Law Journal,* 9 , 61-116.

Ponomarev, Lev A., and A. P. Surkov. 1992. "Conclusion per the results of the open parliamentary hearings 'About the Illegal Financial Activity of the CPSU.'" February 8, Supreme Soviet of the Russian Federation (unpublished in Russian). Translated in *Demokratizatsiya: The Journal of Post-Soviet Democratization,* Vol. IV, No. 2, Spring 1996, 274–276.

Popplewell, Richard. 1991. "Themes in the Rhetoric of KGB Chairmen from Andropov to Kryuchkov." *Intelligence and National Security,* Vol. 6, No. 3, July, 513–547.

Porter, Michael. 1992. "Capital Disadvantage: America's Failing Capital Investment System." *Harvard Business Review,* September–October, 65.

Posner, Richard. 1980. "A Theory of Primitive Society." *Journal of Law and Economics,* 28, 1–53.

Putnam, Robert. 1993. *Making Democracy Work: Civic Traditions in Modern Italy.* Princeton: Princeton University Press.

Rahr, Alexander. 1993. "Kryuchkov, the KGB, and the 1991 Putsch." *RFE/RL Research Report,* Vol. 2, No. 31, July 30.

_____. 1994. "Reform of Russia's State Security Apparatus." *RFE/RL Research Report,* Vol. 3, No. 8, February 25, 28.

Rieber, Alfred J. 1982. *Merchants and Entrepreneurs in Imperial Russia.* Chapel Hill, NC: University of North Carolina Press.

Roe, Mark J. 1993. "Some Differences in Corporate Governance in Germany, Japan, and America." 102 *Yale Law Journal,* 1927.

Romano, Roberta. 1993. "A Cautionary Note on Drawing Lessons from Comparative Corporate Law." 102 *Yale Law Journal,* 2022.

Roosa, Ruth A. 1967. "The Association of Industry and Trade, 1906–1914: An Examination of the Economic Views of Organized Industrialists in Prerevolutionary Russia." Unpublished doctoral dissertation, Columbia University, New York, NY.

Root, Hilton L. 1989. "Tying the King's Hand: Credible Commitments and Royal Fiscal Policy During the Old Regime." *Rationality and Society*, 1:2.

Rose, Richard. 1994. "Postcommunism and the Problem of Trust." *Journal of Democracy*, Vol. 5, No. 3, July.

Rose, Richard, and Evgeny Tikhomirov. 1996. "Trends in the New Russia Barometer, 1992–1995." *Studies in Public Policy*, No. 256, Centre for the Study of Public Policy, University of Strathclyde.

Russian Federation. 1995. *Russian Economic Trends 1994*, 3:4.

Rutland, Peter. 1994. "Privatization in Russia: Two Steps Forward, One Step Back?" *Europe-Asia Studies*, 46:7, 1109–1131.

Saba, Joseph. 1996. "Orphans in the Storm, The Challenge of Corporate Governance in Transition Countries." Paper presented to the Tenth Plenary Session of the OECD Advisory Group on Privatization. Paris, September, 26–27 .

Sachs, J.D. 1995a. "Consolidating Capitalism." *Foreign Policy*, Number 98, Spring.

_____. 1995b. "Russia's Struggle with Stabilization: Conceptual Issues and Evidence." Proceedings of the World Bank Annual Conference on Development Economics 1994. Washington, DC: IBRD/World Bank.

Sachs, J.D., and A. M. Warner. 1995. "Economic Reform and the Process of Global Integration." *Brookings Papers on Economic Activities* 1:108.

Schaffer, Mark E. 1989. "Redistribution of Profit, Financial Flows, and Economic Reform in Polish Industry: Evidence from the Lista 500." Unpublished manuscript. February.

Schelling, Thomas. 1984. "Economics and Criminal Enterprise." *The Economics of Crime*, ed. R. Adreano. New York, NY: The Free Press.

Schmidt, Karsten. 1992. *Gesellschaftsrecht, Carl Heymanns Verlag*. KG, Köln, Berlin, Bonn, München.

Sedaitis, Judith. 1994. "Start-ups or Spinoffs Under Market Transition: The Development of Post-Soviet Commodity Exchange Markets." Ph.D. dissertation, Columbia University, Department of Sociology.

Segodnya. February 23, 1995. "Results of the Work of the Internal Affairs Organs and the Internal Troops in 1994."

Shearing, C.D., and P.C. Stenning. 1983. *Private Security and Private Justice*. Montreal: Institute for Research on Public Policy.

Sheehy, Gail. 1990. *The Man Who Changed the World*. New York, NY: HarperCollins.

Shelley, Louise I. 1995. "Organized Crime in the Former Soviet Union." *Problems of Post-Communism*, January–February.

_____. 1996. *Policing Soviet Society: The Evolution of State Control*. London and New York: Routledge.

Shepelev, Leonid E. 1959. "Aktsionernoe uchreditel'stvo v Rossii (istoriko-statisticheskii ocherk)," 134–82. In *Iz istorii imperializma v Rossii*. Mikhail P. Viatkin, ed. Leningrad: Nauka.

_____. 1973. *Aktsionernye kompanii v Rossii*. Leningrad: Nauka.

_____. 1981. *Tsarizm i burzhuaziia vo vtoroi polovine XIX veka: problemy torgovo-promyshlennoi politiki*. Leningrad: Nauka.

_____, ed. 1995a. "The Commercial-Industrial Program of the Ministry of Finance, 1893: New Documents from the Imperial Archive." *Russian Studies in History*, 34, No. 1:7–39.

_____. 1995b. "Business Organizations in the Russian Empire, 1906–1914." *Russian Studies in History*, 34, No. 1:40–88.

Shklar, Judith. 1986. *Legalism*. Cambridge, MA: Harvard University Press.

Shmelev, Nikolai. 1987. "Avansy I dolgi." *Novy mir*, June.

Shugart, Matthew S., and John M. Carey. 1992. *Presidents and Assemblies: Constitutional Design and Electoral Dynamics*. New York, NY: Cambridge University Press.

Simis, Konstantin. 1982. *USSR: Secrets of a Corrupt Society*. London: J.M Dent & Sons.

Skaperdas, Stergios, and Constantinous Syropolous. 1994. "Gangs as Primitive States." *The Economics of Organized Crime*. Gianluca Fiorentino and Sam Peltzman, eds. Cambridge: Cambridge University Press.

Solov'eva, Aida M. 1968. "Iz istorii vykupa chastnykh zheleznykh dorog v Rossii v kontse XIX veka." *Istoricheskie zapiski*, 82:89–119.

Staniszkis, Jadwiga. 1991. "Political Capitalism in Poland," *East European Politics and Societies*, Vol. 5, No. 1, 127.

Stark, David. 1990. "From Plan to Market or From Plan to Clan." *East European Politics and Societies*, Vol. 4, No. 3.

_____. 1992. "Path Dependence and Privatization Strategies in East Central Europe." *East European Politics and Societies*, 6:1, 17–54.

_____. 1996. "Networks of Assets, Claims and Debts: Recombinant Property in East European Capitalism." In Frydman, Gray, and Rapaczynski (eds.), *Corporate Governance in Central Europe and Russia*. Budapest, London, New York: Central European University Press, Vol. 2.

Sterling, Claire. 1994. *Thieves' World. The Threat of the New Global Network of Organized Crime*. New York, NY: Simon & Schuster.

Surkov, A. P. 1992. "Transcript of Parliamentary Hearings of the Commission to Investigate the Causes and Circumstances of the August Putsch, on the Theme of Illegal Financial Activity of the CPSU." Supreme Soviet of the Russian Federation, February 10, translated in *Demokratizatsiya: The Journal of Post-Soviet Democratization*, Vol. IV, No. 2, Spring 1996, 292–299.

Sustrova, Petruska. 1992. "The Lustration Controversy." *Uncaptive Minds*, Vol. 5, No. 2, Summer, 129–134.

Taniguchi, Yoichiro. 1988. "Japan's Company Law and the Promotion of Corporate Democracy: A Futile Attempt?" *Columbus Journal of Transnational Law*, Vol. 27, 195.

Tilly, Charles. 1985. "War-making and State-making as Organized Crime." *Bringing the State Back In*. Peter Evans, Dietrich Reuschmeyer, Theda Skocpol, eds. New York, NY: Cambridge University Press, 169–191.

_____. 1991. *Coercion, Capital and European States*. Ithaca, NY: Cornell University Press.

Timofeyev, Lev, ed. 1992. *Russia's Secret Rulers: How the Government and Criminal Mafia Exercise Their Power.* Translated by Catherine A. Fitzpatrick. New York, NY: Knopf.

Toman, Petr. 1991. "Collaborators Revealed: The Parliamentary Commissions Report." *Uncaptive Minds*, Vol. 4, No. 2, Summer, 8–12.

Tyler, Tom. 1990. *Why People Obey the Law*. New Haven, CT: Yale University Press.

Unger, Roberto Mangabeira. 1976. *Law in Modern Society: Towards a Criticism of Social Theory.* New York: The Free Press.

_____. 1986. *The Critical Legal Studies Movement.* Cambridge, MA: Harvard University Press.

Vaksberg, Arkady. 1991. *The Soviet Mafia,* translated by John and Elizabeth Roberts. New York, NY: St. Martin's Press.

_____. 1995. *The Soviet Mafia.* New York, NY: St. Martin's Press.

Valuev, Petr A. 1961. *Dnevnik P. A. Valueva, ministra vnutrennikh del,* edited by Petr A. Zaionchkovskii. 2 vols. Moscow: Akademiia nauk.

Verstraete, Maurice. 1949. "Sur les routes de mon passé." Typewritten ms., 2 vols. Hoover Institution Archives, Stanford University.

Vinogradova, Elena. 1992a. "Arbitrazhnaia komissaia pri MTB: Normativniie Dokumenti i Spravochnii Materiali." Moscow, MTB.

_____. 1992b. "Arbitrazhnaia komissaia pri MTB: effektivnaia forma razresheniia sporov." *MTB ezhemesechnii zhurnal,* #5.

_____. 1992c. "Obrashenie v birzhevuyu arbitrazhnuyu kommisiyu: pravo ili obyaztel'stvo." *Khozyastvo i Pravo,* 1992, 3, pp. 106–118.

_____. 1992d. "Tret'eiskii sud: nastoiashoe i budushchee." *Khozyastvo i Pravo,* #2, pp. 85–91.

_____. 1993. *Tret'eiskii sud v Rossii: zakonodatelstvo, praktika, kommentarii.* Moscow: Vek.

_____. 1994. "Pravoviie osnovie organizatsii i deiatel'nosti tret'eiskogo suda." Dissertation, Moscow State University.

Vitransky, V.V. 1992. *Zashchita Imushestvennikh Prav Predprinimatelii.* Moskva: Pravo i Ekonomika.

Vodopivec, Milan. 1994. "Appropriability of Returns in the Yugoslav Firm." *Eastern Economic Journal* 20:3, Summer.

Von Laue, Theodore H. 1954. "A Secret Memorandum of Sergei Witte on the Industrialization of Imperial Russia." *Journal of Modern History,* 26:61–74.

Walicki, Andrzej. 1987. *Legal Philosophies of Russian Liberalism.* New York, NY: Oxford University Press.

Waller, J. Michael. 1994a. *Secret Empire: The KGB In Russia Today.* Boulder, CO: Westview Press.

_____. 1994b. "Post-Soviet Sakharovs: Renewed Persecution of Soviet Dissidents and the American Response." *Demokratizatsiya: The Journal of Post-Soviet Democratization,* Vol. II, No. 1, Winter, 138–147.

Waller, and Victor J. Yasmann. 1995. "Russia's Great Criminal Revolution: The Role of the Security Services." *Journal of Contemporary Criminal Justice,* Vol. 11, No. 4, December, 276–297.

Watters, Francis M. 1968. "The Peasant and the Village Commune," in W. Vucinich, ed., *The Peasant in Nineteenth-Century Russia.* Stanford, CA: Stanford University Press.

Weber, Max. 1978. *Economy and Society,* Vol. 1. Guenther Roth and Claus Wittich, eds. Berkeley, CA: University of California Press.

Webster, Leila M., and Joshua Charap. 1994. *The Emergence of Private Sector Manufacturing Firms in St. Petersburg: A Survey of Firms.* Washington, D.C.: World Bank.

Wegren, Stephen, K. 1994. "Building Market Institutions: Agricultural Commodity Exchanges in Post-Communist Russia." *Communist and Post-Communist Studies,* 27:3, 195–224.

Weingast, Barry R. 1992. "The Economic Role of Political Institutions." *Institute for Policy Reform Working Papers,* 46.

_____. 1993. "Constitutions as Governance Structures: The Political Foundations of Secure Markets." *Journal of Institutional and Theoretical Economics,* 149:1.

_____. 1993. "Constitutions as Commitment Devices." *Journal of Institutional and Theoretical Economics,* 149:1.

_____. 1994. "The Political Impediments to Economic Reform: Political Risk and Enduring Gridlock." Institute for Policy Reform Working Paper, 68.

Williamson, John, ed. 1994. *The Political Economy of Policy Reform.* Washington, D.C.: Institute for International Studies.

Williamson, Oliver E. 1985. *The Economic Institutions of Capitalism.* New York, NY: The Free Press. London: Collier Macmillan Publishers.

Witte, Sergei Iu. 1990. *The Memoirs of Count Witte,* translated and edited by Sidney Harcave. Armonk, N.Y.: M. E. Sharpe.

Wolchik, Sharon L. 1991. *Czechoslovakia in Transition.* London: Ointer Publishers.

_____. 1993. "The Repluralization of Politics in Czechoslovakia." *Communist and Post-Communist Studies,* 26:4.

Wolff, Robert Paul, ed. 1971. *The Rule of Law.* New York, NY: Simon and Schuster.

Woodruff, David. 1992. "The Commodity Fiction and Competition in the Post-Soviet Economy: Theoretical Reflections on Russia's Commodity Exchanges." Ms., Berkeley, CA, pp. 1–40.

Wortman, Richard S. 1976. *The Development of a Russian Legal Consciousness.* Chicago, IL: University of Chicago Press.

Yakovlev, A.A. 1991a. *Birzhi v SSSR: pervii god raboty.* Moscow: Institut issledovaniia organizovannikh rynkov.

_____. 1991b. *Kak kupit' i prodat' tovar na birzhe.* Moscow: Institut issledovaniia organizovannykh rynkov.

Yasmann, Victor J. 1993a. "Corruption in Russia: A Threat to Democracy?" *RFE/RL Research Report,* Vol. 2, No. 10, March 5.

_____. 1993b. "Legislation on Screening and State Security in Russia." *RFE/RL Research Report,* Vol. 2, No. 32, August 13, 11–16.

_____. 1994a. "Security Services Reorganized: All Power to the Russian President?" *RFE/RL Research Report,* Vol. 3, No. 6, February 11.

_____. 1994b. "Domestic Aspects of the New Russian Military Doctrine." Paper delivered to a conference organized by the Hanns Seidel Stiftung, Wildbad Kreuth, Germany, March 21–23.

Zemtsov, Ilja. 1976. *La corruption en Union Soviétique.* Paris: Hachette.

Zhurek, Stefan. 1993. "Commodity Exchanges in Russia: Success or Failure?" *RFE/RL Research Report,* February 5, 41–43.

Zipperstein, Steven J. 1985. *The Jews of Odessa: A Cultural History, 1794–1881.* Stanford, CA: Stanford University Press.

About the Contributors

Anders Åslund, D. Phil. (Oxon), is a Senior Associate at Carnegie Endowment for International Peace, Washington, DC. He has been Professor and Director of the Stockholm Institute of East European Economics at the Stockholm School of Economics, and has served as an economic advisor to the Russian and Ukrainian governments. His latest book is *How Russia Became a Market Economy* (Brookings, 1995).

Timothy Frye is assistant professor at Ohio State University. He received his Ph.D. from Columbia University. His dissertation is entitled "The State and the Market: Governing the New Russian Economy."

Cheryl W. Gray is a Principal Economist in the Transition Economics Division of the World Bank. She received Ph.D. and J.D. degrees from Harvard University and has worked extensively on economic analyses of legal and enterprise reforms in a variety of developing and transition economies.

Joel S. Hellman is Assistant Professor at the Government Department, Harvard University, and Institute Fellow at the Davis Center for Russian Studies. His research focuses on constitutionalism and democracy in transition economies.

Kathryn Hendley is Assistant Professor of Law and Political Science at the University of Wisconsin, Madison. She received a Ph.D. in political science from the University of California, Berkeley, and a J.D. from the UCLA School of Law. She has written extensively on the challenge of building the rule of law in post-Soviet Russia.

Michael Newcity is Coordinator of the Center for Slavic, Eurasian, and East European Studies at Duke University. A graduate of the George Washington University (M.A., Russian Studies, J.D.), Newcity studies the Russian legal system. He is the author of books on Soviet copyright law and taxation and numerous articles on various aspects of Soviet and Russian law.

Thomas C. Owen, a professor of history at Louisiana State University, is the author *of The Corporation under Russian Law, 1800–1917* (Cambridge University Press, 1991) and *Russian Corporate Capitalism from Peter the Great to Perestroika* (Oxford University Press, 1995).

J. Michael Waller (Ph.D., Boston University, 1993) is Vice President of the American Foreign Policy Council in Washington, D.C., and is Executive Editor of *Demokratizatsiya: The Journal of Post-Soviet Democratization.* He is author of *Secret Empire: The KGB In Russia Today* (Westview, 1994).

About the Book and Editors

What impact has Russia's chosen path of reform had on the development of law after the collapse of the communist regime? This collection of essays examines how Russia's distinctive traditions of law—and lawlessness—are shaping the current struggle for economic reform in the country. Nine renowned scholars, chosen from specialties in history, political science, law, and economics, expertly address the question.

Jeffrey D. Sachs is the director of the Harvard Institute for International Development (HIID) and the Galen L. Stone Professor of International Trade at Harvard University. He has served as an economic advisor to several governments in Latin America, Eastern Europe, the former Soviet Union, and Asia, including the Russian Federation, and has published widely on the transition to market economies in Eastern Europe and the former Soviet Union, international financial markets, international macroeconomic policy coordination, and macroeconomic policies in developing and developed countries.

Katharina Pistor is a research associate at HIID and a comparative lawyer. Her research and publications focus on comparative law with special emphasis on legal development in transition economies.

Index

Printed in the United States
by Baker & Taylor Publisher Services